ROUGH MAGIC

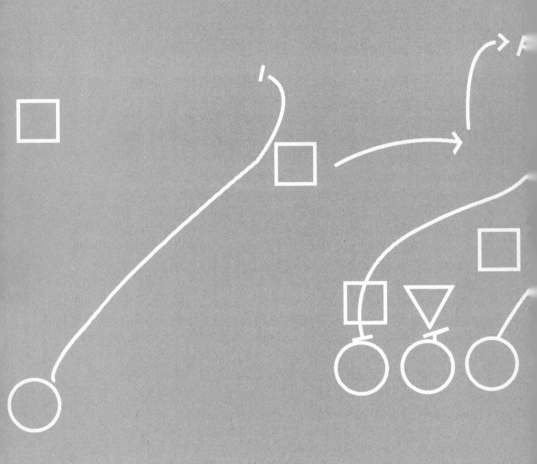

"Triss" pass right. TD vs. Penn State 1993

ROUGH MAGIC

BILL WALSH'S RETURN TO
STANFORD FOOTBALL

LOWELL COHN

HarperCollins*Publishers*

Photographs follow page 152.

HarperCollins books may be purchased for educational, business, or sales promotional use. For information please write: Special Markets Department, HarperCollins Publishers, Inc., 10 East 53rd Street, New York, NY 10022.

FIRST EDITION

Designed by George J. McKeon

Library of Congress Cataloging-in-Publication Data

Cohn, Lowell.
Rough magic : Bill Walsh's return to Stanford football / Lowell Cohn.
    p.   cm.
ISBN 0-06-017043-3
1. Walsh, Bill, 1931– . 2. Stanford University—Football.
I. Title.
GV939.W325C64   1994
796.332'092—dc20   94-8893
[B]

94 95 96 97 98 ❖/RRD 10 9 8 7 6 5 4 3 2 1

For my wife, Dawn, and my mother, Eve Cohn

ACKNOWLEDGMENTS

IN RESEARCHING AND writing this book I had the help of many friends and colleagues. These are a few of the people who advised and supported me: Tom Beckett, Pat Broun, Jim Brungard, Brad Bunnin, Christopher Coats, John Curley, Lawrence Fan, Gary Fanton, Bill Gairdner, Mark Haight, Mike Izzi, Sheila Jennings, Debbie Kenney, Ted Leland, Cheryl Levick, Pat Marcuccillo, Gary Migdol, Chris Norte, Sheri Robinson, Jeff Saal, Jan Souza, Eric Stanion, Bill Tingley, Jane Walsh, and Gene Washington.

I want to give special thanks to Alphonse Juilland for encouraging me to write a book; to my agent, Karen Nazor, for believing in me; to my editor, Eamon Dolan, for taking a chance on me; to my friend Carl Maves for advice and counsel; to the Stanford players and coaching staff, who graciously put up with my intrusions; and to Bill Walsh, who gave me complete access to himself and his team, and had faith in this project from the beginning.

PART

C H A P T E R

TUESDAY, AUGUST 18, 1992. At age sixty, Bill Walsh was starting over and wondering if it had always been this difficult.

It was eight days before the Stanford Cardinal football team was to meet Texas A&M in the first game of the season, the Pigskin Classic in Anaheim, California, and everything was supposed to be coming together on Stanford's squad. But today's practice was a mess. First a fight had broken out between the offensive and defensive linemen, and Walsh had to jump into the middle like a referee and separate the players. He could not tolerate loss of poise. "You've got to be totally impersonal out there," he shouted. "There are no people, just objects. You can't be emotional."

Then Walsh walked back to the sideline, rapidly opening and closing his fists, always a clear sign that he was upset. A few minutes later, he interrupted practice to yell at backup quarterback Mark Butterfield, who had just called the wrong play. "You've got to know this stuff, Mark. I don't want any mistakes." Walsh's voice was petulant, almost a whine. He was worried about Butterfield, a tall, athletic quarterback with a rocket arm. Butterfield was a sophomore who had sat out the previous season as a redshirt. He lacked confidence and was having trouble picking up Walsh's complicated offense. Walsh needed Butterfield. If Walsh's starter, Steve Stenstrom, went down, Butterfield had to take over, but there were times when Butterfield seemed utterly lost.

The team scrimmaged again for about two minutes before Walsh blew up once more. The recipient of his anger this time was Ethan

Allen, a reserve running back. In the last few minutes, Allen had gone the wrong direction on a run play, and then missed a block. Walsh was steaming. His intricate offensive strategy required as much study as any math or political science course at Stanford, and he wondered if his players were doing their homework. "If you don't know the plays, I can't use you," he shouted at Allen. "Either you know it or you don't."

It was not Walsh's style to yell at players on the practice field. He preferred to vent his anger on his coaches, hoping the player who made the mistake would feel guilty for getting his coach in trouble and try harder. But Walsh was unsure about so many things these days, himself included.

He had won three Super Bowls with the San Francisco 49ers and been named the National Football League's Coach of the Decade for the 1980s by the Pro Football Hall of Fame Board of Selectors. But he'd felt burned out in 1988, his last year in San Francisco, and had to get away from coaching. Searching for something to do, he spent three unhappy years as a football analyst for NBC. Being near football but unable to participate, he'd felt discarded, useless.

And then, the previous January, he had amazed the sports world—and himself—by returning to Stanford, where he had been head coach in 1977 and 1978. And now he was wondering if he was washed up.

His voice had become frail after so many years of urgent pep talks, and he wasn't sure the players could hear him, or if he still cut a commanding figure. He was having trouble remembering the names of everyone on the squad—he had about ninety players on the team and found the sheer bulk of bodies daunting. "I've lost something. I know that. I'm just not sure what," he told someone observing practice. "Maybe it's because I'm sixty. I don't know. I'm nervous. I admit it."

When he thought in the abstract about coaching at Stanford, it was easy for Walsh to convince himself he had made the right decision. He could remain in Northern California, a part of the country he loved. He and his wife, Geri, had just bought a home in Woodside, a fashionable suburb near campus, and were spending a fortune remodeling it. The house came with a pool and a hot tub, and even vineyards of chardonnay and pinot noir grapes, from which Walsh planned to produce his own wine. Moreover, he liked the idea of coaching again, of being part of a group with a shared purpose. He had never felt that at NBC, where he was always an outsider.

At Stanford, he would never feel the pressure he'd endured in the NFL—pressure that had ultimately affected his health. He understood that Stanford was unlikely to win a national championship. Admission standards were too high for that. But Walsh entertained visions of going to the Rose Bowl someday.

There were other benefits in returning to Stanford. He was sending a message to coaches around the country that it wasn't important to win at all costs, that a great coach didn't have to work in the NFL or a college football factory to find satisfaction. He saw himself as an educator—he frequently used the word *mentor*—and he'd already had a hand in developing the football coaches of the current generation. Five of his protégés were head coaches in the NFL—George Seifert with the 49ers; Sam Wyche, Tampa Bay; Bruce Coslet, New York Jets; Denny Green, Minnesota; Mike Holmgren, Green Bay. And now Walsh was developing the next generation of coaches, passing on his legacy to five former 49ers he'd convinced to join his staff—Keena Turner, Tom Holmoe, Mike Wilson, Bill Ring, and Guy Benjamin. None of the five had any coaching experience, and hiring them was a risk. So Walsh was involved in at least two experiments—to see if he still had it as a coach and proving he could develop a coaching staff almost from scratch.

From time to time, the Stanford coaches would hear that other head coaches in the Pacific Ten Conference, of which Stanford was a member, objected to the inexperience of Walsh's staff, complaining that he should have hired men who had put in time in high schools and junior colleges. The word was that Walsh had stolen jobs from coaches who had paid their dues. Walsh had no patience with that reasoning; he believed it was the kind of mediocre thinking that led to mediocre football.

But these were all abstractions that gave Walsh no pleasure when he saw his team in chaos eight days before his debut. Perhaps he could have shrugged off the practice as just a bad day and left it at that, but something else was bothering him, and for this, he had no answer.

He wasn't sure he could depend on his defensive coordinator, Fred vonAppen, a huge man whose voice boomed when he yelled at his players—which, during practice, was often. Walsh personally ran the offense on his teams, down to scripting all the plays and installing them during meetings and in practice. He called every play during games. But Walsh had virtually nothing to do with the day-to-day business of the defense, which he saw as another realm. Throughout his career, Walsh had hired men he trusted to administer his defense, most notably George Seifert with the 49ers. Walsh often admitted that he was at the mercy of his defensive coordinator, and it was essential for him and his defensive coordinator to think alike.

VonAppen had him worried. Walsh believed that his offense, which lacked a powerful running back and deep threats at wide receiver, was incapable of running up the score. He planned to control the ball with modest gains, make a series of first downs to keep the opposing offense off the field, and win enough low-scoring games to make his first season respectable—say seven wins and five losses. He did not believe he could compete in offensive free-for-alls. To complement his offense, Walsh needed a defense that played cautiously and did not surrender many points.

And here was vonAppen taking every conceivable risk during practice. He was sending blitzers after the quarterback on almost every down, leaving crucial parts of the field undefended. Walsh was developing a nervous stomach just watching him. Walsh could see vonAppen's high-risk defense getting burned for big plays, giving up touchdowns all over the place.

That wasn't the worst of it. The way vonAppen was running his defense indicated to Walsh that his defensive coordinator didn't understand the first thing about what Walsh wanted. The season hadn't even started, and there was already a potential schism on the coaching staff. Walsh found himself waking up at four in the morning with a pounding heart. Unable to fall back to sleep, he'd pace around his house until it was time to work.

Walsh considered summoning vonAppen to his office, shutting the door, and setting him straight. But two things held him back. First of all, Walsh had a distaste for direct confrontations. He could blow up during a game, chew out a coach. That seemed natural enough. But he could not premeditate a confrontation. Everything about Walsh was diplomacy and nuance. He expected his coaches to pick up cues from general, seemingly neutral comments he made, and if someone failed to catch on, it meant that that coach hadn't understood the message, was not Walsh's kind of guy.

And vonAppen certainly hadn't gotten the message. Any number of times, Walsh had sat in the staff meeting room in the presence of all the coaches and explained the kind of defense he wanted his team to play. He wouldn't necessarily address his remarks to vonAppen or even look in his direction. VonAppen was supposed to understand. He had worked for Walsh a total of eight years—two at Stanford during Walsh's first term as head coach and six with the 49ers. Walsh had great respect for vonAppen, had hired him because he assumed they would be on the same page. And now this.

Even if Walsh had found it in his nature to confront vonAppen, he saw another problem: Walsh was afraid that if vonAppen felt insulted, believed his coaching philosophy was being criticized, he might quit the staff. At the very least, Walsh was fearful of "losing" him—which meant losing control, having a coordinator who no longer was responsive to the head coach and ran his unit like a separate army. When he worried about vonAppen, Walsh obsessively reminded himself that his defensive coordinator, who was only forty-nine, had had sixteen coaching jobs in twenty-eight years. That was entirely too much change and disruption for a normal coaching career. At times like these, when things seemed blackest to Walsh, he thought about Fred vonAppen and the hot dog incident.

In 1980, vonAppen was an assistant coach on the Green Bay Packers. While Green Bay was losing 38-0 to Denver during a preseason game, one of the Packers players abandoned the sideline, walked over to the stands, and purchased a frankfurter from a vendor. There the player stood, happily munching away during the game. The Packers weren't very good, and vonAppen believed that a player eating a hot dog during a game was symbolic of what was wrong with the squad.

The next day, he told management that the player had to be disciplined for the good of the team. He was assured that the player would be suspended without pay and barred from team meetings for a few days.

Later that morning, vonAppen went to the meeting and the player was there.

When vonAppen walked out to practice, the player was there.

VonAppen quit the Packers that day.

Some of his friends warned him he'd be blackballed in football, and he told himself, if standing on principle led to being blackballed, then the hell with football.

The first person to phone vonAppen after he left the Packers was Walsh, who counseled him not to go through with it. VonAppen said there was no way he would back out of his decision. He holed up in Green Bay with no friends and no job. He was miserable. Walsh called again. He told vonAppen he'd created a scouting position for him with the 49ers. Walsh wanted him to check out the local Wisconsin colleges on weekends and inform the 49ers about any hot prospects. The way vonAppen looked at it, the position was completely phony, and he believed—he was certain—the 49ers would deep-six his reports. But that wasn't the point. Walsh, who at various times has had a reputation as a cold man, as a calculating man, had come to vonAppen's aid. From that moment on, vonAppen pledged unqualified loyalty to him.

Walsh had already tested that loyalty. Before Walsh decided to return to Stanford, vonAppen called to say he'd been offered a job in Green Bay by new head coach Mike Holmgren. VonAppen and Holmgren had worked for Walsh on the 49ers, were part of Walsh's elite little in-group of coaches. Walsh told vonAppen it sounded like a good job and advised him to take it. VonAppen told Holmgren he'd be coming to work for him.

A few days later, Walsh called back, said he had taken the Stanford job. Then he told vonAppen, "I would like you to come to Stanford. I think you should reconsider your move." This put vonAppen in an awkward position with Holmgren, but he went to Stanford anyway. He was fond of saying, "It was like the Godfather thing. The Godfather calls and says he has something for you to do. You can't very well decline."

Walsh understood the intensity of vonAppen's loyalty to him. In his calmer moments, Walsh would call him a "grand guy" and a "great coach." But when Walsh was worried—as he was now—he would recall the hot dog, which represented to him vonAppen's pride and hypersensitivity.

At various times throughout the upcoming season Walsh would agonize about vonAppen, although he never confronted him. The vonAppen episodes were like attacks of malaria that would come over Walsh, ravage him, and then vanish.

Not all the preseason days were gloomy for Walsh. In fact, people who knew him when he ran the 49ers said he hadn't seemed so relaxed in years. He'd first called together his entire squad a few weeks earlier at the Holiday Inn in Palo Alto, which was serving as team headquarters until the players could move into their dorm rooms.

The players assembled in a large conference room and Walsh walked to the podium. Standing before them with his white hair and square jaw, Walsh looked more like the president of a university than a football coach. He told the players that hazing was forbidden on the Stanford team and he ordered the veterans to assimilate the freshmen as quickly as possible. "From this point on, everybody is treated as fully mature. Guys your age have done unbelievable things leading other people in warfare, flying bombers. So I know we can do it."

Walsh's voice bubbled with emotion. His face was flushed and his left hand was a fist. He never thought he'd be doing this again—molding a group, filling a team with fight. "Every player in this room is an extension of the other guys," he said. "So if we have a guy in a given game, he's an extension of all the guys who helped him prepare for the game, even those who may not be able to play themselves. We're all an extension of each other."

At the back of the room former 49ers Bill Ring and Guy Benjamin were smiling. Walsh had said those exact words every year to the 49ers, had explained to Joe Montana and Jerry Rice and Roger Craig that they were extensions of the less famous players. Walsh meant what he said. It wasn't only that he didn't want the star players to become egocentric, to place themselves before the team. That was part of it, but he was also revealing his philosophy of play. When Stanford's fine running back Glyn Milburn was streaking down the field, he had to protect the ball for all his teammates—for the offensive lineman who had thrown the block to free him, for the center who had snapped the ball. When Milburn carried the ball, he was representing everyone else on the team, and Walsh expected him to understand the weight of that responsibility.

"We've got to be so good at what we do, so poised, that our opponents can't shake us up, and we cut them apart," Walsh said in a voice as serious as a minister delivering a sermon. "There's nothing better than that feeling when they're confused. They're mad. They take a swing at us. They're swearing at us. They're in our face because they have no idea what we're doing to them. And often you beat them and they don't know they're going to get beat until the middle of the fourth quarter."

The players listened attentively to Walsh. Some wrote in notebooks. By now they were comfortable in his presence, but it had been different when he took over in January. He'd met the team near the weight room then, and most of the players felt a kind of awe being near him. The atmosphere reminded offensive lineman Chris Dalman of a church.

Walsh had tried to break the ice by telling a joke. "The first time I was head coach at Stanford all the players ran around with their finger in the air shouting, 'We're Number One.'" Walsh held up his middle finger, flipping off the team. "I had to teach them which finger," he said, grinning.

No one laughed and the joke died.

The players were scared to laugh, in case, God forbid, he was serious. "This was Bill Walsh, after all," Dalman later said. "No one wanted to be the guy to stand out."

Walsh left that January meeting shaken. "They don't get my humor," he told his coaches. "I'm afraid I can't get through to them."

But by August he had been with his players half a year, including spring practice, and they had come to understand his humor, and he felt comfortable needling them. To running back J. J. Lasley, Walsh had become just another coach, except that he seemed less authoritarian, more laid-back.

Walsh again gathered his team at the Holiday Inn. He wasn't finished indoctrinating. "In dealing with the press, you want to be cordial and responsive. I suggest keeping it short. Typically, if you take an interview further, you say things that are confidential to your teammates."

Tom Holmoe, first-year coach of the defensive backs, and Bill Ring, first-year running backs coach, were taking notes.

"Let's not let anything happen here in town," Walsh said. "Everyone thinks this is a class football team, so let's not wreck that. When anything bad happens, it's always after two or three beers when you've lost your body fluids from practice. It's happened to all of us."

Walsh was pacing back and forth. The players followed him with their eyes. No one spoke. Walsh took a piece of paper out of his pocket and glanced at it. "This I wrote in 1984 for another team." The coaches smiled. "There are no strata or stars. No special head coach. We are all equals in this together. There will be honest competition between dedicated athletes in this room. Don't worry about it. You'll like it. There will be no taunting the opposition."

Walsh looked up from the paper. "I know Texas A&M will demonstrate after a touchdown better than we can. That has nothing to do with the game. Let them demonstrate. Let's knock the hell out of them.

"In top college football everybody hits. Everybody goes balls-out. When San Jose State comes in, they'll play. Northwestern will feel they're representing the Big Ten. Every school is eager to play, especially early in the season. But can they handle a big win or a big loss? A lot of them can't. They strut and then get the hell beat out of them the next week. We'll handle winning and getting beat better than anyone in college football. If we're not quite in sync, it will be there. Have patience."

Walsh took a breath. "Each week is another season to us. This game is a project in our lives. Right this moment nothing is bigger than playing the seventh-ranked team on national television. After that, it's Oregon. Measure yourselves by each play. Each play is an occurrence in our lives, unique to itself. When it's over, forget it. Go on to the next one.

"Don't be awed by anybody on this team or any other team. For the rest of your lives don't be awed by anybody. Don't be awed by Notre Dame. It's you. We play our game. Don't let competition consume you. Thrive on it."

Walsh left the room, allowing assistant head coach Terry Shea to take over. Walsh leaned against a wall in a hallway containing tables filled with apples, oranges, and ice cream for the players. His eyes were hollow and he looked as tired as an actor who had just poured his heart into *King Lear* on opening night. He lurked in the hallway a few minutes, then went home to bed.

WALSH HAD JUST endured several tumultuous years. He stepped away from the 49ers following the 1988 season, even though he had won his third Super Bowl. There had been problems with 49ers owner Eddie DeBartolo, Jr. In fact, Walsh's relationship with DeBartolo had been strained ever since the 49ers lost to the Vikings in an NFC play-off game a year earlier. The 49ers had finished the 1987 season with a 13-2 record, the best in the league, and everyone assumed they would go to the Super Bowl. DeBartolo had begun to define success as a victory in the Super Bowl, nothing less.

But the Vikings beat the 49ers 36-24 in the playoffs, and it was a humiliating experience for the team. In the second half, Walsh pulled Joe Montana from the game and put in Steve Young, which directly led to a quarterback controversy the following season. After the loss to the Vikings, DeBartolo stripped Walsh of his title as team president and bestowed it on himself. It was DeBartolo's feeling that Walsh was on the verge of burnout from doing too many things—Walsh was 49ers president, general manager, head coach, and offensive coordinator. DeBartolo told Walsh he was merely trying to make things easier for him. Walsh felt insulted.

The 1988 season did not start out well. The 49ers had a 6-3 record, then lost to the Phoenix Cardinals 24-23, although the 49ers led 23-0 midway through the third quarter. The next week the 49ers lost to the Raiders 9-3. It was an awful performance—three points for Walsh's state-of-the-art offensive machine, a pathetic 219 total yards.

A few days later, with the 49ers in third place in the NFC West, their record a disappointing 6-5, Walsh met with DeBartolo at the 49ers' headquarters in Santa Clara and offered to quit on the spot or, if DeBartolo preferred, at the end of the season. DeBartolo didn't tell Walsh he wanted him to resign. He also didn't tell him to stay. They would wait and see.

The 49ers won four of their next five regular season games, beat the Vikings and Bears in the playoffs, and defeated the Bengals 20-16 in Super Bowl XXIII. DeBartolo asked Walsh to stay on as head coach, but Walsh resigned anyway.

He had been at it for ten years with the 49ers and needed relief from the constant pressure to win, which regularly made him ill for most of the season with a combination of sinus infections and stomach upsets. He was worn out from serving as a buffer between the volatile DeBartolo and the players. DeBartolo was capable of great loyalty and generosity—he had made Walsh a wealthy man—but he was growing increasingly emotional, especially after losses, as if he himself had fought and bled on the field. After one defeat he ripped a phone off the locker-room wall as the players looked on amazed. Another time he went after Ron Thomas of the *San Francisco Chronicle* for picking the Chicago Bears to beat the 49ers in a Monday Night game—the Bears won 10-9. Afterward in the locker room, DeBartolo told Thomas, "I don't appreciate what you did in the paper today. If you're going to cover the team, you should pick the team."

Thomas told DeBartolo he was under no obligation to pick the 49ers.

"Ron, don't mess with me," DeBartolo said. "I'll kick your ass."

The worst incident, which became legendary among the writers who covered the 49ers, came in 1986 after the 49ers lost to the Saints 23-10 in New Orleans. Joe Montana, who was recovering from spinal surgery, did not play, and neither did second-string quarterback Jeff Kemp. Walsh was forced to use Mike Moroski, third on the depth chart.

DeBartolo, who watched the end of the game on a television set in the locker room, became so incensed that he threw a full Coke can through the monitor. When the players came into the locker room after the final gun, they saw broken glass on the floor and DeBartolo seething. He told Walsh he wanted to give the team a piece of his mind. They were standing next to the coaches' dressing room, a small cubicle with a glass window on the door. Walsh steered DeBartolo into the dressing room, slammed the door, and told him no way was he going to rip the team, especially after a hard game in which the 49ers had played crippled. Walsh called the 49ers "my team," indicating a clear line of demarcation between the owner and head coach. The assistant coaches began to enter the cubicle but saw what was going on through the door window and stayed out.

DeBartolo told Walsh, "You get your attorney and I'll get mine, and we'll see about your contract." That night Walsh flew back to San Francisco not knowing if he still had a job. The next day, DeBartolo's father called Walsh and smoothed things over. Walsh prevailed on that occasion, but he grew tired of keeping DeBartolo at arm's length.

Walsh had other, more subtle problems, and these involved his assistant coaches, most of whom had been his friends for years. Now their relations were contorted, and Walsh was most aware of that during team dinners.

Professional football teams usually stay at a hotel the night before a game, even if they're playing at home. The players need to attend meetings and gather as a group, and in some cases stay away from temptation and out of trouble. At about six o'clock the players and coaches gather in a hotel ballroom fitted out with large round tables that usually seat eight people. Walsh would go to the food line and get his roast beef and mashed potatoes, and he would then take a seat at one of the tables reserved for coaches. Maybe he would be sipping a margarita from a paper cup. Pretty soon, the other coaches would come in, among them George Seifert, who was an assistant at Stanford when Walsh was head coach in 1977 and 1978, and Bobb McKittrick, who had been at the Chargers with Walsh in 1976, and Denny Green, who had been with Walsh at Stanford in 1977 and 1978, and Fred vonAppen and Bill McPherson and Mike Holmgren. They would have plates of food in their hands and would start walking toward Walsh, but, at the last minute, they'd veer away and sit somewhere else—with good reason. Tension leaked out of Walsh's every pore, and the coaches needed relief.

"I don't resent them for not coming over," Walsh once told an acquaintance. "But I wish they had."

At times, Walsh thought of going to sit with them, but he didn't. "They need to be away from me," he would tell himself.

The only one who sat with Walsh was the 49ers' equipment manager, Bronco Hinek. There they would be, alone at that huge table,

Walsh so grateful for Bronco's presence that he would engage him in long, intimate conversations.

Sitting alone with Bronco, Walsh knew he had come full circle. When he was a young assistant in Cincinnati fifteen years earlier, Walsh would eat in a ballroom fitted out with the same round tables, and team owner and head coach Paul Brown, an irascible old man who years earlier had been identified as a genius just like Walsh, would be sitting by himself. No one, Walsh included, went over to Brown. And now Walsh was the one sitting alone.

"I came to realize the isolation of a leader," he once confessed. "People who write these books about leadership don't write about the terrible price you pay, isolation. By that time I knew I had to get away."

After he decided to leave, Walsh lobbied for his defensive coordinator, George Seifert, to become his successor, even though DeBartolo was intrigued by the idea of hiring Jimmy Johnson from the University of Miami. At the time, most observers remarked on Walsh's loyalty to Seifert. And there is no doubt Walsh was loyal. But there was a feeling that Walsh's motives were more complex. One insider put it this way: "If George succeeded, then Bill could say, 'I groomed him. He's my protégé.' That way Bill could still take the credit for the 49ers' success. If George failed, people could draw the conclusion that Bill was the only one who could lead the 49ers."

Walsh remained with the 49ers for a few months as director of football operations, although he did not have that title. Actually, he didn't have any title at all—or a contract, for that matter. He and DeBartolo made a handshake agreement that Walsh would work month to month overseeing the operation.

But even that unstructured arrangement didn't suit Walsh, whose position in the organization was ambiguous and potentially explosive. Already there was talk that he was scheming behind Seifert's back, and some players had come to him complaining about the coaching staff. He needed to get away, and when NBC offerred him the chance to be their Number One football analyst on telecasts, he jumped.

His final parting from the 49ers was painful, and it proved he was correct to leave. Ronnie Lott, Bubba Paris, and Bruce Collie criticized him publicly. They said he had become distant, impersonal, almost icy. He was like royalty, so far above the players that he rarely spoke to them.

Walsh knew there was truth in what they said. At first he had been a players' coach. Wasn't he the one who'd dressed up in a bellhop's uniform and grabbed the players' bags as they got off a bus for their first Super Bowl in Pontiac, Michigan? But over the years such behavior had become inconceivable.

Lott also complained that Walsh was secretive about his retirement, never told the players he planned to leave.

He *had* been secretive. He didn't want to make that last Super Bowl an homage to Bill Walsh, a media extravanganza.

When all this criticism began to appear in the newspapers, Walsh expected someone in the 49ers organization to stand up before the team and say, "Bullshit, you don't talk about Bill Walsh like that." But no one did. "Had I been there, if someone said something about George Seifert or even Eddie DeBartolo, who I had to defend all the time, I'd have stopped it," Walsh once said. "They failed to stand up for me, and they could have done it so easily."

The bitterness of his last few years with the 49ers continued to consume Walsh even after he returned to Stanford. Instead of rejoicing in his achievements, he often found himself dwelling on small, even petty, hurts. For a time, this poisoned his memory of the team he had created.

Walsh assumed broadcasting would be a relaxing alternative to the life of an NFL head coach. He'd only work on weekends, and the rest of the time he'd be semi-retired, playing tennis and golf and enjoying the fruits of his fabulous career. But the three years he spent at NBC became a living death. From the beginning, the network complained about his voice, which sometimes came across the airwaves as tinny and lacking in emotion. Walsh took voice lessons to improve.

On Mondays, Walsh would return to his office in Menlo Park, a few miles from the Stanford campus, and wait for someone from the network to call with criticisms about his tie or his voice, or to grumble about ratings. After he hung up the phone, Walsh often sat with the lights off, staring into space.

NBC wanted him to tell funny anecdotes about his years in football. Walsh can be funny, but he is not a stand-up comedian. He uses irony. He is a verbal counterpuncher. In a room of ten people, he delivers the undercutting remark with a twinkle in his eye, and people laugh. But on the air, Walsh came off rarefied, almost didactic. When he told jokes, he seemed to be trying too hard.

Television requires a broader kind of humor than Walsh provided. Television requires John Madden shouting "Oops!" or "Boom!" Talkative, loud, chubby, folksy John Madden and Middle America were made for each other. Walsh, who seemed like a refugee from a think tank, didn't have an "Oops!" or a "Boom!" and Middle America didn't know what to make of him.

Given time, Walsh might have been able to come up with anecdotes, but he never wanted to. For him, football was not funny stories. It was an art form, his passion. He wanted to explain strategy on the air, the beauty of a trap play at the line of scrimmage, but whenever he'd begin to analyze what was happening on the field, a voice in his headset began buzzing about amusing anecdotes. Walsh felt as if they wanted him to be Jack Benny.

On weekends, Walsh found himself hanging out with executives from NBC, not football people. He was cut off from his life source, had become as frustrated as a harem eunuch: a coach who couldn't coach. His entire adult life had been devoted to drawing up offensive plays, but now he could not even fantasize about designing formations and pass routes. What was the point?

"It's like when someone in prison doesn't draw pictures of his favorite cars," Walsh said after leaving NBC.

Walsh was always bored with announcing, took no pride in it. In his three years with the network, he never watched a tape of his telecasts. At times, Walsh wanted to tell the NBC executives just how he would do the broadcasts. But he never did. He is assertive in the world he knows—football. In other contexts, he can be curiously passive. While at NBC, he would frequently call friends and complain, "Television is not my arena." With the 49ers, Walsh might blow up at any minute. At NBC, he allowed himself to be pushed around. When he wanted to run an off-season quarterbacks' camp, just to dabble in his element, NBC said no. Walsh acquiesced.

At one press conference, an NBC executive remarked publicly that Walsh was "improving." This was during Walsh's third year at the network. Walsh thought he had already arrived, that his work was just fine. Walsh came home and got on the phone to several friends. "Am I some kind of neophyte that I'm improving?" he asked in a voice shaking with emotion.

Jeff Saal, one of the Stanford doctors, examined Walsh during this time and was alarmed at Walsh's condition. Walsh was so tense it seemed to Saal that he might explode. He advised Walsh to make drastic changes in his life. A few months after Walsh had taken the Stanford job, Saal saw a different person. The color had come back to Walsh's skin and the fire had returned to his eyes. Saal believes leaving NBC and returning to Stanford prolonged Walsh's life.

During Walsh's third year at NBC, the Tampa Bay Buccaneers expressed an interest in having him run their football operation and become head coach. Walsh said he would consider the job, but NBC asked Walsh not to speak about the offer on the air. Walsh spoke about it.

After that he phoned NBC to apologize. His executive producer refused to take his calls for almost a week, and the relationship became chilly.

Late in the 1991 season, Walsh was sitting in the television booth at Candlestick Park just before kickoff, working on last-minute details for a broadcast, when he got a call from an NBC producer in New York directing him to interview Joe Montana, who was not playing because of injury. Montana was mulling over his future and had made it known that he refused to speak to the media. Journalists and television people from all over the country were trying to leverage interviews with Montana through Walsh. Even television reporter Maria Shriver, part of the Kennedy clan, had asked Walsh to help set up a Montana interview. Walsh never cooperated with these requests.

But now NBC had ordered him to interview Montana, and Walsh was caught between conflicting loyalties to his employer and the great quarterback who had been his pupil. Walsh's deepest code of behavior told him that Montana was family. They had gone through the wars together, while he wasn't even sure if he and NBC were on the same side or how loyal the network would be to him in a crisis. He respected Montana, believed he deserved his privacy while he healed.

In his reluctance to approach Montana, Walsh was thinking like a football man. The problem was—and this became painfully clear to him at this moment—he no longer was a football man. He was an announcer, wearing a suit, a tie, and loafers. He was being paid by NBC, not the 49ers.

So Walsh took the press elevator downstairs, walked across the field and into the 49ers' locker room, where he no longer felt comfortable. Montana refused to let Walsh interview him.

Walsh went back up to the booth, called New York, and explained what had happened. He assumed that would be the end of the issue.

He received another call from NBC. "You owe us one," he was told. "If you don't do this, your ass will be in a sling."

Twelve minutes remained before the broadcast, and Walsh had things to prepare. Still, he took his time, walking slowly to Ed DeBartolo's private box, where Montana would be watching the game. On the way, he kept telling himself he was the top football analyst at his network, not some flunky errand boy. As he approached the door to the box, he hesitated. "Madden wouldn't have to do this," he said to himself bitterly.

Montana refused Walsh a second time.

Walsh walked back to the booth and sat down. He picked up the phone and told NBC what it didn't want to hear. He couldn't deliver Montana. A voice over the phone said, "Did you talk to him?" As if Walsh had been lying.

After that, things changed. Terry O'Neil, executive producer of NBC sports, flew out to the Bay Area from New York, took a motel room, and arranged to have lunch with Walsh. O'Neil told him he was no longer the Number One analyst. Walsh assumed this was a subtle way of firing him—that he would be so upset by the demotion he'd quit.

By now, it didn't matter. Walsh already was in serious talks with the 49ers.

A few months earlier, he had gone to dinner with DeBartolo, and the 49ers' owner talked to him about returning to the organization. At the time, the conversation was casual. DeBartolo phoned team president Carmen Policy and said Walsh might ease his way back into the 49ers in a low-profile capacity. DeBartolo told Policy that Walsh had assured him he'd have no problem working for Policy.

"Can you imagine Bill Walsh working for me or working for anybody?" Policy gasped. "You can't be serious."

But DeBartolo was dead serious. He told Policy that Walsh didn't want the pressure of coaching or of running an organization. They had talked about his returning as a consultant. DeBartolo told Policy, "I don't know that I could say no to Bill, to the guy who put together the franchise."

Policy believed DeBartolo was motivated by more than loyalty. DeBartolo was worried about the team. The 49ers had begun the 1991 season poorly, and DeBartolo was concerned that the 49ers' staff was not strong at evaluating personnel. Walsh always had been brilliant at drafting and trading. He was an extraordinary coach, but he may even have been more gifted at spotting and developing talent. The list of his football draft picks is dazzling: He got Joe Montana in the third round, Dwight Clark in the tenth, and then there were Ronnie Lott, Roger Craig, John Taylor, Steve Wallace, Eric Wright, and Harris Barton. After Walsh left, the 49ers' drafts had been ordinary.

Policy was fairly certain Walsh would return to the 49ers if the team could find a place for him: "Bill wanted out of broadcasting. Bill wanted back into football, and Bill wanted to stay in Northern California." But the more Policy thought about Walsh, the more problems he ran into. Basic problems. Like, which office would Walsh occupy? Would Policy have to move someone out, or would Walsh function as an outside consultant, working from his own office in Menlo Park and visiting the facility in Santa Clara just like the team doctors? Walsh could be the 49ers' "football operations doctor." The concept amused Policy.

In another scenario, Walsh could be an on-site consultant with his own office and secretary, an independent contractor working in the building.

However he tried to find a place for Walsh, Policy kept running into the fact that Walsh "cast such a large shadow." He was becoming worried. But not DeBartolo. As time passed, DeBartolo decided he absolutely needed Walsh. The 49ers had just missed the playoffs for the first time in nine years, and DeBartolo was desperate for new leadership. "If it can't work," he told Policy, "you're going to have to use whatever finesse you can to explain to Bill that it won't work. If it will work, let's go with it."

Policy decided Walsh couldn't be associated with the 49ers merely in a ceremonial capacity. He had to work on the premises twelve months a year, answerable only to Policy. To explain Walsh's role, Policy came up with a metaphor. Walsh would be separate from the other coaches and administrators, but he'd be available to them like a reservoir. The department heads could go to the reservoir and draw from the water of knowledge as often as they liked.

But when Policy thought about the reservoir, the water of knowledge kept spilling down the halls of the 49ers' headquarters, flooding the stairs, inundating the other executives and the coaches. No matter how carefully he might try to structure Walsh's duties, "Bill just flows over all that," Policy told himself. He was afraid that Walsh would drown everyone else in the organization, even if he didn't intend to.

Policy and Walsh met several times at Walsh's Menlo Park office, never at the 49ers' facility. If it had come out that Policy was talking to Walsh, people in the organization might have drawn the conclusion that management was panicking, desperately seeking a savior. Policy also met continuously with head coach George Seifert, who felt threatened by the idea of Walsh's return. Seifert wondered what would happen to his authority with Walsh in the building. Policy was trying to establish a balance between Walsh's ego and Seifert's ego, but it was hard work.

One day DeBartolo called Policy and said, "What do you think?"

Policy answered, "I think it's capable of causing havoc. It wouldn't be Bill's fault and it wouldn't be the organization's fault. It's just the mixture of elements—it's the chemistry. You have one element that's stable and proper and nonharmful, and mix it with another similar element, and the two of them are capable of causing a reaction that's volatile. I just fear that this is a distinct possibility."

"Well, are you going to deep-six it?" DeBartolo asked.

"I don't know," Policy said. "I don't think I can do that either."

Walsh remembers things differently. According to him, an informal agreement was reached that Policy would take care of the financial and legal aspects of the franchise. Walsh would be responsible for all football operations, except coaching, which would be Seifert's domain. Walsh never thought he would be a mere consultant.

Walsh had no doubt that his appointment as the 49ers' football czar would make Seifert uncomfortable. The players might think Walsh was making the football decisions, and this could dilute Seifert's power, but it didn't bother Walsh a bit if Seifert felt edgy. It might do Seifert good to confront his own shortcomings—that he was not as skillful as Walsh in acquiring personnel, and needed help. Walsh was sure Seifert would come to understand he was no threat.

But it was not that easy. Seifert began to fear that Walsh would be working behind the scenes, getting Policy's ear, maneuvering for more power. Seifert met with Policy and DeBartolo, and the next thing Walsh knew, DeBartolo pulled back on his commitment to him, started talking about Walsh coming in as a consultant. Seifert, not Walsh, would have the final say about the roster. To Walsh, this was unworkable. If Seifert had final say, then Walsh couldn't make a trade unless he got Seifert's permission, and if he had to ask Seifert's permission, then Seifert's judgments, not Walsh's, would make the difference. The whole thing seemed cockeyed.

It became obvious to Walsh that he would be the one always making concessions. This made no sense to him. He was still viable in the NFL. In addition to Tampa Bay, the Vikings and Eagles had offered him jobs as general manager and coach in the last few years, and he didn't see why he should return to the 49ers as a petitioner.

And then, in one reckless, dramatic moment, Walsh slammed shut the door at the 49ers—perhaps intentionally, perhaps unconsciously.

He was in Buffalo to broadcast the AFC championship game between the Bills and the Denver Broncos on Sunday, January 12, 1992, when he ran into Ira Miller of the *San Francisco Chronicle*. Even though he had not officially been hired by the 49ers, Walsh spoke on the record about what the team needed. He said keeping Joe Montana, Steve Young, and Steve Bono on the same team could be "a major distraction." He said Montana and Young had a "semi-frosty relationship," which was not good for team morale. He suggested trading Young. He said the 49ers' first priority would be to get a quality running back. With such a back the 49ers would be playing in the NFC championship game instead of watching it on television.

Walsh was speaking like a team president, not a part-time consultant, but he didn't care. NBC had changed its mind and indicated he could come back as the Number One analyst. The network would even let him run his quarterbacks' camp. So he had a job.

As he looked back months later on the interview with Miller, he said, "In my remarks with Ira I just said some things I felt. My intent was to lay it on the table for the 49ers. If the response wasn't real positive and supportive, well, then it was easy for me to decide not to go back, because at some point it had to be stated where I would be as part of the 49ers. There just wasn't a way I could go back as a consultant who would come in and work four hours a day and sit in my office and be available if someone had a question. I wasn't ready for that. If I were ten years older that would have been an ideal kind of work. But I had far too much energy and vigor and competence to be able to do that. I had to test the waters, test how I felt. If they didn't respond well, that would be OK."

It's safe to say the 49ers didn't respond well. They were furious. Policy and Seifert specifically had asked Walsh not to act as a spokesman for the team, and they thought Walsh had agreed. And now he had shot off his mouth, before he'd even signed on with the organization. He had acted out their worst fears, giving Policy and Seifert the feeling there was no way they could control him.

Seifert stormed into Policy's office after he saw Miller's article. Policy suggested Seifert and Walsh meet with no one else present, to see if they could work things out. By now, though, Policy was completely pessimistic. He told himself that despite Walsh's talent, bringing him back would be a "lose situation." Still, he did not want to call off the deal. Either Walsh or Seifert had to call it off.

Policy was reasonably sure one of them would, probably Walsh. He perceived Walsh as being hurt that Seifert hadn't welcomed him back with open arms. "I think Bill felt like, 'I was his coach. I'm the guy who brought him along. There were people who said George would never make a good head coach—he's too narrow.' I think Bill was just hurt."

When Walsh returned from Buffalo, he phoned Seifert. With his voice breaking, Seifert said he had been lying in bed the previous night watching the news when a sportscaster said Walsh was taking over the team. Then he woke up and read Miller's story.

"Am I the coach or what?" Seifert asked.

Walsh invited Seifert to lunch. Walsh drove down to Santa Clara, and on the way, as he liked to explain later, he experienced an epiphany, his entire future flashing before him whole and complete. Dennis Green had just announced he was leaving Stanford to become head coach of the Minnesota Vikings, and it hit Walsh like a surge of electricity that *he* wanted to be Stanford's new coach. He was surprised at the intensity of his desire; he hadn't felt this serious about a project since his last Super Bowl season. He saw himself aided by Terry Shea, the head coach at San Jose State, whom he would lure to Stanford by bestowing on him the title of Assistant Head Coach.

"Goddamn, with Terry Shea working with me at Stanford, it would be a bridge back to college football," Walsh said out loud. "Terry Shea could be the bridge. He can join me, and then I'll get some of my original guys. I can get Keena and Tom and Mike. I'll get Fred."

So now a new Walsh, fresh from a freeway conversion, went to meet Seifert at a local delicatessen. Seifert looked terrible. Feeling euphoric after his decision to go to Stanford, Walsh walked over to his old friend and put his arm around his shoulder. Shocked at Seifert's appearance, struggling for a way to break the ice, he heard himself saying, "George, why don't you have some fun? Right now. Go home to your wife and take the phone off the hook. Relax. For God's sake don't let this bother you."

As Walsh remembers the scene, Seifert laughed. But then Seifert said the strangest thing. "If you want to be the coach, Bill, I'll step away."

Walsh looked at him as if he were crazy. Walsh said coaching the 49ers was the last thing he wanted to do. "You know what, George? I'm thinking of going back to Stanford."

Walsh is sure Seifert never heard what he said, and that he left the meeting convinced Walsh was campaigning for his job.

Meanwhile things were happening at Stanford. Walsh had remained close to the university while he was at the 49ers and NBC. The previous year Stanford had asked him to be athletic director, but Walsh declined. And just a few days earlier, Stanford supporter Tom Ford had asked Walsh to recommend a new head coach. Walsh suggested Terry Shea, and then blurted out, "Don't forget me."

Ford was flabbergasted. He asked if Walsh was serious, and Walsh, stunned by what had just popped out of his mouth, said he needed time to think it over. Then Walsh flew off to Buffalo to announce the AFC championship and spill his guts to Miller about what changes the 49ers needed to make.

Thinking about the meeting with Ford several months later, Walsh said, "It was almost like I was propelling myself toward Stanford. I was forcing myself to consider the job."

While Walsh was flying to Buffalo, Ford was on the phone with Stanford athletic director Ted Leland, who was on the verge of hiring a new head football coach. Ford breathlessly told Leland to put everything on hold. There was a chance Walsh might come back.

When Walsh returned from his lunch with Seifert, Leland was at his house discussing the Stanford job with Geri, who wasn't sure her husband should go back to coaching. Walsh told Leland he wanted to see his old office again. Leland drove Walsh to the Stanford Athletic Department, and they walked up the dark stairs, through the huge double doors into the football offices. Walsh walked into the conference room and gazed at the long table and the greaseboards where he had drawn plays so many years before. He headed for his old office, but Green was there packing up, and Walsh and Leland quietly left the building.

Stanford made a formal offer the next day. Leland was surprised that Walsh agreed to the first figure, didn't even try to negotiate. The salary was $350,000, laughable compared to the million he was making at NBC. Stanford also threw in a forgivable loan to help with the remodeling of Walsh's new home.

On January 16, 1992, only three days after Miller's article appeared, Stanford held a press conference at the school's Burnham Pavilion announcing Walsh's return. It was like a coronation. A captivated crowd of six hundred Cardinal alumni, fans, and employees had turned out, including about seventy-five reporters from all over the country. It was larger than the crowd that had come to see Mikhail Gorbachev at Stanford a few months earlier. Walsh walked past them, got up to speak on a makeshift platform, and, quoting Joseph Campbell, said, "This is my bliss." His face glowed. He was in his element. He had come home.

Sitting in the front row were Carmen Policy, George Seifert, and Eddie DeBartolo, Jr. They were smiling broadly—probably with relief.

C H A P T E R

3

WALSH'S FIRST TEST would come August 26 against Texas A&M at the Disneyland Pigskin Classic. It was the earliest college football game in the country, and it would give him a chance to evaluate his personnel, his staff, and himself—to find out just how much he had left after three years as a civilian.

The Texas A&M Aggies were the seventh-ranked team in the country, and although their offense was primitive by Walsh's standards, they had a fast, mobile defense that might give Stanford's offense trouble. Throughout training camp Walsh complained about the scarcity of good athletes on his offensive unit—a theme he would revert to before every game of the season.

A few days before Stanford was scheduled to fly to Anaheim, Walsh held his team's first practice in Stanford Stadium. The Cardinal had been working out for several weeks on Stanford's three practice fields, but today Walsh wanted a run-through simulating game conditions. That meant he would be putting on the headphones, standing on the sideline, and talking to Terry Shea, who would be up in the press box going over offensive calls with Walsh.

The team left the gym and walked a quarter of a mile to the stadium past eucalyptus groves where tailgaters partied on game days. This is "The Walk," traditional at Stanford. Bob Mathias did it and so did John Brodie and Jim Plunkett and John Elway.

It was a glorious sunny day, dry and warm. When they arrived at the stadium, Walsh gathered his players outside their locker room. He began to jump up and down like a boxer limbering up before a fight. He turned to his players. He hadn't planned on saying anything, but he was overcome with the joy of the moment. "I want you to smile before you go on the field," he said. "This is not a grim team."

His mind skipped back to the last time he had stood in that place, another team gathered around him. It was January 20, 1985, and the San Francisco 49ers were about to crush the Miami Dolphins 38-16 in Super Bowl XIX. "We once stood here before a Super Bowl," he said. "We were smiling and jumping up and down. The other team was grim and, of course, we killed them."

The Cardinal players ran onto the field, Walsh jogging after them. He jogged awkwardly, raising his knees high, pumping his arms like someone with arthritis trying to imitate Roger Craig. He jogged to the sideline, put on the headset, and began calling out situations to his players and coaches. Punt. Holding on the right tackle. Fourth and one.

For an hour, Walsh prowled the perimeter of the field, snapping his fingers with excitement and talking a mile a minute to Shea in the press box. It was Walsh in the one universe he completely understood, his head filled with the beloved sounds of football.

For as long as Walsh could remember, his imagination had been like a fountain. Football plays kept gushing and gurgling to the surface of his consciousness, and it was his gift and his curse that he could not turn off the flow. He used to tell a story of going to dinner with Geri. He affectionately put his arm around her shoulder. Suddenly he thought of a new play and began to punch it out with his fingers like a code on her back. When he was done, Geri turned to him and asked, "Did it work?"

Other times, he'd be sitting in restaurants with her and close friends, and inevitably he'd drop out of the conversation because the fountain was flooding and he had to draw up a new play before he lost it. Sometimes he didn't have a pen, so he'd grab his fork and start pressing tiny dots into the tablecloth while his friends stared in amusement.

When he took the NBC job the fountain went dry. No new plays flowed. But after Walsh returned to Stanford, the fountain gushed again. Quarterback Steve Stenstrom saw it firsthand when he and Walsh attended a banquet together. Stenstrom got up to speak first, and when he finished, he sat down, and then Walsh went to the microphone. Stenstrom noticed Walsh's napkin. While Stenstrom was speaking, Walsh had drawn two plays on it.

* * *

On August 22, Walsh planned to bring the team to the stadium one more time. It was a Saturday, the day before the Cardinal would fly to Anaheim, and Walsh wanted to reexperience the excitement of the stadium, but he also had a practical reason: He wanted privacy. Only one of Stanford's practice fields is closed to the public. The others are surrounded by short chain-link fences, and everything that goes on during practice is completely visible to anyone who wanders by. Each day, spectators lured by the thrill of seeing Walsh would drive up in cars, pull out lawn chairs, and relax near the sidelines. Walsh was certain that Texas A&M coach R. C. Slocum had dispatched a spy to sit among the retirees and the sunbathers and the executives on lunch break to dope out Stanford's game plan. Walsh did not fault Slocum for this. He wouldn't have respected the A&M coach if he let a perfect setup slip through his fingers. "Their coach would be childlike not to have someone at our practice taking notes," Walsh told his coaches. "I'd sure as hell do it. He'd be a real gentleman not to."

When Stanford practiced, administrative assistant Al Matthews constantly eyed the sidelines for someone who looked suspicious. One day, he spotted a man behind a truck taking notes. He ran over and asked to see the man's notebook. It contained Stanford formations. Matthews ordered the man to leave. A few minutes later, the man returned with Stanford Sports Information Director Gary Migdol, who verified that he was a sportswriter from Houston. Matthews said he could stay if he didn't take notes.

Walsh entertained fantasies of sending one of his own staff members as a secret agent to Texas A&M. But when he played out the scenario in his mind, the whole thing seemed unrealistic. First of all, the Aggies' workouts were closed to the public. But even if they weren't, Walsh saw other problems. The minute someone with a California credit card checked into a hotel in College Station, Texas, word would get around that a Stanford scout was in town.

But he had been busy in other ways. The previous May, he'd sent Terry Shea and offensive line coach Scott Schuhmann to confer with the coaching staff at Florida State. The Seminoles had beaten A&M 10-2 in the last Cotton Bowl, and Walsh wanted to make sure he knew how they prepared for the game.

Gene Washington, a former wide receiver at Stanford and for the 49ers, and now a special assistant to Athletic Director Ted Leland, was amused when Walsh dispatched Shea and Schuhmann to Florida. Walsh was publicly portraying himself as an older man who'd stopped at a way station on the road to retirement. In the newspapers, stories proclaimed how "laid-back" Walsh appeared. The truth was he already had been working four months on the A&M game plan. "Bill wants to kick their ass," Washington said.

Before Walsh took his team to Stanford Stadium, he met with his coaches in the conference room and explained he was going to work on two-minute drills, the no-huddle offense, plays in the red zone (inside the twenty-yard line), and two-point conversions. Then he thought of something, looked over at Terry Shea and asked, "Is there a twenty-five-second clock in college football that you see?"

Shea said there was.

Walsh gathered the players in the Hall of Fame Room, the football team's primary meeting room, a long, dark, narrow oblong space, its walls covered with black-and-white photos of Stanford football greats—Glenn "Pop" Warner, Ernie Nevers, Darrin Nelson, Brad Muster, Jim Plunkett. A crew of Pacific-10 officials was there to explain various new rules to the players and then work the practice under game conditions. Before Walsh spoke, Pat Marcuccillo, the Stanford equipment manager, addressed the team. Marcuccillo was normally a soft-spoken, businesslike man, but today he was boiling. When he spoke, his voice was a shout, his face the color of uncooked liver. "There are only thirty-eight lockers in Anaheim. I don't give a shit what year you're in, I give out the lockers. I'm tired of seeing you kick each other's ass. Now I want to see you go out and kick somebody else's ass."

When Marcuccillo was done, Walsh walked slowly from the back of the room to the front and ascended the stage, which was raised about a foot above the floor. He was grinning.

"That was Pat, our equipment man," he said dryly.

The remark was addressed to the players and the Pac-10 officials, and it was a comment on Marcuccillo's overheated rhetoric. Walsh almost never gave speeches like that. He believed a team was in trouble if it had to work itself up to play a football game. Walsh always stressed what he called "our standard of play," and that involved unemotional precision.

The head official, dressed in striped shirt and cap, joined Walsh on the stage. He said players were forbidden to shoot anyone after a big play. He held out his forefinger like a pistol and pretended to put a bullet into the head of Steve Stenstrom, who was sitting in the front row. The official said all taunting was forbidden. "And don't do a dance," he said. "When you score a touchdown, put the ball down and go back to the huddle."

"What if the coach does a dance?" Walsh said, grinning.

The official chuckled, but he didn't answer. He said players couldn't wear bandannas.

Walsh interrupted again. "The nine other Pac-10 coaches don't want bandannas," he told the players. "They voted against them, so I raised my hand, too."

And so it went. Walsh was impish because he wanted his team relaxed. He'd already established a series of gags related to the stage in the Hall of Fame Room. Sometimes he would walk up to the stage and trip on purpose, or go over to the edge and pretend to do a swan dive, or fall to one knee and spread his arms like Al Jolson. He tried to cut tension with humor, but if his manner in public was carefree, in his private moments, he worried. It wasn't only that he was unsure about himself—if he still could think quickly under game conditions, if he had the stamina to run the offense for three hours. He also had doubts about his team, which, all things considered, was odd, because Dennis Green had left him with a fine squad with sixteen veteran starters.

The season before Green arrived on campus, Stanford's record was 3-6-2, but under Green, progress was steady. In 1989 the Cardinal was 3-8, the next year, 5-6, and in Green's last year the team went 8-4 and was invited to the Aloha Bowl, losing to Georgia Tech 18-17. It was Stanford's first bowl appearance since 1986. Green drove his team hard; he would yell at players on the field and at his coaches in the conference room.

But the team leaders—Glyn Milburn, Ron George, Tom Williams, Estevan Avila—worshiped Green because he had transformed them from losers into winners by the sheer force of his will. They were confident about the Cardinal and expected to play in the Rose Bowl on January first.

Walsh wasn't so sure. Here he was, the so-called guru of the passing game, and he didn't have one wide receiver fast enough to outrun the coverage. When he thought about his split ends and flankers, which was often, he would tell himself that defenders intuitively would know they could handle the Stanford receivers. Walsh liked to make an analogy to basketball. "You're guarding someone and, suddenly, it dawns on you that the man can't beat you to the hoop. When that happens, he's yours."

Walsh preferred to extend the football field by having a player like Jerry Rice who could go deep, and now the field was shrinking on him. Four men were competing for the two starting spots at wide receiver, and among them they had caught only fourteen passes the previous season. Not one had caught a touchdown pass.

Running back was only slightly more promising. All-American fullback Tommy Vardell, who'd rushed for 1,084 yards the previous season, was now a rookie with the Cleveland Browns. J. J. Lasley had taken over for Vardell, but Lasley was undersize for a fullback, and his backup, Ellery Roberts, had missed the entire 1991 season because of neck surgery. Walsh didn't know if Roberts could hold up to the constant hitting at the line of scrimmage.

He had more confidence in his halfback Glyn Milburn, the one legitimate star on his offense. Milburn had breakaway speed and brilliant moves, but he was only 5-9, 175 pounds, and Walsh perceived him as vulnerable. The previous season, Dennis Green had shifted the focus of the offense from Milburn to Vardell, and now Milburn had something to prove.

When he looked at his team dispassionately, Walsh wondered if he'd be able to win half his games. Fred vonAppen, a habitual worrier like Walsh, was painfully aware of the lack of depth on his defense, and in the last few weeks, he obsessively told the press and anyone else who would listen, "We're one or two injuries away from being average."

In the three days the Cardinal spent in Anaheim before the Pigskin Classic, Walsh participated in five press conferences, a parade down Disneyland's Main Street USA, and a Kiwanis kickoff luncheon at the Disneyland Hotel. He shook hands with Mickey Mouse, sat next to Goofy dressed as a football referee, and spoke to the press outside Sleeping Beauty's Castle.

As he rode back to the hotel one day after making several public appearances, he fell asleep in the backseat of his car. He seemed fragile. Walsh's face could look like two different faces. From the front, he had a square jaw and rugged lines around his mouth and along his cheeks, which made him appear weathered and tough. But from the side, he sometimes looked tired and sixty years old. In Anaheim he had on his fragile face.

He privately complained about the demands on his time: "I feel uneasy sometimes because I don't like the idea of working the room or being a politician or a public relations man. But I'm sort of forced to represent the university. So I do far more things now with the public and the press than I ever did with San Francisco. I don't want to be too quotable. I don't want to be too visible. But in this game, to sell tickets, you have to do everything that is requested. And I don't do it grudgingly, I just do it. But I'd hate to think that for the next game I'll have to go through anything like this. I can't do it. I feel guilty just leaning back in bed for ten minutes. That's the downside of coming back, the hype."

At dinner the night before the game, Walsh alternated between euphoria and worry. Over coffee, he said to Terry Shea, "Well, I think we're prepared. I think we've done everything we can do. Do you think we're prepared? Do you think we've done everything we can do?"

Shea said he was sure they had.

Then the team filed into a meeting in a large ballroom in the hotel. This would be the last meeting before everyone arrived at the stadium the next afternoon, and Walsh wanted to set the tone for the game and then go over the first twenty offensive plays. During the last few weeks he'd installed thirty pass plays and twenty run plays. That might seem like a manageable number, but in his offense each play could be run out of four or five formations, and that meant the team had to memorize upward of two hundred plays. With the 49ers it would be double that amount. Some coaches believed it was better to limit the number of plays to ensure that the team could execute them perfectly. To Walsh that was uninteresting. He insisted on stretching the capacities of his players, thinking they'd eventually rise to another level if that's what was required of them.

By scripting the first twenty plays as he had done with the 49ers—the first would be a pass to Glyn Milburn—Walsh took a burden off his team, limited what they were responsible for, at least in the early part of the game. He also intended to use the scripted plays to test the A&M defense. He would run his first four plays out of entirely different formations to see how the A&M defensive coordinator reacted, to see if he'd react at all. He expected to force A&M to adjust to one play while it was confronted with the next, and then to adjust to the next when Walsh sprang something entirely different. Walsh literally wanted to put A&M on the defensive. At least, that was the theory.

At the team meeting, Walsh gave his usual pep talk. "So we understand how we play the game. Every week there's a standard of performance that we have, come hell or high water. No matter what the score is we keep the pressure on, and everybody goes balls-out until the last play of the game. If you're a backup, don't go in with a sort of tepid feeling about playing football—'I wasn't supposed to play. The coach didn't say anything to me all week and here I am. I don't know what I'm doing.' Bullshit."

Walsh walked to the side, and Fred vonAppen announced he was going to show a film of defensive highlights from the previous season. "It won't go to the Cannes Film Festival," vonAppen said. Accompanied by the rock song "Takin' Care of Business," the film showed the Stanford defense making bone-crushing hits on the University of California, USC, UCLA, and other Stanford rivals. Each time an opponent went down, the Cardinal players cheered hysterically and leaped out of their seats. When the lights came on again, Walsh stood with his back to the team, and it was a while before he could speak. Finally he said, "We're not bad, are we? We're pretty darn good. These guys will find out tomorrow."

The defense filed out, and Terry Shea read the game-day schedule to the offense. Walsh walked to the back of the room, sat wearily in a chair. He hung his head and stared at the floor. A few minutes later, he looked up at a friend sitting near him. Walsh's mouth was dry.

"My nerves are shot from football," he whispered in a tone of disgust. "It's not that I can't stand up to the pressure. I can. It's when things are going well that I have a problem. I get sentimental and maudlin. Like after that film. I had tears in my eyes. I couldn't speak to the team."

"Is that bad?" his friend asked.

"Well, if I start crying before the first game, they'd wonder, 'What's wrong with this guy? Oh, he's off his rocker. That's why he's here.' It might be OK if I did it once, like after the last game."

The idea of crying before the first game suddenly struck Walsh as absurd, and he began giggling uncontrollably, his shoulders shaking. Some of the players turned around to see where the noise was coming from. The giggling was bothering Shea, who stared at Walsh. Walsh lowered his head like a mischievous schoolboy and tried to pull himself together.

This was not the first time he had been overwhelmed by nerves. When he finally made up his mind to return to Stanford, he broke down in his living room and cried in Geri's arms. When the sobbing subsided, his daughter Elizabeth, an undergraduate at the University of Colorado, walked into the room. Walsh told her of his decision and broke down all over again. Elizabeth had to comfort him.

Walsh felt embarrassed about his lack of control but could do nothing about it. He believed all those years of calling plays and cutting players and managing the press and fencing with Ed DeBartolo had affected his nerve fibers. He resigned himself to crying at inappropriate times.

The coaches ate lunch silently the next day. They sat in a big room while Walsh roamed from table to table trying to keep up their spirits. Fred vonAppen was reading a piece of paper. "You want to see a telegram from an interested parent?" he asked Terry Shea. The telegram said: I HOPE YOU GUYS HAVE A GREAT FIRST GAME OF THE YEAR. I KNOW YOU HAVE WORKED HARD. WILL BE WATCHING AND PULLING FOR YOU. It was from Joe Gibbs, head coach of the Washington Redskins. His son Coy was a linebacker for the Cardinal.

VonAppen put away the telegram. "You go over all these scenarios," he said to the others. "What if we can't stop them?"

No one answered. Running backs coach Bill Ring, who routinely vomited before 49er games, looked as if he might dash to the bathroom. "This is the part I hate the most," vonAppen said. "There's nothing you can do anymore."

Walsh sat down next to vonAppen. "What are you doing tomorrow?" Walsh asked in a serious voice. "Cleaning out the garage?" Then he left. VonAppen smiled. He'd seen that particular manifestation of nerves before. Walsh was projecting right past the game and into the next day.

VonAppen walked into the hotel lobby where Stanford supporters, all wearing red, milled about. VonAppen called them the Lobby Team. "All the boosters, trainers, equipment people, assistant athletic directors—it's nice, but it's superficial. They try to give us strength, but the strength comes from within. We teach the team you can't get strength from the outside. Finally only the players are accountable and we coaches who line them up."

Next to Walsh, vonAppen was the most complex member of the coaching staff. He looked tough and mean and, with his huge, wide body, could have passed for Mike Ditka's younger cousin. During practice, he wore his cap with the bill in the back and would routinely scream, "You're pissing my ass off!" His voice sounded like tires on gravel.

The Stanford defensive players, some of whom vonAppen had coached in 1989, the last time he was part of a Stanford staff, gladly would walk through a wall for him. He was fair and honest and he kept returning to Stanford—this was his fourth tour of duty—because, like Walsh, he believed in the ideal of the student-athlete. Graduate assistant Guy Benjamin, who was Walsh's quarterback in 1977 at Stanford and later played for him on the 49ers, considered vonAppen the perfect defensive coordinator for the Cardinal. "Stanford has a bunch of overachievers on the football field," Benjamin once said. "Yelling at an overachiever isn't the best approach. So Fred will yell to motivate them, to make them take football seriously, but he knows not to cross the line. You'll never see Fred grab a guy's face mask. You'll never see him insult or degrade somebody. But he will be tough and he will be demanding. And quite frankly, I think for some Stanford athletes, that's a good thing."

When he was away from the practice field, vonAppen exhibited the most refined taste. He created the defensive game plan while the music of Bach and Mozart wafted around his office. He was generally reading three or four books at a time. Poetry was his favorite. He read Sylvia Plath and John Berryman and William Butler Yeats and William Carlos Williams. He'd collected more than nine hundred books, many of them rare volumes, and when he moved from job to job—which was often—he lugged all nine hundred around the country with him. On the chalkboard in his office he had written this line from James Joyce's *Ulysses*: "Hold to the now, the here, through which all future plunges to the past." He wanted his players to understand that few of them ever would go on to the NFL and had to make as much as possible of their "now," their "here," the Stanford experience.

At this moment, however, the now, the here was no picnic. VonAppen was in agony, and would be until the game finally started and he was actually calling defensive plays. He took an early bus to Anaheim Stadium and dressed quietly in front of his locker. When Terry Shea walked by looking grim, vonAppen said, "Your asshole a little tight?" Shea didn't answer.

Walsh had been installed in a small dressing room with an even smaller bathroom. He sat on a three-legged stool reading the sheet that contained his first twenty plays. Once he came out to the locker room and said to Shea, "I wish I could be casual about these things. I still get the rush." A few minutes later, he joked to Mike Wilson, "Anyone got a drink?"

Walsh ate a banana. He would go silent for minutes at a time studying plays or staring into space. He was in a pregame trance. None of the coaches approached him. He would get up and wander around the locker room, a faraway smile on his face as if he were pre-playing the game in his head. He walked by Bill Ring, who had been a tough little running back for him with the 49ers. "Are you going to put on eyeblack, Billy?" Walsh asked. Ring smiled. For no apparent reason Ring said to Walsh, "Coach, I once stood on the sideline when I was hurt and said, 'Gee, those guys are fast. Am I that fast?'"

The game was supposed to start in a few minutes. Walsh walked to the center of the room and told everyone to surround him. The players dropped to one knee and looked up at Walsh, who stood there, his posture erect, his white hair gleaming in the glare of the overhead lights. He looked like a hero. He launched into his pregame speech, his left hand clenched into a fist.

"There should be no worries in your mind right now. You can't wait to play, you're ready to play, you've prepared yourself. We're not going to be an up-and-down ball club. We're going balls-out on every play, regardless of the score. You act like it's zero-zero, and you keep putting pressure on. Anything can happen early in the game. We go way ahead. We go way behind. It doesn't affect how we play football. Remind yourself of that. OK. Don't worry about a hell of a lot of celebrating for your first touchdown, just start making a number of first downs."

Walsh finished. It was a good speech. He hadn't lost his touch after all. The players stood up, grabbed their helmets, and got ready to raise a shout and charge out the door behind Walsh, who was going to lead them.

Someone informed Walsh that five minutes still remained before his team was due on the field. Walsh sagged. His timing was off; he'd missed the moment.

"Now what do I say?" he asked vonAppen with an embarrassed smile, while his team lingered in a state of anticlimax.

Steve Stenstrom was sacked on the very first play of the game. He was in trouble throughout the first quarter because the Texas A&M defense was too quick for Stanford's offensive line. This was something Walsh did not anticipate. He had worried about his running backs and his receivers, but he assumed his offensive line was a strength, even though Bob Whitfield, an All-American left tackle, had left Stanford after his junior year, and had been chosen by the Atlanta Falcons in the NFL draft the previous spring.

Dennis Green had selected his offensive linemen to block for Tommy Vardell. "Selected" is not the accurate word. He *bred* them. In 1991 the linemen averaged three hundred pounds and ended up as the largest offensive line on the planet, excepting the Indianapolis Colts. Green taught them to drive block—simply to push back the defensive linemen—and Vardell did the rest. But Walsh no longer had a big strong running back and depended on deception instead of power. He had asked his offensive linemen to slim down to gain speed, but Stanford's five starters still averaged 6-7, 294 pounds, an aggregate 1,470 pounds, almost three-quarters of a ton.

The Aggies' quick, attacking defense was running through and around Walsh's line with ridiculous ease, which meant Stenstrom was running for his life on almost every play.

Stanford managed a touchdown on the first play of the second quarter, a five-yard run by J. J. Lasley. But the story of the first half, which ended with Stanford leading 7-0, was Fred vonAppen's defense. VonAppen was having a good time. He called a safety blitz on the Cardinal's first defensive play and he did it again on their third. If Walsh had talked to vonAppen about being cautious, the message hadn't sunk in. VonAppen was calling blitzes like crazy, and in the first half his players held A&M to exactly thirty-three yards of offense.

At halftime, the defensive team went to one side of the locker room, the offense to the other. The players sat on bridge chairs as if they were attending a lecture on the evolution of the English sonnet. Walsh wrote quietly on a blackboard, detailing for the offense the plays that had worked and the ones he would emphasize in the second half. Although he was disappointed with the way his offense had performed, his voice was calm, almost bland. "We've got to score," he said as his team got ready to return to the field. "We can't win this game seven to nothing."

Stanford went the first twenty-one minutes of the second half without making a first down. Walsh couldn't believe what he was seeing. He'd gained a reputation as a great play-caller, but everything he called turned to failure. He knew college players would be more limited than the 49ers, but he didn't expect *this*.

Stanford inside linebacker Tom Williams did. Williams had a bad feeling coming into the game. During training camp, the defense had its way with the offense, dominating it every day. It got so bad that Walsh would ask vonAppen right in front of the players not to apply defensive pressure. It was embarrassing. The defensive coaches began to tell their players not to be competitive in practice, and, above all, "Don't go for interceptions." Sometimes the coaches would tell the defense, "This is an offensive drill," which was code for, "Go easy on the offense." Williams and the others smirked when they heard that.

But surely things would be different in a real game, Williams thought. The offense was bound to get rolling as soon as Walsh got a taste of battle. When Stanford couldn't convert a first down in the entire third quarter, Williams looked at the new head coach and allowed a heretical thought to cross his mind: Where's this Bill Walsh magic?

In their first offensive series of the fourth quarter, the Aggies drove to Stanford's 21-yard line. On the next play, quarterback Jeff Granger dropped back to pass, but was chased out of the pocket by a horde of Stanford defenders. Fred vonAppen was proud of the pursuit. Granger ran to his left and somehow got away from Stanford linebacker Dave Garnett. "We've lost containment," vonAppen whispered to himself. It was like a condemned man saying, "Gee, they're slipping the noose around my throat."

Granger threw the ball downfield. It was a long, high, lazy pass, the kind someone might improvise in a pickup game. When Granger threw the ball, he happened to be standing a few feet in front of von-Appen.

"Surely he won't complete that pass," vonAppen told himself.

But he would, and he did for a touchdown, and the score was 7-7 with twelve minutes to go.

A few minutes later, the Aggies scored a field goal, set up by Granger's 33-yard run to the Stanford 29. By now the Cardinal defense was exhausted from spending so much time on the field.

Stanford got the ball back with 4:25 to play and still a chance to pull out a victory, but Stenstrom was sacked twice more, bringing the grand total to five. The game ended Texas A&M 10, Stanford 7.

As the Stanford team walked back to the locker room, Walsh took Fred vonAppen aside and whispered, "It was the offense's fault, Fred. One more first down and we'd have won the game."

Walsh felt responsible for the loss because he hadn't understood the limitations of his personnel. He hadn't understood its strengths, either. It was as if Walsh were the conductor of a symphony orchestra that he had met for the first time that day. He didn't know what to expect from the first violins or the brass section, and what was worse, what frightened him, was that his players could not understand his music, could not play all the beautiful notes he heard in his head.

Aside from the aesthetic issues, there was a more practical consideration: If his offensive line couldn't protect any better, Steve Stenstrom was going to get killed.

Walsh told his players to kneel in the center of the locker room. His voice was confident. He never revealed his fears to his team.

"OK, men, I'll tell you, I'm impressed with our defense. It gave one hell of an effort, as good as I've seen. Whatever was built with spirit and determination and will-to-win is here. Offensively, we failed to do anything with the ball all night. All we can do is go back to work, because we just couldn't get anything on track, we couldn't hit people, we couldn't protect, we couldn't run with the ball, and we sort of broke down. It's that simple."

Walsh gave his personal pledge that the offense would improve by the time the Cardinal played its next game against the University of Orgeon in two and a half weeks. The players went to the showers, and Walsh escaped into his tiny dressing room. When he did, his face fell. He sat down and sipped an orange juice, his hands shaking. So much had been made of his debut all over the nation, and he'd lost. His offense had lost the game, because, after all, vonAppen's defense had been brilliant, holding the Aggies to 196 net yards.

"Nothing worked," Walsh told a visitor to his dressing room. "Absolutely nothing worked. I tried everything and then I tried things I ordinarily wouldn't do. And nothing worked." It galled Walsh to lose to Texas A&M, whose offense, by his standards, dated from the Mesozoic Era. "Their offense was just awful," he said.

He slipped his game plan into his briefcase and began to undress. Players and coaches were walking out of the locker room and beginning to board the buses for the trip to the airport. Walsh took his time. Stanford boosters would be waiting outside to console him, and Walsh was in no hurry to work up the energy to appear cheerful.

He took a long hot shower, toweled off, and used a blow dryer on his hair. He slowly put on his suit and carefully knotted his tie. By now the locker room was deserted except for Walsh and a visitor and several hundred yards of used adhesive tape the players had cut off their arms and legs and thrown on the floor. Walsh gathered his things and slowly began to walk out the door.

Suddenly, he stopped. "It was so much easier on the 49ers," he finally said, sounding bemused. "You put Wendell Tyler, Roger Craig, Russ Francis, and Dwight Clark out there, and just give the ball to Joe."

CHAPTER

4

IN THE DAYS following the loss to Texas A&M, Walsh admitted to himself that he had not yet come together with his team and new coaching staff. Walsh was used to winning games by virtue of his coaching, and while it couldn't be said that he had lost the game for Stanford, he certainly didn't pull it out. He hadn't understood his personnel, hadn't even understood Steve Stenstrom, and this was the hardest to swallow. No one had intuited the quarterback position better than Walsh, but during preseason practice he had not grasped the essential fact that, despite great cunning and courage, Stenstrom ran slowly and could not always get away from trouble. Sometimes he would make things worse by throwing unwisely under stress—he'd thrown an interception that led to A&M's winning field goal.

Walsh did not fault Stenstrom for any of this. It's hard to blame a quarterback for occasionally losing his composure when he's getting blasted after almost every throw. Walsh knew it was his job to work around Stenstrom's limitations. Even Montana was flawed, didn't have a great downfield arm, and Walsh had found ways to emphasize other parts of Montana's game.

The staff took off a few days after A&M and then met early on a Saturday morning in the conference room of the Stanford football offices. The windowless room, where the staff came together to plan practice and hammer out the game plan, contained a long wooden table, one large-screen television, and a VCR. Walsh always sat at one end of the table, Fred vonAppen at the other. All the defensive coaches sat near vonAppen, and the offensive coaches migrated to Walsh's end. Terry Shea positioned himself directly to Walsh's left. Without intending to, the staff had divided the table as if it were a football field, and each side, offense and defense, seemed to be defending a goal.

On this Saturday morning, no defensive coaches were present. In the room sat Walsh, Shea, offensive line coach Scott Schuhmann, running backs coach Bill Ring, special teams coach Bill Singler, receivers coach Mike Wilson, and graduate assistant Guy Benjamin. The lights were off because Walsh was going over the tape of Stanford's offensive plays from the A&M game. The mood was tense in the dark room. Walsh would run a play, then back it up, sending players spinning backward, skidding across the ground, sprinting backward to the line of scrimmage. And then he would run it again. Sometimes he repeated a play four or five times.

His jaw was tight and his eyes looked hollow. Mostly he didn't speak, and no one spoke to him, but when he spoke his voice was angry. Plays that Stanford had practiced in the spring and again in preseason weren't working. Walsh wondered out loud how a team could put in so much time preparing and then lose its composure. One time, Stenstrom was sacked because the offensive line failed to protect and, on the TV screen, the Texas A&M defenders raised their arms in celebration. "Jesus Christ," Walsh burst out, "they think they're playing good defense."

Walsh criticized himself. This was important. He intended to critique his coaches during this session, and he had to show that he shared the blame. The quickest way to polarize a coaching staff is for the head man to accuse the assistants of letting him down. Several times, he pointed out that he had gotten the exact defense he'd expected, and didn't call the right play to take advantage of it. He was rusty. Near the end of the tape, Walsh winced at one of his calls. "I'm groping because I've lost confidence in everything."

The session lasted a few hours. Receivers ran incorrect patterns. The offensive linemen let defenders through untouched. Steve Stenstrom threw to the wrong receivers. Running backs failed to cut upfield with the ball. After watching Glyn Milburn give ground and lose yardage, Walsh stopped the tape, turned on the lights, walked to the greaseboard, and, with a blue marker pen, hastily diagrammed the play. "This is how the play should be run," he told Bill Ring. "Either he goes upfield or he slides the other way." Ring copied the diagram into a notebook.

Walsh was most critical of the offensive line. He ran a certain play over and over, and watched in disgust one offensive lineman who didn't lay a hand on anyone.

"The offensive linemen are nice. They're very pleasant, real gentlemen," he said sarcastically. "My God," he burst out in the dark, "you don't have to apologize for playing football."

"I know," Scott Schuhmann whispered in a guilty voice.

Walsh glared at him. "They're too goddamn nice, Scott."

Schuhmann put up his right hand like a policeman stopping traffic. He was warding off the verbal blows.

Schuhmann was a veteran coach who had been on Dennis Green's staff for three years, and, along with defensive line coach Dave Tipton, he was one of only two men Walsh had retained from the previous staff. Schuhmann was aware that Walsh could be indirect, and sometimes Schuhmann would sit in meetings when Walsh threw out a generic criticism and say to himself, "I wonder if that was meant for me." But today, Schuhmann didn't have to wonder if he was being criticized. He knew it.

When Walsh turned on the lights, his coaches looked pale, as if they had the flu. Walsh didn't look any better. He dictated specific personnel changes. He wanted another offensive left tackle against Oregon. Justin Armour was promoted to starting wide receiver. Freshman Eric Abrams would be the place kicker. Freshman running back Kwame Ellis would now play defensive back. Reserve running back Ellery Roberts would see more action. Walsh was decisive—a general making hard, necessary decisions. The coaches took notes.

Walsh began coughing and clearing his throat. He had developed a sinus infection that would last all season and seemed to get worse during periods of stress. He left the conference room, walked into his office, and shut the door.

Bill Ring stared at the television screen. One of his running backs was getting clobbered behind the line of scrimmage. "It makes you want to vomit just looking at it," he said.

On Tuesday, September 8, four days before Stanford's home opener against the University of Oregon, Walsh made the team practice for two hours in the morning. It was an unusually hot day—September and October are the warmest months in Northern California—and it was humid. Red-faced players had to break frequently to drink water, and underneath their uniforms their sweat-soaked T-shirts stuck to their skin. Many of them wondered why in this, the fifth week, Walsh chose to work them so hard. With Denny Green, practices never dragged on like this. But Walsh was such a perfectionist, always making the team go over plays again and again.

Some of the players were angry with Walsh. The previous day was Labor Day and many of them had been invited to barbecues and picnics. The players had consulted the schedule, and, as far as they could tell, the afternoon was free. But at the last minute, Walsh announced a P.M. practice. Senior running back J. J. Lasley found this embarrassing. He'd agreed to spend the day with a local family, and now he'd had to call and cancel. The players privately complained that Walsh did not stick to the printed schedules, didn't even come up with a schedule sometimes. It seemed as if everyone connected with the team was edgy on this Tuesday.

Walsh wasn't aware of any of it. When the practice ended, he headed off to the Hall of Fame Room for his pre-Oregon press conference. He felt lighthearted and lingered in the room, eating a turkey sandwich and joking with the writers, many of whom he had known from his 49er days.

At that moment, a potential tragedy was unfolding in "The Fort," Stanford's enclosed practice field. Strength and conditioning coach Fernando Montes, a compact man built like a middleweight boxer, was disciplining John Sims, a freshman linebacker. This seemed like a routine matter. Sims had missed eleven o'clock curfew the night before, and the defensive coaches discussed the situation and decided Montes ought to give Sims extra work. Ordinarily the coaches would require a player to get up early the next morning, which was punishment in itself, and work out at 5:30 A.M. But even the fact that the discipline came after a hot, hard workout didn't seem important to Montes and linebackers coach Keena Turner, who had brought Sims to Montes. Sims would sweat a little, and then he'd take a shower and head off to lunch. The situation seemed so trivial that the assistant coaches didn't bother to tell Walsh about it.

A sandpit runs for twenty-five yards alongside the practice field in The Fort. After Montes told Sims to perform exercises on the grass, he ordered him into the pit for bear crawls, which required Sims to scurry back and forth on his hands and knees. Montes and Keena Turner were joined by several players who had come out from the weight room to watch.

At first, team members J. J. Lasley, Estevan Avila, and Dave Garnett shouted encouragement to Sims. But soon they grew quiet, uncomfortable with what they saw. Sims, who had a history of asthma, was having trouble breathing, and began to make whimpering sounds. Sand was smeared on his face, his legs and chest hurt, and he was slowing down. "I couldn't move," Sims said later on. "My arms and my legs were so tired, I couldn't put one in front of the other. I froze. The coaches were like, 'Come on, John, you're not finished.' I burst into tears because it hurt and I couldn't quit."

J. J. Lasley recalled, "Not to say he's weak or anything, but he was in the sand, clawing, trying to crawl. You could see he had no energy left, and he's mad that he has to do this. So he's crying—one that he was hurt, and two, that he couldn't get up and strangle somebody like I'm sure he wanted to."

The players got scared. They told each other that Montes should stop the exercise. Estevan Avila said to linebacker Tom Williams, "I'd never go that far for Fernando." Then he called over to Montes, "That's enough. You've made your point," but Montes continued to make Sims work. Looking at what was taking place, Williams thought Montes was on a power trip. Earlier in the day, he had heard Montes say, "Sims, I've got you after practice."

When he decided Sims had done enough, Montes told him to quit and return to the locker room. Then Montes and Turner left. Sims did not hear it that way. What he heard was that he wasn't through, and he went on for a few more minutes.

When he finally left the sandpit, Sims began to feel dizzy. He put his arms around the shoulders of Williams and Garnett, and they guided him to the locker room while Lasley carried his helmet. As the lightheadedness grew worse and his chest began to burn, he told himself that if he could make it to the locker room, he'd sit down and relax.

Lineman Chris Dalman was appalled when he saw John Sims enter the locker room. "He was barely walking," Dalman later recalled. "He was stumbling down the row to his locker, and he was crying. The worst part was that he was covered head to toe with sand. It was a weird look. Sand was in his hair, on his shirt, on his skin. It looked like someone had dunked him in a vat of the stuff."

Sims stumbled toward his locker, knocking over several wooden stools in his path, then tried to sit on a bench, but misjudged the distance and crashed to the floor.

Several players ran to the trainers' room and got team doctor Gary Fanton. He hurried to the locker room, where he found Sims on the floor in "a total body shiver." All of Sims's muscles were contracting, his body was clenched, his hands were fists, and his legs were curled. Fanton immediately determined that Sims was not clinically dehydrated; in fact, he was sweating heavily, his temperature was normal, and he was not wheezing or having trouble taking breaths.

What struck Fanton was that Sims, who was conscious the whole time, seemed scared out of his wits. In the past, Fanton had noticed that fright or extreme upset could cause a person to hyperventilate. "John, just relax. Everything's fine," Fanton told Sims. Fanton sent someone for a paper bag. He placed it over Sims's mouth, telling him to breathe slowly. After a few minutes, Sims's carbon dioxide level rose, the spasms ceased, and he calmed down, recovering rapidly.

He did not recover rapidly enough to save Montes's reputation. Word of what Montes did quickly spread through the team. He was not popular with the players to begin with, and now many were outraged. Some of the veterans thought Montes, who had been a staff sergeant in the army, acted as if the Stanford football team was boot camp.

Montes believed the players' dislike for him was proof he was a good coach. "I'm not here to be a player's friend. I have a job to do. Whether they like it or not, I have a job to do."

He had been brought into the program by Denny Green when the Stanford football team was soft, a loser, and he had tried to instill a sense of pride and discipline. He was convinced he hadn't gone too far with Sims. "He wasn't breathing hard," Montes was to say later. "He was definitely tired; he was fatigued. The stress level—if at any given time myself or even Coach Turner would have felt that it was out of control or he was not responding back to our talk, then I would have stopped it, immediately."

Turner said, "I didn't feel he was in any trouble while he was doing it, but I did feel as though he was getting his ass worked on."

As the story of what had befallen Sims made its way from player to player, it snowballed. Sims had gone into shock. The doctor had to treat him with an I.V. drip while he lay unconscious on the locker-room floor. None of this was true. In the locker room, the players began chanting, "Kill Fernando!"

Linebacker Ron George, leader of the defense, was not one of them. He believed the players disliked Montes the *man* because

Montes the *coach* would push them during workouts. "Put Mother Teresa in his job, people would be saying, 'Kill Mother Teresa!'" George said.

Some of the players went in search of Walsh. They were members of the Committee, a group of eight seniors Walsh had selected before the season. Walsh had explained that the Committee was to serve as a liaison between the team and the coaching staff. It could air grievances and discuss problems, but the players were skeptical of its usefulness. Walsh, after all, was Walsh, the most famous football coach in America. They perceived him as distant, as Olympian, and they had trouble believing he would listen to them. Dennis Green had been more down-to-earth, although he'd never appointed a Committee.

Walsh was not around when the first wave of Committee members arrived at his office. The team went to lunch in Branner dormitory, and Montes was there. Estevan Avila confronted him, said he had been out of line, but Montes said he had not overworked Sims. After lunch, J. J. Lasley, Chris Dalman, and Tom Williams set out for Walsh's office. From across the lunchroom Montes watched them go. Dalman glanced back at Montes and told himself that Montes looked scared.

Walsh had already talked to the trainer when the players arrived at 1:30. He knew Sims had collapsed but didn't know what led up to it. He invited them in, shut the door, and all four sat around a small rectangular table on which he wrote his game plans. The players filled in the details, while Walsh listened calmly. J. J. Lasley said, "Fernando degraded Sims. He made him crawl in the sand like a dog." As Walsh learned more, his face flushed and his brow crinkled. "I am repulsed by corporal punishment," he told them. "I'm sorry this happened." That was all he said. The players didn't know that his heart was exploding in his chest. This was exactly the kind of disaster he feared. He had visions of Sims suffering a seizure or a stroke from working too hard in the heat, and he saw the Stanford football program and his own comeback going down in disgrace. He told himself that what Montes had done was "disgusting."

What bothered him most was the scene in the locker room, Sims crying in front of the team and then collapsing. Walsh told the three players Montes had broken Sims, and he feared such humiliation could ruin an eighteen-year-old.

"If it was up to me, I'd have Fernando's bags packed, and he'd be out of here this afternoon," Walsh said. "At the 49ers, he'd be fired on the spot. But at the university, he's not totally under my jurisdiction. I'm not sure how to handle this."

At 3:30 Walsh entered the Hall of Fame Room for the daily team meeting. The players were waiting to see what he would do, and Walsh knew that. If he glossed over the incident, they would conclude that the Committee was a sham, and he was just another hardass football coach who didn't give a damn about his players.

Ironically, the veterans didn't even like Sims. At the beginning of each season, the upperclassmen were required to run laps across the stadium field—it was a ritual that the whole team witnessed. Ron George noticed that Sims casually observed the run while sitting in a camp chair and told him to stand up and show respect. Sims shrugged as if to say, "Who are you?" It was unwise to tick off George, whose opinion carried great weight. Because of that incident, Sims was the last player the upperclassmen would have defended. Yet now the seniors were waiting to see what Walsh would do, because they interpreted Montes's actions as an offense against all of them.

Walsh stepped onto the stage, a black frown on his face. "I don't run guys until they puke," he told the team. "I want you to know that. I don't believe in that sophomoric military-style bullshit. The team owes an apology to John Sims, but John owes one to the team for coming in late."

Then Walsh tried to ease the tension. He said that from now on anyone who broke curfew would have to read the Scriptures. He said curfew would be a minute after Sims got into his room, whenever that was. Everyone laughed. He upped the curfew from eleven to midnight.

Walsh changed the subject. The Committee also had complained about the lack of a schedule and the difficult two-a-day practices. "This is the time to bitch," Walsh announced. "I have no problem with that. Good teams bitch all the time. It brings them closer together. Bitch all you want. Bitch about the food and the beds and the schedule."

He walked to the front of the stage. "But I don't want at the end of the season for everyone to say we had the best schedule in the Pac-10—of course, we got our asses kicked. Just get pissed off. What we have to have against Oregon is a Stanford explosion. Now let's go to practice."

It wasn't much of a practice. Walsh let them work out in street clothes, mostly shorts and T-shirts. Glyn Milburn was running pass routes in a pair of sandals, everyone was lighthearted, and the practice didn't last more than fifteen minutes.

Walsh's performance had been brilliant. He'd taken the team's anger about Montes and the schedules and exhausting workouts and used all that to his advantage. He'd publicly sided with a player against a coach and had proven to the team that he would listen to its complaints, that he had been sincere when he established the Committee.

Beyond that, the players now saw Walsh as a moral man. He enjoyed that role—it was such a refreshing change from professional football. If a guy in the NFL broke the rules, he would be fined or cut, and that would be the end of the story. It was business, and vengeance was swift and primitive. No one ever argued about justice. But in college, where the players were studying Plato and Locke, the whole point was to be fair and evenhanded. Walsh liked to make fine distinctions; he was sick of a coaching ethic that depended on mindless, authoritarian rules: "My way or the highway." He insisted on fitting the punishment to the crime.

One other benefit derived from the incident. The upperclassmen had stuck up for a freshman, shown that the Cardinal was one unified team, not a caste system. At a time when the Cardinal players were down, plagued by self-doubt, unsure of their ability, the Sims episode bonded them in an almost magical way. Months later, when the players looked back on the season, many defined this as the day the Cardinal finally came together.

Walsh never forgave Montes, who wanted to speak to him that day. Walsh made him wait, and then Walsh was icily distant. A letter detailing the incident appeared in Montes's permanent file. Walsh blamed Montes for going too far, for not understanding the spirit with which he ran the team. Montes insisted he did not overwork Sims, that something must have happened between the end of the workout and the collapse in the locker room, perhaps hazing by Sims's teammates, but neither Walsh nor the players bought that.

"So in the long run, I call myself Ollie North," Montes once said. "I'm the guy who did the dirty work that was asked to be done, and I'm the one that got laid out and hung for it. It wasn't my call. I was asked by somebody else to do this. My assumption was it had already been cleared through [Walsh] by the position coach."

Walsh had no patience for that line of reasoning. Months after what came to be known as the Sims Affair, Walsh would flash anger if it was suggested that Montes inadvertently had been set up, had suffered for doing a job that got dumped on him. "That's like saying, 'Why didn't you tell me I shouldn't have shot the guy when he stole the money out of the phone booth? Nobody told me I shouldn't shoot him.' There's some decency involved. So no, he didn't have anything to stand on whatsoever, not a thing. He was wrong, and he was indulging himself in his authority, and the weakness of the freshman."

Montes stayed with the team for the rest of the season but afterward went to the Cleveland Indians as their strength coach. At the time he received the offer from the Indians, he met with Athletic Director Ted Leland and asked for a raise. Montes told Leland the Indians would double his salary. Leland offered an increase of $2,000, and Montes took that to mean Stanford didn't want him around.

Walsh was forgiving to linebackers coach Keena Turner, who had stood by without doing anything while Sims struggled in the sand. "Keena didn't assert himself," Walsh was to say later. "He was new to coaching and he didn't appreciate his authority. He could have stepped in and stopped things, but he learned from that experience."

John Sims didn't carry a grudge. "What's done is done," he said months later. "I don't know if that is the way it could have been handled or should have. I guess it served as an example. I don't really like being someone's example."

The veterans finally accepted John Sims after the Sims Affair. They even gave him a nickname—Sandman.

AS THE GAME drew nearer, Walsh clarified his game plan. He had tried to attack the perimeters against Texas A&M because the Aggies were more powerful and quicker than the Cardinal, and he did not think he could beat them by running up the middle. The Ducks of Oregon were something else entirely. Walsh wanted to run the ball right down their throats. To do this, he planned to make greater use of backup fullback Ellery Roberts, although he didn't know much about him. Roberts was bigger and probably faster than starter J. J. Lasley, but he'd missed the entire 1991 season and spring drills because of neck surgery for a herniated disc—for a time it seemed he might never play again. Although he was healthy now, the coaches weren't sure if he would attack the defense. In preseason practices, he sometimes would hesitate at the line of scrimmage as if protecting his neck.

Roberts was a fifth-year senior who had begun his football career at the University of Miami in 1988. Although he was scheduled to be the starting fullback at Miami his sophomore year, he transferred to Stanford, even though it meant he'd have to sit out one season. He didn't like the separation of academics and athletics at Miami, the peer pressure to hang out only with football players. "I didn't want to be pigeonholed because I was a black athlete at Miami, didn't want to conform to the black stereotype of a football player listening to rap and walking with a swagger. I'm not saying that's bad, but I didn't have the persona of a Miami player, and it wasn't worth changing who I was to become a great player."

He started the transfer process before Dennis Green was hired at Stanford. At the time, Stanford didn't even have a head coach. "People in Miami thought I was crazy," Roberts said. He'd graduated from high school on Long Island with a 3.89 grade point average and was a semifinalist for a National Merit Scholarship. When he wasn't practicing football or watching tapes in the Stanford football offices, he was usually reading. He was an English major, and he would read novels and classics in hotel lobbies and dark buses traveling back and forth from the games. But because of his powerful running, his teammates called him "L Train."

Walsh wanted to see what Roberts could do. He was an adaptable coach and would use a power game if he had to. But he wasn't in love with power football, saw no beauty in smashing a fullback into the line of scrimmage twenty times a game. He wanted a diversified offense, even if it was more difficult for his players to learn. He had contempt for coaches who depended on a big back and the strength of the offensive line to push back defenders. If a coach like that ran into a team with bigger and stronger players, he'd lose. Walsh never wanted to leave himself without options, didn't believe he could beat Notre Dame, UCLA, Washington, or Southern California merely by giving the ball to Ellery Roberts.

Walsh worried continually about his offense. One day, he told a visitor, "Until we move the ball effectively against somebody, I'm going to be really anxious." He saw Oregon as a middle-of-the-road football program with limited resources, just the kind of team Stanford should handle. "You like to think you're just strong enough to go out and play and win the game. But until we do that once, I have no way of judging how well we can do. I just don't know yet. If we can't win this game, it'll be a tough year because we will collapse."

It didn't help that practices were still erratic—some effective, some unbelievably bad. One day, Walsh stood on the sideline observing his players bump into each other as some ran the wrong way. "Jesus Christ. Fuck," he muttered to himself out of earshot of the players.

"This is the worst practice we've had in a while, bad practice," he told a friend on the sideline. "There are three or four players on this team who I don't understand how they got into this place. They can't learn our program. I don't understand that. I'm going to have someone do profiles on them to see how they're doing in their classes. I don't see how they can't learn our program and still do well in school."

Walsh walked down the row frowning, then said, more to himself than to anyone else, "We'll be a really good team in three years. We'll have better athletes and they'll have three years in this program. We'll be a Rose Bowl champion. But this is a learning year."

More than anything, Walsh worried about the offensive line. It was one thing to block straight ahead for a back like Tommy Vardell, but now Walsh was asking the linemen to perform any number of complicated moves with which they were unfamiliar. Sometimes Walsh would become impatient with offensive line coach Scott Schuhmann in practice. One day he observed an offensive line drill for a few minutes, then yelled to Schuhmann, "It's not fast enough. Too routine."

Schuhmann screamed at his players, "I told you to go faster."

Once in a staff meeting, Walsh put Schuhmann on the spot. The coaches had taken a break, but Walsh remained in the conference room, slouched in his chair, his right leg casually draped on the table top. Schuhmann, a tall, easygoing, good-natured man, got up to leave, but Walsh stopped him.

"How would you start the Oregon game, Scott?"

The mood in the room grew tense. Walsh never had done this before, not in full view of the other coaches. This was a test and Schuhmann knew it and so did everyone else. Schuhmann thought a moment, then said he would start the game with a toss to Glyn Milburn for a run. Walsh barely acknowledged the answer; he seemed preoccupied. Later, he admitted to someone who had been there why he had put Schuhmann in the hot seat. "I want him to be decisive, want him to say something. He was OK for the job he has and the role he plays. There have been others who would be quicker to answer, but no, he's OK. See, I need that during the game, too, need his input."

As it turned out, Walsh was to begin the game with three straight runs by Ellery Roberts.

Administrative assistant Al Matthews was worried about Walsh, who, in trying to balance his commitments as coach and spokesman for the university, had become dangerously overextended. Matthews didn't see how even a young coach could maintain Walsh's pace. "Bill's concerned with calling the right play, with down and distance, with getting back the rhythm. He's been away for three years, and he's constantly taken away from the game by university duties."

Walsh had given four speeches in one day in the week prior to the Oregon game, and, to this point in the season, he had become something of a mini-media factory, giving interviews almost daily. Already he had been profiled in *Time, Newsweek, Sports Illustrated, The Sporting News,* the *New York Times, Los Angeles Times, Chicago Tribune, Philadelphia Inquirer, Boston Globe, Newsday, Dallas Times Herald, Orange County Register, San Diego Tribune, San Francisco Chronicle,* and *San Francisco Examiner,* and on ESPN, ABC television network news, CNN, and NBC television.

Walsh was tired. His sinus infection acted up all the time now, and he was constantly blowing his nose and coughing. He'd already had one operation to fix the problem, but obviously it hadn't worked. Now he was taking medication to dry up his chronic nasal drip, and the medication was making him sleepy. At an afternoon coaches' meeting, Matthews had watched Walsh's eyes roll and his head begin to droop. Matthews thought Walsh's head was going to hit the table. Finally, Walsh pleaded, "Can we get this over with before I fall asleep?"

Matthews, who was a year older than Walsh, was as protective of Walsh as if the head coach were his little brother, which, in a way, he was. They had played on the same football team at San Jose State in 1951 and 1952. Later, Matthews was a graduate assistant at San Jose State under coach Bob Bronzan. Bronzan's other graduate assistant was Walsh. The two had remained friends ever since, Matthews becoming a lifelong high school football coach in the San Jose area. During Walsh's years in Cincinnati, he often would phone Matthews and say, "I'm thinking about you. I'm having a beer and reminiscing about our past with some good country western music."

When he coached the 49ers, Walsh would phone Matthews and ask him to drive up to 49er headquarters for lunch. Walsh needed relief from football and 49er politics. The two old friends would sit in Matthews's truck eating sandwiches, talking about the past. When Walsh decided to return to Stanford, he called Matthews, who was retired, and asked him to be a graduate assistant. "I'd like to have you come up here and be with us," is how Walsh put it. Matthews accepted. "Hey, Bill, I'm absolutely flying high right now," he said.

Matthews had gotten out of coaching in 1990 because, after thirty-four years at it, he felt burned out. He would stand at his team's practices and wish they would end. But he was too young to retire, tried unsuccessfully to fill his time. He went to the driving range, golfed, had lunch with friends if they were available. And mostly he felt old, useless, discarded. Matthews was in exactly the same situation as Walsh—looking for another chance at life.

During the preseason, Walsh often told visitors to the Stanford football offices that Matthews was the oldest graduate assistant in the country. That amused Walsh. Later, Matthews's title changed to administrative assistant, but his duties remained the same. He handled clerical jobs, kept intruders away from the practice field, made sure the staff didn't violate the rule limiting players to twenty practice hours a week.

But mostly he was there as Walsh's ally, someone from Walsh's past. At sixty-one, Matthews was well conditioned and energetic. He only needed five hours of sleep a night and sped around the football offices on permanent fast-forward. He had the chest and large biceps of a boxer and was the picture of health, except that he was suffering from a hernia. He would refuse an operation all season because he believed it was his duty to be there if Walsh needed to talk. Some days, Matthews would come to work in obvious pain, his face white and sickly. He never complained. He would occasionally go to the coaches' locker room and lie on a couch just to regain his strength. If the lining of his intestine was pushing through the ruptured wall of his groin, he would shove it back, slap cold water on his face, and go about his business.

Once, on a walk back to the locker room after practice, Matthews said, "I just feel I want to be with Bill. When we walk down to the field and back, I want to be part of his life—because of our age and the past. I'm extremely proud of him, and I want to make sure everything is right for him. I want him comfortable. At times, I'm almost reading his mind. Something's going on and I'll look over there, so I'll make my appearance in front of him and he'll point at me and say, 'Al, I want you to do this for me and do that for me.' So I'm kind of reading him."

To show how he read Walsh, Matthews opened his eyes wide and bent his knees like a defensive back anticipating the snap of the ball.

"I even watch Bill on the practice field," he said. "I can see the practice situation going along and I know that he's got something on his mind. So I'll get over there close to him and I'll look at him, and many times something will come up and I'll relay that message or take that information from him and do what I have to do with it. Sometimes I stand there at practice and I can see him working his way toward me. I'll say something funny and crack him up, and then he won't speak to me for another twelve hours. It's not that it's an ego thing with me. It's just that I have a feeling that he includes me in his thinking and his life."

Just then Fred vonAppen came hurrying by on his way to the coaches' locker room, and as vonAppen drew within hearing distance, Matthews stopped talking, stared at his shoe tops.

When vonAppen left, Matthews was almost whispering. "I have to say this, I consider Bill above me. Even when we were in college, he was a leader—so focused. If I have a problem, I ask him and I know he has the answer. I can look up to him and I'm proud of him, and I think he's proud of me. I think he is. I haven't done what he's done in a lifetime. I mean he's the greatest coach *ever*. He was far ahead of everyone else when he even began. And I could see it develop. I could see the thinking. I could see the changes in the sport through the years, too. He talks about Sid Gillman doing it. He talks about other coaches. And I don't know what ideas he got from them, but all I see are Bill's ideas. I mean, the defenses have had to change because of his philosophy. You can tell with the 49ers. Damn, he won Super Bowls with just inferior athletes."

Matthews was smiling now, his face flushed with happiness. He had stopped in front of the Hall of Fame Room, was in no hurry to get back to the office.

"The 49ers were a big thing with me," he said, his words coming quickly. "If I didn't go to a ballgame I'd have it on TV, and watch Bill's reaction on the sideline and try to read what he was going to do. That's all been part of my life. Most guys would sit down and watch what's going on on the field, but I would watch him. And there are times, even now, when I'll look at him and I won't say, 'Do this,' but I'll say, 'Open it up, Bill.' Which means, 'Take chances, don't be afraid, don't be conservative, go ahead and do it!' That's the point I'm trying to make to him when I'm telling him that, but I just say, 'Open it up, Bill, open it up.' I don't know if he's listening to me or not, but he just kind of nods a little bit."

Someone said it sounded as if he loved Walsh.

"Yeah, I love that guy," Matthews said. His eyes filled with tears, his chin trembled, and, for a moment, he couldn't speak. The love he felt for Walsh transcended brother-to-brother affection. It was almost as if their relationship dated from another era, from the medieval age of kings. Walsh was the liege lord, and Matthews pledged absolute fealty, unconditional devotion.

Matthews and Walsh did not often see each other away from the football team. Matthews had remarried after a long first marriage, and he and his wife Rita had a nine-year-old son named Troy. Matthews spent most of his nonworking time with his son. Aside from Stanford football, Troy represented Matthews's other second chance at life. Sometimes, Matthews would lie in bed at night and pray for the world to be safe for his son.

On Friday, September 11, the day before the Oregon game, Walsh held a noon practice at the stadium. It was a warm, lazy day, and Walsh let his players work out in shorts. He had given them Thursday off, and he kept reminding them that they were "fresh." It was an important part of Walsh's coaching philosophy to keep his players rested. If he worked them hard a few days in a row, he would back off after that. At a school like USC the players might be required to scrimmage several times a week, but Walsh rarely had his players wear pads more than once a week, and he kept contact to a minimum. It was the same on the 49ers. He wanted his players to explode during games, not practice.

At the end of practice, which merely consisted of jogging through various plays, he told all the players to sit in the end zone and, one by one, called on every special teams unit—punt, return team, field goal team, etc.—and had the players stand in formation in front of the others. The mood was lighthearted. When one of the special teams would gather in formation, the others would hoot and yell. To an outsider it might have seemed that this exercise had little purpose.

Walsh had often done the same thing with the 49ers. Special teams players usually worked out after practice, after the starters had left for the day. By calling them out in front of everyone, Walsh was giving them credit for doing a hard, anonymous, thankless job, emphasizing that they were absolutely essential to the team. But there was more than that. With Walsh, seemingly simple acts were often complicated and usually contained a psychological component.

By telling the players on each special team to stand up, Walsh was singling them out, holding them accountable. Stanford's special teams were not nearly at the level Walsh demanded, and this was a way to motivate his players. Standing on the side, watching the exercise, defensive backs coach Tom Holmoe felt pleased. Holmoe recalled exactly when Walsh had begun calling out the special teams. It was 1984 and the 49ers' special teams had performed poorly in a game. The next day at practice, Walsh said, "Let's see who these guys are who did that." They had to stand there in shame. At the end of the week, after they had practiced well, Walsh said, "OK, let's see them again," and then they were proud. He had turned the situation around.

As it turned out, standing in front of the team was not enough motivation to improve the Cardinal special teams. Walsh would have to resort to other measures, but that was to come later.

That night the team stayed at a hotel in Palo Alto called Rickey's Hyatt House, a sprawling, one-story complex with a large ballroom where the team ate and several meeting rooms where the coaches went over the final game plan with the players. While Walsh was explaining the first twenty plays to the offense, something unexpected was happening in the defensive meeting.

The night before the Texas A&M game, Fred vonAppen had asked his players to set goals for the game. He went to the front of the room and induced the players to reach a consensus on passing yards allowed, run yards, total yards, sacks, fumbles, and points. Then he wrote the numbers on a chalkboard. After the game, he compared what A&M actually got with what his team had projected.

Things worked differently the night before Oregon. VonAppen asked linebacker Tom Williams to come to the front of the room and lead the meeting, while the coaches killed time outside in a breezeway. "I'm turning the meeting over to the seniors," vonAppen had said. "Tom, why don't you come up here?"

Williams, a fifth-year senior whose academic endeavors included working on the Martin Luther King, Jr., papers, was called "Old Man" because of his maturity and the way he grew cantankerous when he was hungry. "Can you give me yardage?" Williams would yell. He asked the defensive backs for passing yards, the linemen for rushing figures, working out a consensus before moving on.

Even after they had written down all the numbers, the players didn't invite the coaches back in, not right away. Something was eating at them, but they weren't sure how to get started. Williams stood quietly in front of the room, then had an idea and asked his teammates to say what was on their minds. At that instant, the meeting began to take on a life of its own.

Estevan Avila, the senior member of the Cardinal defensive front, stood up and said the unmentionable. Proud to be a winner after the Cardinal had been so bad his first year in 1988, going 3-6-2, his voice now was filled with disdain. "We can't depend on the offense to score points. Let's do it on our own."

The room went silent. Players experienced a secret, almost illicit, thrill at what Avila had said. It was what everyone in the room was thinking. Avila challenged the others to "stand up and say what you think."

Tom Williams jumped in. "Let's not count on the offense to do anything."

Dave Garnett, usually quiet, studious, rose from his chair and shouted, "Let's do it ourselves. If the other team can't score, it can't win."

Estevan Avila, grinning, said, "Let's be accountable only to ourselves."

Walsh had emphasized that the Cardinal was one team united, but there it was, the defense didn't have confidence in the offense, and it was best just to admit it, to get it into the open, without the coaches present. The players talked passionately about how they would have to make interceptions, recover fumbles, and set up the offense with excellent field position. Some felt angry at the offense for how it had played against Texas A&M, for how it couldn't hold its own in practice, and it felt good to get that out. By the time the meeting ended, the defensive players had promised each other to "do it ourselves" until the offense got itself together.

After that, the defense always requested time alone the night before games. VonAppen didn't object. He recognized that when his players worked up the nerve to ask him to leave, they had become a team.

At least one member of the offense thought he could make a difference. Running back Glyn Milburn, who'd rushed for only fifty-nine yards against Texas A&M, had to excel for Stanford to beat Oregon. He had the magic, was almost impossible to tackle in the open field. Yet he was an oddity for a football player, only 5-9, 175 pounds, a normal-sized man in a game of giants. His face was youthful and his skin smooth, and if it weren't for a mustache that filled out his upper lip, he could have passed for an adolescent.

In his first year at Stanford, Milburn had been a phenomenon. That was in 1990. He was the Number One all-purpose back in the country, gaining 2,222 yards by running, catching passes, and returning punts and kickoffs. Before the 1991 season, Stanford Sports Information Director Gary Migdol mailed a flyer to the national media pushing Milburn for the Heisman Trophy. But the 1991 season was a mass of confusion for Milburn. He sprained his knee in Stanford's second game and was not healthy for several weeks. In the meantime, fullback Tommy Vardell, who had been projected as Milburn's blocker and a short-yardage runner—strictly part of the supporting cast—vaulted into stardom, eventually gaining 1,084 yards and scoring twenty touchdowns, a school record.

When Milburn recovered, he expected the focus of the offense to shift back to him. But Dennis Green had found a good thing in powering Vardell up the middle behind his big offensive line, and Green pushed Milburn to the side. Milburn didn't score a touchdown until the seventh game of the season.

When Milburn realized he wasn't the star of the offense, he began to take risks on the field; he would do something extra to try to score a touchdown. He never had been like that before. He was unassuming, a team player, and now he found himself obsessed with making an impression so he could gain back what he had lost.

"When the attention was not placed on me it was troubling," he explained. "I felt that I wanted to go all the way for a touchdown instead of doing what the play was designed to do. I found myself trying to do the unexpected, something that nine times out of ten would not work, but just might score a touchdown."

He went to Green's office and asked how to win back the coach's approval, but Green said Milburn was doing just fine, and Milburn left the office even more confused.

But all that was behind him now. Green and Vardell were gone, and Milburn was once again the brightest star in Stanford's offensive firmament. Throughout the spring and preseason, Walsh had promised that the attack would focus on him, utilizing his speed, his ability to deceive.

Milburn was a serious man who, at times, almost seemed glum. If he passed an acquaintance at the team's hotel, he often dropped his eyes, turned his head, and walked on without a word. He was thinking about football, and he had to concentrate harder than everybody else, because he was smaller than everybody else. All his life, he'd been dogged by the feeling that he was cheated by his size. When reporters asked if he was "durable," he knew they were suggesting he was too small.

When he was eleven, he would lie in bed while his mother sat next to him. "What do you see?" she would ask, and he would say, "I can see myself running down the sideline and scoring a touchdown." The fantasy hadn't changed since then, except that now he could picture himself scoring against Notre Dame or UCLA or USC. Usually he'd be sprinting around the end, dazzling a linebacker or safety with his moves, and then breaking free to the end zone. The sensation was glorious. "It's great," he once said, "feeling yourself in the open and hearing the cheer of the crowd." His elusiveness on the field was a perfect metaphor for his personality—distant, shy, unknowable, almost impossible to pin down.

He considered it something of a miracle, an act of grace, that he attended Stanford instead of the University of Oklahoma, where he started out. He had been accepted at Stanford during his senior year of high school in Santa Monica, California, where he set a state rushing record. He arranged to sign a letter of intent to go to Stanford, was at school with the principal and his coach waiting for his parents, who were required to sign as well because Milburn was only sixteen, but his parents never showed, and Milburn went home with nothing decided.

Milburn's stepfather, who had played football in junior college, was an avid Oklahoma fan and wanted his stepson to play for the Sooners. The Oklahoma people continued to come to Milburn's house the next three nights, pushing hard, emphasizing Oklahoma's tradition, its history of placing players in the NFL, its use of smaller backs. The Stanford recruiters, thinking Milburn was theirs, had stopped putting on the pressure. As Milburn began to vacillate, the letter of intent remained unsigned. His stepfather was afraid Stanford's mediocre football program would be an impediment to the NFL. Milburn ended up changing his mind and committing to Oklahoma, primarily to keep peace at home. "I was only sixteen, so I really didn't have much of a say in what I did."

Oklahoma head coach Barry Switzer had been persuasive. Five years earlier, Milburn had attended football camp at Oklahoma, and now, when Switzer came to the house on a recruiting visit, he was as comfortable as a favorite uncle, calling them all by their first names. "My, you've really grown since camp," he told Milburn.

At Oklahoma, Milburn ran back punts and kickoffs, thrilling the Sooner fans with his speed and moves. Switzer told him he would be the starting tailback the next season, but Milburn wanted out, knew he had made a mistake. He lived in a football dorm, segregated from the rest of the student body, whom he'd only meet in class. He was stereotyped as a jock, even though he had a 3.8 GPA.

"Once the season was over, I saw a lot of players who had aspirations to play in the NFL not being drafted and not having any other alternative, not knowing what their next move would be. And I just didn't want to get caught in that same position. I was motivated academically, too, and I didn't want to feel I was losing out on all I could get out of college. I thought, I can probably do the same thing in football at Stanford that I can do at Oklahoma, but maybe not get the same education at Oklahoma that I could at Stanford."

His mother had told Switzer her son would leave in a year if he didn't like Oklahoma, and Switzer agreed. After spring ball, Milburn went into Switzer's office to tell the coach he'd decided to transfer. He was nervous. Switzer became emotional, acted shocked, saying, "You've got a starting position. What more could you want?"

Milburn tried to explain, but he wasn't sure Switzer understood. "I hung tough," he said a few years later. "I knew this was my one chance."

He came to Stanford in 1989, the same year Ellery Roberts defected from Miami, and like Roberts he had to sit out his first season because of NCAA rules governing transfers. For almost two years, he felt he had betrayed his family, especially his stepfather, and although their relationship seemed cordial, Milburn sensed an unspoken chill, a subtext of disapproval until the Cardinal improved and Milburn gained national recognition.

In the spring of 1992, he ran for the Council of Presidents, the four-person group that represents the Stanford student body. Although he lost the election, Milburn found the experience fascinating. At Oklahoma he might have won because he was a football hero. Not at Stanford. All along, he had wanted to be treated like any other student, and now he'd been granted his wish.

On the Saturday of the Oregon game, Walsh went down to breakfast at 8:45. He was always cheerful on game day, even if he felt nervous. He wanted to create the right mood for the team and the other coaches. Early in his career, when he was starting out as a college coach, he had worked for a head coach who insisted the players begin to psych themselves up for the game at breakfast. No one was allowed to talk unless the conversation directly related to the game. Walsh thought that was the right way to instill discipline until he went to the Oakland Raiders for one season as an assistant coach. On the morning of the game, Raiders players would be sitting at breakfast with their feet over chairs or on the table, and they'd be talking about what bar they'd be going to that night. The game never entered their conversation. Then they'd go out and beat the crap out of the other team.

After that, Walsh wanted the atmosphere at breakfast to be light-hearted. This morning, he was sitting with running backs coach Bill Ring and defensive line coach Dave Tipton, and a visitor who mentioned that someone had broken into his house the day before. That reminded Walsh of what had happened to Jim Mora just after he'd taken over as head coach of the New Orleans Saints. Walsh put down his cup of decaf and wiped his mouth with a napkin. "Mora moved to New Orleans and had been living there about sixty days. One night he and his wife go out and when they come back there's a van backed into their driveway with the back door open. They go into the house and they hear noise. All of a sudden, they see a man carrying out their TV.

"Mora starts to wrestle with him. They're rolling around on the floor. The guy pulls a gun, and Mora, who's in an absolute panic for his life, desperate for any sort of advantage, yells, 'Don't you know who I am? I'm the head coach of the Saints.' The robber stops struggling for a moment, stares at him, and says, 'Gee, I thought you looked familiar. Hey, Coach, I'm really sorry this had to happen, but you've got to do something about the Saints. They're terrible.' And he left with the TV, stereo, and everything else he could grab."

By now, Walsh had risen from his chair and was standing next to the table acting out the parts of Mora and the burglar. Ring's eyes were wet with laughter, and the players were staring across the room at Walsh, who temporarily seemed to have lost his mind.

During the preseason, Walsh had spent one entire lunchtime telling Bubba Paris stories. Paris was a good-natured, immensely gifted left tackle for the 49ers who ate himself out of the league. The tales of his food consumption fell into the genre of the tragicomic.

Walsh constantly tried to get Paris to lose weight, but Paris found ways around him. "One year, we were checking out of training camp and the maid came to see my secretary. She wanted to know what to do with all the chicken bones. My secretary came and got me. We went to Bubba's room. We looked. Bubba secretly had eaten Colonel Sanders after dinner and hid the bones in boxes in the back of his closet. There were dozens of them. When Bubba left, he forgot to get rid of the evidence."

Walsh was laughing. "One year at training camp everyone sees him eating a salad and a Diet Coke at every dinner. We feel sorry for him. One night some players go to an out-of-the-way pizza place in another town. It must have been in Loomis, somewhere down a dirt road. The guy who owns it says, 'You guys from the 49ers? That big guy comes in here every day.' It turns out Bubba had been sneaking there for two large pizzas after workouts."

As he talked, Fred vonAppen and Scott Schuhmann came over to hear the Bubba stories. Walsh had one more.

"After a while, we had a rule that Bubba would be fined if he came in over three-twenty-five. Every week for nine weeks in a row he was three-twenty-three. I was encouraged. Everyone said he was working hard. The scale was kept next to a Coke machine and there were wood boxes for empties next to it. One day a delivery man moved the boxes a foot. Bubba gets on the scale and tries to lean his left elbow on the boxes, and almost falls off."

Walsh got up from the table, trying to imitate Paris, who must have looked like an elephant prancing on one foot. "It was too far for him to reach. His weight instantly goes up to three-thirty-six. He'd been keeping his weight down by leaning his elbow on the empties. So I fined him."

Walsh was in his element, swapping yarns with football people. He was relaxed and funny, and the stiffness he projected on television vanished.

After breakfast the players bused back to the university, but Walsh didn't stay with the team. He went up to his office and studied the game plan and made phone calls to prospective recruits. Later, he hung around the courtyard in front of the gym making small talk with a few high school players who had come to visit the campus. Fred vonAppen, who was taking in the scene, glanced at Walsh. "Look at him standing there with his white hair," vonAppen told a bystander. "He's special. Even if he weren't Bill Walsh, you'd still notice him."

The team made the quarter-mile walk to the stadium, past Stanford fans dressed in red who lined the street or were picnicking in a nearby grove. VonAppen never liked "The Walk," didn't enjoy making the polite effort to fans so close to the start of the game. His mind was elsewhere. He wished there were an underground tunnel that would take him directly from the gym to the stadium.

After warm-ups, Walsh met with the team in the locker room, actually a large shed just the other side of the running track. He paced back and forth in front of his players, who were seated on chairs. He was shouting, "Explode all over people. Beat them to the punch. Finish them off." He walked over to Chris Dalman and Steve Hoyem and the other offensive linemen. "Offensive line, this is your day to dominate. Get started with it right now." Walsh walked away. He was pacing again. "Execute. Execute. Precision," he shouted. "It's a machine today, a relentless machine that knocks them down and knocks them down until they have to go to the shower."

But the machine wasn't exactly relentless, at least the offense wasn't. Although Oregon was on a seven-game losing streak dating back to the previous season, the Stanford offense still could not dominate, even though Glyn Milburn managed to bust loose for a 68-yard touchdown run in the second quarter. In the first half, Stenstrom was besieged by blitzers who seemed to have no trouble faking out Stanford's offensive linemen and getting past them. Stenstrom was constantly throwing off the wrong foot or throwing on the run or throwing the ball just to get rid of it. He was intercepted twice and Ellery Roberts fumbled once, and although Stanford gained more yards than Oregon, the Cardinal only led 13-7 at the half. This was not a good sign. If Stanford had trouble with the Oregon Ducks, how was it going to do against Notre Dame or Washington or USC?

Walsh was angry at halftime. He rarely showed the team his temper, but now his face was red and his voice loud. "Hold on to the goddamn ball," he shouted at the offense. For a moment, Walsh stared at the greaseboard, on which he had sketched the plays he would emphasize in the second half. "We're going to cut people down. We've got to score two touchdowns the second half or it's not a performance. It's got to happen. We've got to go after their ass physically. They're tired. You can tell that already."

The players listened impassively. They were gulping water to replace fluids and they were just as tired as Oregon. While Walsh was lecturing the team, an old man, apparently lost, wandered into the locker room. No one knew how he'd got in, because a guard at the door was supposed to keep strangers out. The old man walked right past Walsh, who was reaching the high point of his passion. Walsh tracked him with his eyes but continued. The old man urinated in the restroom and washed his hands and face, and again shuffled into the locker room where Walsh was trying to regain his momentum. Walsh was frantically scribbling on the greaseboard and talking as fast as he could, and now the old man was standing between him and the team, inspecting Walsh's work.

Walsh stopped. For a moment, it was unclear what he would do. If he were Mike Ditka, he might have heaved the man through the skylight. Then the merest smile creased Walsh's lips. It was so absurd to have an old man loitering during halftime. Certainly nothing like that ever happened in the NFL. Walsh turned his back to the team and laughed. He regained his composure. He faced the team again. The old man was still there, staring as if trying to get the gist of the play. "Oh, do you want to get through?" Walsh asked solicitously, as if he were the intruder. The old man got himself together and left, probably still wondering why all those oversized men were crowded into such a small locker room.

Stanford scored one touchdown, not two, in the second half. Stenstrom found Milburn in the end zone with a nifty pass over the middle. After a two-point conversion, Stanford went ahead 21-7, which turned out to be the final score.

The Stanford offense had outgained the Ducks 496 yards to 244, and Steve Stenstrom, fighting off pressure the whole time, threw for a career-high 331 yards. But, in addition to throwing the two interceptions, he had been sacked three times and once he fumbled the snap from center, blowing a chance at converting a fourth-down play. The Cardinal defense, on the other hand, had handled Oregon, and in two games gave up only 17 points.

When the game was over, Walsh began to walk out of the stadium with Al Matthews. At the gate, a mob awaited him. One woman was yelling, "We love you, Bill." He made his way into the crowd like a swimmer easing into the surf and tried to walk back along the lane to the gymnasium. But he could hardly move. People wanted to touch his shoulder, his sleeve, or shake his hand. He walked slowly forward, a smile locked onto his face. Stanford fans thrust at him programs, notebooks, footballs, photographs—anything for him to write on. He signed as he walked.

Al Matthews looked concerned. He hovered over Walsh like a worried aunt, trying to clear a path. The crowd followed Walsh as if he were the Pope dispensing blessings. Walsh whispered to Matthews, "There are signs we could be really good if we could just eliminate the mistakes." Walsh grunted in disgust. "Drop the ball from center."

Matthews didn't hear a word Walsh said. He was scurrying around him, making sure people didn't come too close. Finally Matthews quit trying. "I'll leave him alone," he told a friend. "Look at his face. He's enjoying it."

When Walsh finally walked into the coaches' locker room, the others had showered and some had already left. Fred vonAppen was studying the game summary at a table in the center of the room. Someone asked vonAppen if he was going to celebrate that evening. VonAppen smiled. "Nah," he said. "I'm going home and watch a football game."

CHAPTER 6

WALSH DID NOT seem in the least worried about Northwestern, Stanford's next opponent. Why should he be? The Wildcats—one San Francisco sportswriter called them the Mildcats—had one of the most grotesque records in college football. In the last four seasons, they had won seven of forty-four games. That included 1989, when they won no games. The last time they'd enjoyed a winning season was when they went 7-4 in 1971, before many of the current Wildcats were even born. They already had played two games, losing to Notre Dame and Boston College by a combined score of 91-7.

Walsh had little sympathy for them. Northwestern was supposedly handicapped by high admission standards, but Walsh was quick to tell local reporters that Stanford's requirements were even tougher. "They don't have the admissions problems we have," he said at his weekly press conference. "Besides, there's a spirit at Stanford that crosses over to all sports—men's and women's. There's been a spirit of sports that's dramatically different at Stanford than at Northwestern."

Part of Walsh's irritation with Northwestern related to Dennis Green, who had been head coach there from 1981 to 1985, but managed to win only ten games. Green was a Walsh protégé, worked for him at Stanford and with the 49ers, and Walsh considered him one of the brightest young coaches in America. If Green couldn't win at Northwestern, no one could. The way Walsh saw it, the university was the recipient of lavish income from the Big Ten Conference, including a hefty annual share of Rose Bowl loot. But Northwestern didn't funnel enough of that money into the football program, which Walsh considered grossly underfinanced. During Green's tenure at Northwestern, the two friends had been on the phone constantly, discussing the problems a football coach confronted at Northwestern. Walsh concluded they were insurmountable. He did not see how a coach could be successful there.

This did not mean he felt the slightest sympathy for Northwestern's first-year coach, Gary Barnett, who had a sense of humor about his situation. At the weekly press conference, the Bay Area media first interviewed Barnett over a speakerphone, while Walsh ate a sandwich and listened quietly. Someone asked Barnett if there might be a conflict between him and factions at the university who didn't think Northwestern should stress a quality football team.

This question apparently came as a complete surprise to Barnett, who said he wished he had such a problem. Based on getting blown away in his first two games, he didn't think he posed any threat to the integrity of the university.

Everyone listening to Barnett in the Hall of Fame Room laughed. Everyone except Walsh, who sat there with a blank look on his face. Barnett's problems were of no concern to him. He wanted to win big before he entered the hard part of his schedule against San Jose State, Notre Dame, and UCLA.

As the week wore on, Walsh began to relax. Practices were going well, and he was confident of beating Northwestern. By Friday, he was downright casual. When he convened the coaching staff in the conference room early Friday morning, he had one thing on his mind. Should he tell the team to dress for practice, or forget all about it? At times like these Walsh always spoke in interrogatives. "What do you think?" he said, as if he were just any other coach in the room. Most everyone agreed there was no reason to suit up, except for Keena Turner.

Turner was the only former 49er Walsh had brought on as a first-year assistant who had been an outstanding player, a mainstay at outside linebacker on all four 49er Super Bowl teams. The other former 49ers—Bill Ring, Mike Wilson, Tom Holmoe, and Guy Benjamin—were backups, and Walsh liked them because they were smart and observant, much like Walsh himself. Although Turner's playing credentials were impeccable, he was reluctant to speak up in coaches' meetings. Al Matthews used to get on him, reminding Turner that

Walsh respected coaches who had opinions and the courage to make them known.

Tom Holmoe understood this better than all the others. He had been a defensive back with the 49ers—intelligent, hardworking, not as gifted as others. But he talked all the time in meetings, sometimes drowning out senior coaches like Scott Schuhmann or Dave Tipton. No one was offended by Holmoe because brashness was a good sign in a young coach. The other first-year assistants were amazed at how quickly Holmoe asserted himself, and among themselves used to say that Holmoe was Walsh's favorite.

But this morning it was Turner, not Holmoe, who spoke up. Maybe it was because of what Al Matthews had said. "Just be yourself, Keena. Bill may disagree, but that's OK."

Turner usually had a giggle in his voice and a shy half-smile on his face, as if he didn't expect people to take him seriously. His good friend Joe Montana was exactly the same way. But now Turner wasn't smiling, and when he spoke, there was no hint of the giggle. "I think the players should put on uniforms today. They've seemed complacent to me all week, and I'm concerned how they'll react to the idea of *not* suiting up. Dressing the day before games always seemed important to me on the 49ers."

Walsh listened attentively, his head cocked to one side, and then he overruled Turner.

Matthews muttered under his breath, "It gives the team the wrong message not to suit up."

But Walsh didn't hear him.

That night Walsh felt giddy at dinner. He and Terry Shea were inventing trick plays, cracking themselves up. Walsh was talking like some kid who was diagramming a play in the street—you run past the fire hydrant, and I'll hit you with a pass behind the green Buick.

"On kickoff returns, we can have a guy pretend to flub it in the end zone," Walsh was saying. "Another guy is motioning furiously for him to down it in the end zone. Meanwhile, the kicking team is running like crazy toward the flubber. At the last second, he picks up the ball, laterals to Glyn, who runs a hundred and five yards for a touchdown."

Walsh clapped his hands for effect.

"Has anyone ever done this?" someone asked.

"I don't know," Walsh said, "but we're going to practice it."

They lingered over coffee. The night was warm. Everyone was feeling content. No one was in a hurry.

After a while, Walsh, Shea, Ring, Schuhmann, Wilson, and Benjamin—the entire offensive brain trust—strolled over to one of the hotel meeting rooms to look at film. It was not unusual to study film the night before a game. The team meetings didn't start until eight, and that gave the coaches an hour. It was unusual that the coaches weren't looking at Northwestern film. They were watching San Jose, whom Stanford wouldn't be playing for a week.

While they watched the film, Walsh quizzed Shea about San Jose's defensive tendencies. Shea had been head coach at San Jose the two previous seasons, and having him there was like getting insider trading tips on the New York Stock Exchange. Every once in a while, Walsh would walk over to the greaseboard to draw plays, and when that happened, one of the coaches had to jump up, run to the wall and flip the light switch. Otherwise, Walsh would have been scribbling in the dark. He became disconnected from his surroundings when he was creating, would become so excited with his ideas he'd wipe off the greaseboard with his hand, leaving smudge marks all over his palm.

After a while, Walsh made a mental leap right past San Jose to Notre Dame, which Stanford would be facing in two weeks. The game against Notre Dame and the confrontation with head coach Lou Holtz were the culmination of the first part of the season. At this moment, Northwestern was a million miles away. Walsh was saying he wanted to emphasize his Amtrak formation the next two weeks. Amtrak was a backfield configuration similar to ones he'd used with the 49ers, which featured 218-pound Ellery Roberts as the ball carrier. Blocking for him would be 245-pound defensive end Nathan Olsen, son of former Rams star Merlin Olsen, and freshman offensive tackle Jeff Buckey, who weighed in at 290. This alignment was supposed to come at defenders like a runaway freight train, and it was pure power, the flip side of Walsh's finesse. A variation of Amtrak was "Heavy Load," consisting of Roberts as a runner and Olsen, who could take out two defensive linemen all by himself, as the blocker.

Walsh was aware that Holtz would study the films from the Northwestern and San Jose games, and he was not above trying to mislead Holtz. He wanted to show Amtrak on the tape, have Roberts chug right up the middle for good gains. He expected Holtz to plan ways to neutralize the train. That was fine with Walsh, because when he went to South Bend, he intended to fake the handoff to Roberts, and after the Irish defense made a mad dash toward the ball carrier, Steve Stenstrom would throw a downfield pass.

Walsh was pleased with the concept. Mike Wilson took notes like the recording secretary at a lodge meeting. The lights still were off.

"The warm-ups in South Bend should be short," he told the others, as if they were playing Notre Dame the next day and needed to work out a few last-minute details. "I don't want the players lying around the field hearing people in the stands chant 'Rockne!' It's a lot of fun, but they don't need to hear it. Just get out and play."

Walsh leaned back in his chair, crossed his legs in front of him. His remarks made Terry Shea think of what happened to the University of California when he was an assistant coach there in 1989. The Bears visited the University of Miami, and while the players were on the ground performing calisthenics before the game, the Miami Hurricanes ran right through them and kicked their helmets.

"Talk about intimidation," Shea said.

"They're a sorry bunch. They really are," Walsh said of the Hurricanes.

Benjamin turned on the lights. They still had time to kill. Walsh said he wanted to give backup quarterback Mark Butterfield some work against Northwestern in the first quarter to get experience in case Stenstrom was ever injured and couldn't play. Walsh planned to give Butterfield two plays in a row, a sprint around end, then a rollout pass. Walsh grinned at Shea.

"Afterward, the press will ask, 'Why Butterfield? Why did you lose confidence in your starter after eight plays?'"

The coaches laughed at the denseness of the media. Walsh looked at Shea and said, "If we're way ahead, Terry, you should call plays. You've been calling them for ten years. I'm sure you can do it."

Shea beamed.

When the Cardinal players assembled in the locker room, Walsh gave a brief speech. His voice was strong and he oozed confidence, stressing that Stanford had to be a machine, had to play its own standard of football no matter what Northwestern could or couldn't do. As the Cardinal left the locker room and began running toward the field, one of the Northwestern coaches was leaning against an outside wall, vomiting into a garbage can.

But Stanford wasn't a machine, or if it was, it had loose parts. Although the Cardinal finished the first half with a 21-10 advantage, and although Stenstrom had been precise with his passes and found his receivers with regularity, Walsh was dissatisfied. In the second quarter, the Wildcats' Lee Gissendaner ran back a punt 53 yards to the Stanford 30. The Cardinal punt cover team, which had worried Walsh before the game, had missed tackles and run after Gissendaner in a trance. Northwestern scored a touchdown four plays later, and the half ended with Walsh cranky.

As the team gathered in the locker room at halftime, it looked as if Keena Turner had been right all along. Maybe the players were too nonchalant. Walsh took off his hat, ran a hand through his hair. When he addressed the team, his voice was strained. "We're going to run the ball this half. There isn't a way in hell we should have to pass the ball to win this game. If we're going to be a great team, we've just got to take it to them physically, take it to their ass."

It was an intriguing little speech. Walsh, the acolyte of sophisticated offense, was telling his team to forget finesse—nothing fancy, just cram it down the Wildcats' throats, or whatever orifice was handy. Then he turned to the special teams. His face grew red, his voice angry. His eyes seemed to bulge. He was Al Capone in *The Untouchables*, normal one second, crazed the next.

"Listen up, special teams!" he shouted. "Get your act in gear. It's embarrassing to get manhandled by this team. If we have to make changes, we will." Walsh cleared his throat. "The first fifteen minutes I thought, boy, do we have a football team! Then the whole damn thing starts wobbling on us. We've got to establish it right now, because we have a series of tough games after this."

To begin the second half, Walsh called seven straight runs for Ellery Roberts, the last for a touchdown from two yards out. When Milburn made it into the end zone from the ten-yard line on the Cardinal's next possession, inflating the lead to 35-10, it looked as if the game was over.

It wasn't. Although Stanford had come in as a 35-point favorite, and although Northwestern had managed only 75 yards of total offense the previous week against Boston College, the Wildcats inexplicably began to creep back, closing the gap to 35-16 late in the quarter.

Stanford's next drive failed after Stenstrom got sacked and began to see double. The offensive line had broken down again, especially at left tackle where Scott Schuhmann had already used three different players in three games. He was finding it impossible to replace the previous year's starter, Bob Whitfield. "Bob gets paid five million to play left tackle for the Atlanta Falcons," Schuhmann once explained. "The people who are playing that position now may never get paid anything."

Stanford had to punt, and this time Lee Gissendaner ran it back seventy-two yards for a touchdown. After a successful two-point conversion, Northwestern trailed 35-24 with more than thirteen minutes remaining. Walsh was appalled. Twice the failure of Cardinal special teams had brought Northwestern back.

After that, Walsh tried to control things with his running game, but that didn't work, and the Northwestern offense got more chances, too many chances. The game petered out with the score 35-24, mostly because the Stanford defense finally shut down the Wildcats.

It was a win for Stanford but it didn't feel like a win—to be brought to the brink by Northwestern was an embarrassment. All the coaches seemed worried. Walsh waited by the locker-room door as the players silently filed past him. He waited longer than he wanted to because some of the players were outside socializing with the Northwestern team. Walsh showed no emotion. When the last of the Cardinal made it into the locker room, he shut the door and walked to the front of the room, where the players awaited him on their knees for the Lord's Prayer. He put his hand on the shoulder of the player closest to him, defensive end Tyrone Parker. And then he flashed.

"When the game's over from now on, get in here, especially the fucking freshmen," he said, his voice seething. "You didn't play and you're out there shaking hands." He took his hand off Parker's shoulder and began pacing. "I'm going to ask for changes on special teams. Some of you guys are not doing it. We won a goddamn game today, but there are all sorts of things we need to improve."

He was touchy with the press a few minutes later. He often had been this way when he ran the 49ers, especially after victories. In those days, he could be condescending or acid, but so far, he'd been relaxed and conciliatory with the writers who covered Stanford. He perceived them as younger practitioners of their craft, beginners, and he felt an obligation to be polite. But when someone asked if he was satisfied with the progress of his team, that pushed all his buttons. "I'm not as concerned as some of the writers," he answered, his voice full of sarcasm. "I feel good that we're making progress. We'll be a solid team. I appreciate your concern."

As he made the long walk back to the coaches' locker room, he told

Al Matthews, "Northwestern was the worst-looking outfit to come into Stanford Stadium in a long time. They had just enough fast guys to screw us up."

Observing Walsh, Matthews said, "Bill won't sleep tonight. He'll have that scowl in the meeting tomorrow to let the coaches know he's not pleased."

Back in the coaches' locker room, Terry Shea was glad for any kind of win, even an ugly one. He never once complained that he didn't get to call any of the plays.

The coaches met at 1:15 Sunday afternoon in the conference room. Most had been in their offices since early in the morning. Scott Schuhmann had arrived at ten to grade the performance of his offensive linemen. He gave them a detailed critique of their work after each game. Terry Shea had already graded Steve Stenstrom, giving Stenstrom comments and pluses or minuses for each play. Shea stayed away from numerical grades because he had learned from experience that grading a quarterback numerically could turn out to be dangerous. If a backup came out with a higher score, the team could find itself in the middle of a quarterback controversy.

Walsh, who was scowling as Matthews had predicted, showed the coaches the film of the special teams' plays from the day before. They were a mess. He drummed his fingers ominously on the table when Gissendaner returned the punt for a touchdown. When the lights went on, Walsh said, "Maybe it's a blessing we see all this and we still won a game."

Walsh was sitting in his usual spot at the head of the long table. Near the other end was thirty-nine-year-old Bill Singler, who coached the special teams. Singler was nervous. This was his first year as a Stanford assistant. When Walsh took over, he wanted a Stanford graduate to coach special teams, and vonAppen and Dave Tipton recommended Singler, a three-year starter for Stanford at wide receiver, 1973–1975. He'd earned a bachelor's degree from Stanford in psychology and a master's in education. After graduating, he worked at seven different schools, most recently as head coach at Pacific University, a small Division II school in Oregon.

This was the first time Singler had been in charge of special teams, a thankless job because the best athletes never participated in the grunt work of punt coverage and punt returns and field goals. At every level from high school to the pros, harried and unappreciated special teams coaches knew there would be breakdowns and embarrassments no matter how hard they prepared.

Singler was an earnest, enthusiastic man who worked late each night watching films and planning. He was thin and youthful with neatly trimmed hair that dipped across his forehead. He wore large glasses. He looked like someone who might have devoted his life to missionary work, not football. When he was excited or nervous, he jiggled his right leg, and he was jiggling it now.

Walsh asked Mike Wilson to put the special teams rosters on an overhead projector, and then all the coaches began the tedious process of deciding who would stay on each team and who got dumped. Walsh asked each coach to recommend at least one new player for special teams play.

Walsh walked to the screen and pointed at the rosters with his finger. Sometimes, when he strayed in front of the projector, the rosters would flash across his face. The work was boring and took three hours. "I know this is taking a lot of time," Walsh said when he saw Bill Ring yawn, "but we've got to do it."

When the teams finally were set, Walsh asked Singler to read the changes back to him. Singler looked stricken. There were so many names involved that Singler had lost track. Tom Holmoe saved him. He had copied down each new name and read them off while Singler looked relieved. Then Walsh went around the table asking each coach to give Singler his impression of special teams' play and any helpful suggestions that came to mind. Some of the criticisms were severe. "The players aren't staying in their lanes on kickoff coverage," Dave Tipton said. "You've got to have your two backs stand together on kickoffs, so the other team can't always kick away from Glyn," Tom Holmoe said.

When he saw that the other coaches might tear down Singler, Walsh stepped in. "I want to remind you that we are not teaching Bill. Obviously he knows these things."

Walsh's voice was calm, unthreatening. Another head coach might have told Singler his job was on the line, either his teams improved or he was history. Walsh did none of that.

"I have no quarrel with how it's been coached," Walsh told Singler in front of the others. "Lately your buddies have let you down." Walsh scanned the room, letting everyone know with his eyes the responsibility was communal. "Early on I thought this was the best I'd ever seen it coached. Now we're into game plans and we've let it slide a little. That's understandable. Now we've got to come back."

Only once did Walsh lose his temper, but the object of his anger was Fred vonAppen, not Singler. After Walsh had gone around the table, soliciting names for special teams, vonAppen complained that too many of the candidates came from defense. VonAppen's defense was thin to begin with, and he was afraid of losing players to injury.

"Do we have to go around the fucking table again?" Walsh snapped.

VonAppen sat there stone-faced. He understood what was happening. Walsh would not attack Singler, who was vulnerable, so he took out his frustration on vonAppen, his old friend who would absorb it without feeling insecure.

Later, vonAppen shrugged it off. "It'll pass," he told a friend. "I still love the guy. Because he says 'fuck' in my presence doesn't mean that our relationship is over. He gets annoyed with me because I'm bulldog persistent about some things to a fault, but that's the way I am. Sometimes I suffer from overkill and he lets me know it."

One other issue developed during the discussion of special teams. As the coaches watched the film, Walsh noticed one player who seemed listless on almost every play. He stopped the tape and asked the others what they thought of him. Bill Singler informed Walsh that this player had a twenty-eight-year-old girlfriend a few miles up El Camino Real from Stanford. Keena Turner told everyone that the player had spent the summer in Australia where he got someone pregnant. In fact, the player had just received a letter from the girl explaining the situation. Fred vonAppen said the kid's hamstrings hurt, too. "He's hobbled." Everyone agreed he was "distracted," coaches' talk for "potential disaster." This player was a freshman. Classes hadn't even begun and already he seemed lost.

Walsh stood quietly in front of the room, his head listing to one side, his left hand at his chin, his eyes wide. "Let me get this straight," he said. "He has a twenty-eight-year-old girlfriend. He's got someone in Australia pregnant, and his hamstrings hurt." The coaches nodded. "I'd say let's not suit him up, but he'd love that. He'd be in Atherton or wherever she lives in a shot. I can see I'll have to visit with him."

Then Walsh got back to the special teams' problems, but every few minutes, he'd think about the freshman and interrupt what he was doing.

"He's a freshman, right? If he's doing this now, he'll flunk out in a month. I need to talk to him tonight. He doesn't have a clue what's about to happen to him in school, let alone in football."

He got back to the meeting, but a few minutes later, he again returned to the freshman. "This is a disaster about to happen."

Walsh walked out of the conference room and phoned the player, who peeked his head into the room an hour later. Walsh escorted him into his office and closed the door. They were in there for fifteen minutes.

When he returned, Walsh didn't say anything. He had done what he could, which, as things turned out, was enough. Although Walsh was afraid he would flunk out, the freshman made it through the year, and became a valuable player as a sophomore.

At six o'clock, Walsh peeled a hundred-dollar bill from his wallet and told running backs coach Bill Ring to order pizzas and soda. Ring asked the coaches what they wanted as he jotted down notes on a pad—pepperoni but no anchovies; mushrooms and green peppers; sausage with extra cheese.

Walsh started to laugh. "Gee, Billy, I take you from being a Wells Fargo executive to ordering pizza for a whole football staff."

Ring smiled. At thirty-five, he still had the innocent look of a teenager, resembling the young, handsome Mickey Rooney. He had played for Walsh on the 49ers from 1981 through 1986, participating in two Super Bowl victories. Although never a starter, he won the team's Len Eshmont Award for "courageous and inspirational play" in 1983. It was the most prestigious award on the 49ers. After the 1986 season, Walsh, who never let personal feelings influence professional decisions, cut Ring from the team.

Ring knew it was time to go. There were only so many times he could run down the field full speed on kickoffs and absorb monster hits. The very first time Walsh had asked him to be a blocker on kickoffs, he got knocked cold. When he woke up he felt numb from his head to his toes. On the plane ride home he told himself, "I could have been in a wheelchair."

After he left the 49ers, he became a vice president with Wells Fargo Bank and was happy with his life. But the previous winter he was vacationing with his family in Hawaii and Walsh called. Would Ring join his staff as an assistant coach? Ring was torn, took six weeks to decide. If he went with Walsh to Stanford he would be earning less than one-fifth of his Wells Fargo salary. Finally he told Walsh he couldn't afford to join him. As soon as he said that, he felt plagued by remorse. The next morning he went to mass, and the priest's sermon was about the hollowness of material possessions. Sitting in the church, Ring believed the sermon was directed at him. "I've got to give it a shot," he told his wife.

So he had come to Stanford for the adventure of coaching, but when he thought about the downward mobility of his job move, he had to admit that he wouldn't have done it for anyone but Walsh. Attaching himself to Walsh was like grabbing hold of the third rail of life, and Ring wanted a jolt.

But tonight, Ring's duties consisted of ordering the pizzas and lugging back a case of sodas from the coaches' locker room. If he minded the work, he didn't complain.

After dinner, the offensive staff began to go over the Northwestern film. Walsh's face was pale and he was coughing. The coaches were hours behind schedule and this was shaping up as a long night. As he watched tape, Walsh lapsed into a conciliatory mood—the exact opposite of how he had been after Texas A&M. He pointed out several good blocks by offensive linemen and told Scott Schuhmann, "Just what we've been trying to develop, Coach." When one of Ring's running backs whiffed a block, Walsh was understanding: "He'll learn."

When they finished the film, the coaches began to work out the game plan for San Jose State. Shea wrote on the greaseboard all of San Jose's defensive sets. He even had with him San Jose playbooks from his two years there. This was an advantage, although not as great as it seemed. Ron Turner, San Jose State's new head coach, had been Stanford's offensive coordinator the previous three years. When Turner went to San Jose and Shea came to Stanford, the two men literally had exchanged offices, and whatever inside information Shea had about the Spartans was no better than what Turner had about Stanford.

Walsh told his coaches he wanted to keep his offense basic against San Jose, not reveal anything. He was already planning ahead for Notre Dame. "Notre Dame will look for very little from us, and I'd like to win this game without showing a lot." That included not giving away the Cardinal's Apache formation, its no-huddle offense. Walsh called a significant number of plays from Apache. The play would end, and his players would run to the line of scrimmage and immediately start the next play, catching the defense unprepared.

Walsh didn't want Notre Dame to know how often he was using the no-huddle, and he was sure he could keep the Irish in the dark. He explained this to Terry Shea, and his reasoning was coy. When Notre

Dame, or anyone else, watched Stanford game films, they saw the Cardinal at the line of scrimmage as they began a play. After Stanford ran the play, there would be a break in the film, and then the next play would start. The film always left out the players getting to their feet, assembling in a huddle—all the irrelevant movements on a football field. No film ever showed how Stanford got to the line of scrimmage, so Notre Dame would have no reason to be thinking no-huddle. Walsh seemed pleased with that.

His mind worked in circuitous ways, and he was wandering down strategic backroads now. He wondered about San Jose outside linebacker Ray Bowles, a quick, powerful pass rusher who might disrupt the shaky timing between Steve Stenstrom and his offensive line.

"Is it unsportsmanlike to come in motion and just hit Bowles right under the chin with Nate Olsen?" Walsh asked with no emotion in his voice.

"Bowles is hurt already," Shea said. "He might just curl up and go home."

Bill Ring was smiling. He said that reminded him of the time Russ Francis ran down the line of scrimmage and knocked hell out of Dexter Manley. Manley was a stud for the Washington Redskins at that time, and he was disarranging the 49er offense all by himself, so Walsh decided to take him out of the game.

Walsh smiled back at Ring. "Dexter's feet just went right up into the air," Walsh said, laughing. "He's not a real bright guy to begin with. He's lying there trying to piece together what happened. 'Now what in the hell was that?'"

The coaches swapped a few more stories, and then they broke for the night. Scott Schuhmann seemed worried. San Jose had a fast defense, similar to Texas A&M's, and what his offensive line couldn't handle was speed.

"I always say I'd rather play Notre Dame twice than San Jose once," he said, leaning against the door of the conference room. "Notre Dame isn't as fast."

Viewed in the long term, Schuhmann's point was moot. His line would have to face San Jose *and* Notre Dame, one right after the other.

NOT ONE PLAYER currently on the Stanford football team had ever participated in a victory over San Jose State. This was a source of embarrassment to the players and coaching staff. San Jose, after all, was just a state school twenty minutes down the Bayshore Freeway, and Stanford was one of the elite universities in the world, yet San Jose had won the last two meetings, and three of the last four.

The most recent victory for the Spartans against the Cardinal came in 1990 at Stanford Stadium. San Jose won 29-23, and afterward, the Spartan players paraded around the stadium chanting "Our house" to their 25,000 fans, who had driven up from San Jose and saw this as their big game of the season. San Jose had a dinky, uninviting stadium, and its attendance was poor, and the Spartan players were saying Stanford Stadium belonged to them. Stanford linebacker Dave Garnett remembered how he'd felt that day. "It's like your next-door neighbor coming over and saying, 'This is my house' and knocking over anything he wants to."

Terry Shea was San Jose head coach during the "Our house" episode. In his two years at San Jose he won fifteen games, lost six, and tied two, and after his second season, he applied for the vacant head coaching job at the University of California at Berkeley. Everything came together on January 14, 1992. That morning he received a call from Berkeley saying he would not get the job. He was disappointed, but he reconciled himself to staying in San Jose. Then Walsh phoned and asked him to be his assistant head coach, saying he would not take the Stanford job without him.

So within the space of a few hours, Shea had gone from rejection to nirvana. He was forty-six years old and before his two years as head man at San Jose, he had been a lifelong college assistant. He agreed to come to Stanford because he could not pass up the chance to learn from Walsh, and there was always the possibility—implicit, never promised—that when Walsh finally stepped away, Shea could take over as Stanford's head man.

He had attended the University of Oregon, earning a bachelor's in sociology and a master's in counseling psychology, and there was no denying that, when he spoke, he had the calm, reasoned, supportive tone of a therapist. His first coaching job had been at Mount Hood Community College in Oregon, and the only reason he was able to get that appointment was his ability to double as a counselor for undergraduates. He was a gentle man, who had no desire to coach in the NFL. In this, he was wise. Walsh admired Shea's manner with the players, depended on Shea to install most of the offense during daily team meetings, but did not see Shea as someone who could flourish in the National Football League. "The pros might eat him alive," Walsh once said.

Some of the assistant coaches saw Shea's manner as amateurish. He led cheers and patted players on the back and was relentlessly cheerful. "I know some of the others think Terry is too rah-rah," Walsh once said. "Of course he's rah-rah. This is college."

A certain irony attended Shea's position at Stanford. Although he was the offensive coordinator, he understood Walsh's offense less than the assistants. Guy Benjamin had been Walsh's quarterback at Stanford and had played for him on the 49ers along with Mike Wilson and Bill Ring. All were familiar with Walsh's pass routes and run plays and his way of thinking. Shea was an outsider, which he freely admitted. For Shea this was a learning year the same as it was for quarterbacks Steve Stenstrom and Mark Butterfield and anyone else exposed to Walsh for the first time. Sometimes at staff meetings he would have to ask basic questions while the rest of the coaches were ready to move on.

The problem for Shea was that Walsh's approach to football was idiosyncratic and far removed from the mainstream. Shea was bewildered by the sheer abundance of what Walsh threw at him and the team. For example, Shea had always worked in systems where certain pass routes were designed to beat zone coverage, and others were designed for man-to-man situations. Very simple. Very neat. But many of Walsh's routes were fluid and multipurpose. He expected his receivers to read the coverage in mid-play, and if they were facing a zone, they would do one thing; against man-to-man, they would do something else. In this way, Walsh could dismantle whatever defense he faced. Because the quarterback had to read the defense at the same instant as the receivers—usually with an all-out blitz in his face—the whole scheme was delicate and required incredible precision. Shea rarely had thought about pass routes in this way, and as he learned, he felt old assumptions slowly breaking down in his mind.

He was also baffled by Walsh's terminology. Shea had always worked at places where colors denoted pass protection codes. If the quarterback called out "brown," that color would tell the offensive linemen and running backs whom to block on a pass play. Not so with Walsh. In his system, colors told the backs where to line up for running plays. So Shea had to forget a lifetime of training and habituation when he heard "blue" or "brown" or "red."

Shea's problems with terminology ran deeper than colors. He could discover no rhyme or reason for the names of Walsh's plays. The creative fountain in Walsh's brain always was bubbling, and just as fast as the plays came, Walsh would assign names to them. Double post, for example, was a Dino. Why? It just sounded good. The Stanford playbook was crammed full of Bims and Bams and Bobs. It had a Bingo Cross, and a Shallow Cross, an Okie, a Hank, Dragon, Drift, Texas, Knife, Cowboy, and Denver. At first, Shea tried to reason all this out, to find the hidden order in the nomenclature. When Walsh realized Shea was doing that, he had to explain that there was no hidden order. It was a matter of committing the entire organism to memory. So no wonder Shea felt overwhelmed—here he'd spent his whole life in football, had been a successful coach, and sometimes he had only the vaguest notion what Walsh was talking about.

Walsh, of course, had a reason for his system of terminology. To him, every play was a discrete creation unlike anything else in the playbook, and Walsh wanted the name of each play to describe it and nothing else. If you had a horse and a zebra in a corral, you wouldn't call the zebra "Horse-2." It would be a zebra. Walsh worked hard to keep his horses and zebras distinct.

He once explained, "We might say, 'Pass 31-0, X-Slant,' and the Raiders might say, 'That's a 727.' Ours may seem a little cumbersome, but when you start dealing with just numbers, you lose your focus on the play itself. You just add another number. 'If the 727 doesn't work, let's run 728.' In some systems it's just a matter of, 'Have the receiver go over here this time. Have this guy do this.' Ours is timing, discipline, and execution. Theirs is just, 'OK, try this. OK, try that.' And they lose track of the discipline it takes to make it work."

In theory that was all very interesting, but Shea was taking a crash course in this approach to football and he was finding it mind-bending. What he had to realize at some point was that he wasn't really learning a football system. He was learning Walsh. In this sense, Stanford football was like a medieval guild or a religious initiation that the master coach imparted to his apprentices.

Aside from trying to learn the offense and teach the quarterbacks, Shea performed administrative duties for Walsh—filling out the week's schedule, dealing with the Athletic Department, teaching the players the nuts and bolts of the offense Walsh had drawn up for that week, a fatiguing task that would have taken too much out of Walsh at this stage of his life. Shea freed Walsh to be creative, and in that sense they were like two sides of a single personality. Walsh was the dreamer, Shea the realist. Walsh took Shea into regions he had never imagined, and Shea pulled Walsh back to earth and kept him grounded. Stanford's offense, as it was evolving, was a dynamic tension between the world-views of Walsh and Shea. Walsh strove to expand it without the concept of a horizon or limit, and Shea preferred to contract it, reduce it to its essence, get the players to perform perfectly a limited number of plays. The Stanford offense existed somewhere in between the two concepts, although much closer to Walsh's end of the spectrum.

At the start of the team meeting each day, Shea read the week's itinerary to the players, although every player had his own copy of the schedule. He would read from the sheet telling the team when to practice and attend meetings, and when the buses would leave campus for the airport on travel days. It might have been necessary to read the itinerary at San Jose State, but this was Stanford. Each time Shea started reading, the players dropped their heads and rolled their eyes. He never noticed. Before long, the players took to calling him "The Itinerary Man."

Walsh was tired and grumpy on Friday morning, the day before the game. He had been up late the night before at a San Jose State alumni dinner that stretched on endlessly. He faithfully attended functions at his alma mater, even though it still burned him up that San Jose had twice passed him over for the head coaching job. He went to these dinners and fundraisers at San Jose State because, the way he saw it, his generation was the last to care about the place. He suspected that San Jose's recent crop of football players had little school loyalty. He privately believed that they were paid mercenaries who went to the school to play football.

Aside from needing sleep, Walsh was ticked off by an article from that morning's *San Francisco Chronicle* that made him think some of his players were apologizing for going to Stanford. To him, it was as though they were ashamed of being at a better school than San Jose. Linebacker Vince Otoupal had said, "They think we're a bunch of pansies with BMWs and Mercedes Benzes. I'd probably think the same way if I were those guys."

Walsh was also ticked off by some quotes from the Spartans. Safety Anthony Washington said, "Their assets off the field don't have anything to do with football. . . . We feel we're in the same echelon they are." Starting quarterback Jeff Garcia said, "Stanford is the school with all the prestige. It kind of seems like everything has been given to them." This may have sounded incendiary, but Garcia also said, "Everybody would like to be part of Stanford. Those who aren't are jealous. I wish I was at Stanford, and I'm sure most of our players do, too."

Walsh walked into the 12:15 team meeting brandishing the sports section. "You worked hard to get here," he shouted at the players, waving the article. "The guys who didn't work aren't here. Just because you worked hard, you shouldn't fucking apologize. We have no apologies to San Jose State. Because you went to school to make something out of your lives we have to say we're sorry. Why the hell apologize?"

Walsh's face was the color of a beef tomato and his eyes threatened to pop out of their sockets.

"I want guys decked in this game!" he shouted, changing the subject. "This team we can intimidate. They think they can come in here and point their fingers and brag. Well, I want you to deck people. It's a great feeling." He grinned. "I hope they're looking the other way, but if they're not, I don't care."

Anyone listening to Walsh would have understood that he was portraying San Jose as a team from the wrong side of the tracks, reinforcing the idea that this was a game between the good boys and the bad boys. There was a certain amount of truth in what he said. In 1990—Shea's first year as San Jose's head coach—the *San Jose Mercury News* uncovered some disturbing crime statistics about the Spartan team. Nearly one of every five players on the 1990 squad had faced criminal charges in Santa Clara County in the past five years. Most of the charges were misdemeanors, many involving drunken fights, but there were felony arrests, one for threatening a motorist with a gun, another for stealing a pizza from a delivery driver who was dragged by the neck from his car.

So Walsh's speech had a foundation in fact. But what was more interesting, what made his little tirade provocative, at least from a personal standpoint, was that Walsh himself was originally San Jose, not Stanford. He may have cultivated an aristocratic image, he may have planted vineyards on his new spread in Woodside, he may have used words like *salient* when he talked to the players, but he was a product of San Jose. In his undergraduate days, he'd come up to Stanford Stadium to play football like someone visiting another planet and found himself chasing the great Bob Mathias all over the field in a losing cause. As he railed against the Spartans, Walsh sounded like someone who not only wanted to distance himself from San Jose State but, perhaps even more touching, from a part of himself.

This was the second time today he had exploded about the newspaper article. Earlier, at the staff meeting, he went through a similar performance—like a one-man show opening in Philadelphia before moving to Broadway. Walsh, who was among other things theatrical, was testing out his approach with his coaches, seeing if it would work. After he had waved the article over his head and worked himself into a lather about his players apologizing for going to Stanford, he shouted, "I'm sick and tired of hearing how Stanford players have things handed to them, that they don't have to work for anything. Hell, Stanford players are the ones who worked hard to get here."

Walsh's eyes were bugging out and he was screaming and the coaches were wondering where all this anger came from. Fred von-Appen laughed to ease the tension and said, "Hey, slow down, Coach. Take it easy."

The coaches and players would have been surprised to know that Walsh's bluster was mostly for effect. At least that's what he privately explained to a friend in a calm, reasonable voice a few minutes after the team meeting.

"There really wasn't much in the article. Don't get me wrong. I felt what I said, but I had to work myself up to it."

Walsh giggled as he remembered his performance in front of the coaches and players.

"It takes that approach to get this team ready for San Jose State.

They're not a traditional rival and typically Stanford is flat playing them. So you've got to have something to grab hold of. So I grab hold of the fact that they taunt us a little bit. They strut around. They want to ridicule us and make fun of us. They don't have the class we have. I try to build a scenario there. It's probably not that valid. But that's the way you have to get ready for these guys. It's got to be a mean, miserable kind of thing, if I can get that engendered, because otherwise, there isn't anything to hang my hat on as a coach."

Later, Walsh said to Guy Benjamin, "Do you think I overstated the 'deck them' stuff?"

Benjamin assured Walsh he had done exactly the right thing. He reminded Walsh that in 1977 he'd used the same approach against Berkeley, urging Stanford to "Start one fight." Benjamin enjoyed the memory, recalling that Walsh had said, "If you hit a guy, don't stay there and jaw. Just run back to the huddle."

Walsh was not above inciting his team a third time, just to make sure the message took. When the players appeared for the evening meeting at the hotel, Walsh immediately worked himself up—the red face, popping eyes, the whole bit. By now, he could slip in and out of character in a millisecond. "If you deck a guy, don't stand over him and mouth off. Disappear. Let him wonder who did it. Do it at the whistle. After the whistle, no."

The players took a break before going into separate offensive and defensive meetings. They milled outside in a courtyard, passing around copies of the offending article, working themselves up. Steve Stenstrom and wide receiver Mike Cook were sitting at a picnic table, turning the article this way and that, trying to catch a shred of light filtering through the window from one of the meeting rooms. Cook read out loud Jeff Garcia's statement about the Stanford players: "It kind of seems like everything has been given to them."

"What a stupid thing to say," Cook grumbled.

Stenstrom read the quote, then threw down the newspaper. "I feel insulted," he said.

That's exactly what Walsh wanted.

Walsh based his game plan for San Jose partly on a scouting report Guy Benjamin had put together after attending San Jose's first game against California, which the Spartans lost 46-16. Pac-10 teams are not allowed to scout each other, but San Jose State was not in the Pac-10, so Walsh had called up Berkeley's new head coach Keith Gilbertson and asked if Benjamin could sit in the press box in Berkeley to observe San Jose State. Gilbertson agreed because Cal and Stanford wouldn't be meeting for more than two months, and it was too early for Stanford to get a line on Cal.

Walsh did not ask Benjamin to write a typical scouting report, which might delineate plays and formations or the strengths and weaknesses of particular players. That, Walsh could get from game films. He was more interested in what the film would *not* show, in what went on between plays, in San Jose's psychological state.

Benjamin wrote:

SJS came out semi-enthusiastic for an opening game: I don't want to say intimidated, but a better word would be unsure or not as confident. SJS talked some trash but not a lot. After the first two TD's, which came early, they started to fade as a team. SJS recovered a fumble in the 2nd qtr and only two or three guys showed any enthusiasm. The coaches were obviously trying to get the players "up" from the beginning of the game on. Offense moved the ball in the first half but ran out of steam in the second. SJS really didn't come out and hit nor look like they wanted to hit with Cal. On one kickoff in 3rd qtr SJS did not have one guy on the ground. SJS just didn't match up physically or emotionally with Cal.

Benjamin was interested in how Stanford could steal offensive play signals from San Jose's wide receivers coach Ed Buller:

Offense gave signals to QB very quickly. Signal caller was Eddie, who wore a distinctive blue shirt and stood on the right. Eddie always signaled, never used player shuttle, even on substitutions. QB uses finger signals like our guys do to signal routes—this should be easy to steal.

And finally, Benjamin observed the San Jose defense:

Def LE #99 quit early in 3rd qtr or is really out of shape. LOLB #40 didn't look like he quit but was really tired. Both #99 and #40 were sucking wind by the middle of 2nd qtr. Def line quit rushing passer with 6:19 to play in 2nd qtr.

It was no accident that Walsh had sent Benjamin to dope out San Jose State. In many ways, the two men thought alike. At thirty-seven, Benjamin was a tall, handsome man with black hair and an irreverent manner who, unlike some of the other assistants, did not seem in awe of Walsh. He knew when to approach him and when to leave him alone—when he would see Walsh at his desk with that glassy look in his eyes, Benjamin understood the coach was in conference with his muse, and he left quietly. He once compared Walsh to Einstein: "There are probably certain times when Einstein's approachable, when you're able to talk to him and his mind's not on it. And there are probably times when he's thinking, even in a restaurant, and it's not a good time to go up to him and talk about anything."

When he could sense Walsh wasn't deep into his thoughts, Benjamin would burst into his office and demand to be heard about some player who couldn't get the right courses or some problem with the administration. Walsh always listened carefully to what Benjamin had to say. Benjamin was the one intellectual on the staff in addition to vonAppen, and like vonAppen he was absolutely loyal to Walsh.

Benjamin still ranked fourth at Stanford in career passing and career total offense. In 1978, he was a Miami Dolphins' second-round draft pick. He played with the Dolphins in 1978 and 1979, New Orleans in 1980, and with the 49ers from 1981 through 1984. He was not a fast runner, and by the end of his career, four knee operations had slowed him down even more. His throwing arm was ordinary, but he survived on cunning, on knowing how to place his feet when he threw, how to position his hips, and how to follow through with his arm. He was the ultimate apostle of Walsh's offense and knew every nuance, every variation of every play. Even now, when the quarterbacks had a problem and didn't want to disturb Walsh or Shea, or when they simply wanted to shoot the breeze, they would go to Benjamin's office.

Benjamin had never been comfortable in the NFL because among other things, it wasn't Stanford, operated at a lower intellectual level, was venal, hardhearted, corporate. One night during his first season with the Dolphins he came home, crawled into bed next to his wife, and felt tears spilling down his face.

"What's wrong?" she asked.

"It's not what I expected," he said.

When Walsh released him from the 49ers after the 1984 season—"I would have cut myself," Benjamin said—he decided to get out of football entirely. For as long as he could remember his identity had been "quarterback," and now he wanted to be someone else. It was painful, this casting off of his old personality, but he was detaching himself from football, at first running a travel agency that arranged cultural exchanges with the Soviet Union. And then one morning Don Tobin of the Chicago Bears called and said he wanted Benjamin to play quarterback for them. It was 7:30, and Benjamin hadn't even gotten out of bed yet. Tobin told Benjamin the Bears had a plane ticket waiting for him at San Francisco Airport for a flight that morning.

"I don't know. I'll have to think about it," Benjamin said.

He went for a jog, came back, and told his wife, "When Tobin calls back, tell him, thanks, but Guy isn't interested."

Then Benjamin went to work. For years after that, he cut himself off from football, even from his friends. He hated the idea of being identified exclusively as a *former* football player, of going to banquets and wearing a blue blazer with the NFL Alumni patch. Later on, he took a full-time faculty appointment at New College in San Francisco, teaching the political economy of sport and recreation. He also set up a program helping professional athletes and former college athletes complete their undergraduate degrees.

Through it all, he stayed in touch with Walsh, even arranging a banquet for Walsh and all his quarterbacks. Kenny Anderson attended and so did Greg Cook and Dan Fouts and Joe Montana. Walsh, who is nostalgic about his players, who has told his executive assistant Jane Walsh (no relation) to put through phone calls from former players instantly, no matter what, appreciated what Benjamin did for him.

After Walsh decided to return to Stanford, he asked Benjamin to come with him, and Benjamin thought, yes, this would be the perfect opportunity to discover if he had a vocation for coaching. But he wasn't interested in a staff position. He told Walsh he wanted to get an advanced degree, and so it came about that Benjamin took a leave from New College and found himself at Stanford working on a master's in education and helping out as a graduate assistant with the football team. Like vonAppen, Benjamin had come to Stanford to be with Walsh.

Despite Benjamin's scouting report and the way Walsh worked his team into a frenzy, the Cardinal offense did not dominate San Jose State. Walsh wanted to run right through the Spartans, to show from the beginning that the privileged kids from Palo Alto could beat the punks at their own game, but it didn't work out that way. Stenstrom fumbled the very first snap from center, and the Cardinal couldn't get anything going. The only touchdown Stanford scored in the first half came on an interception by cornerback Vaughn Bryant, which he ran back twenty-eight yards into the end zone. Freshman placekicker Eric Abrams kicked a field goal to put Stanford up 10-0 at the gun.

Stenstrom was lucky to be alive. He'd been knocked for a loop twice, and both times he had to lie on the grass and catch his breath and wait until the pain went away. Each time he'd come out of the game until he could pull himself together. The pass protection was still awful, and after Stenstrom went down for the count the second time, one Stanford defensive player shook his head in disgust and told another, "Our offensive line is pretty bad. There's no way Steve's going to make it through the season."

The defense, on the other hand, was having its way with San Jose, beating hell out of quarterback Jeff Garcia, who seemed confused and frightened. As the San Jose State team passed by Stanford's locker room at halftime, some of the Spartans yelled "Our house!"—but their tone was halfhearted, and it was clear they said it because that's what was expected, not because they had any faith in their cause. The Stanford defense had already received proof of San Jose's demoralized state when Cardinal linebacker Ron George strolled into the Spartans' offensive huddle and announced, "You guys can't touch me." Instead of throwing him out, the Spartans dropped their heads.

Stanford did not score its first offensive touchdown until the fourth quarter, and by then it was clear that Walsh had not yet found a way to communicate his genius to his offense. Throughout the game the defense had given the offense good field position, and when the offense didn't do much with it, Estevan Avila felt "pissed."

Finally, San Jose State, which was playing with only fourteen men on defense, caved in from sheer fatigue. Stanford scored three touchdowns in the fourth quarter and won 37-13, but the Cardinal offense had not been impressive.

The Cardinal and Spartan players shook hands when the game was over. After all, there hadn't been animosity, except once when San Jose's Anthony Washington stood in front of the Stanford sideline grinning and waving his arms. Scott Schuhmann walked over to him then, and yelled to Washington, who was only five-seven, "Fuck you, Shorty. Go play."

But that was the only incident. There was too much inbreeding between the two coaching staffs for lingering bad feelings. In the locker room after the game, Cardinal players started yelling "big game," a reference to next week's trip to Notre Dame, but Walsh, who was smiling, brought them back to the moment. "Defense, you guys are the best in football. Our offense still isn't in sync, but we won. We did just what we said we would do. We kicked their ass. So far we're on schedule, and our best football is ahead of us."

When Walsh opened the locker room to the press, Terry Shea slipped out the door and walked over to the San Jose room. He talked to players and coaches, and then he went looking for quarterback Jeff Garcia, whom he had tutored and brought along just as he now was working with Stenstrom. But Garcia was taking a shower. Shea waited. Garcia emerged wet and distraught over the three interceptions he had thrown.

"Coach, I didn't play very well," he told Shea.

Shea hugged him and said, "I love you, Jeff."

Garcia began to cry.

Walsh's coaches didn't know that he had worn a wireless microphone during the game so that NBC, his former employer, could put together a feature catching Walsh in the act of coaching. NBC planned to air the film, complete with a Walsh interview and background on his return to Stanford, before the Notre Dame–Stanford game the following week.

The microphone picked up the conversation over the headsets between Walsh and Terry Shea, who sat on the third level of the Stanford press box, an old wooden structure without elevators. By the time the coaches climbed all the way up there, they felt as if they'd gone into oxygen debt. The coaches inhabited a tiny room with a ceiling-high window through which they watched the game. In addition to Shea, Mike Wilson, Guy Benjamin, Tom Holmoe, Keena Turner, and Al Matthews worked in the press box, each performing a specific duty. Benjamin, for example, would track the opponent's defensive fronts and report them to Walsh and Scott Schuhmann on the field.

It was Shea's job to tell Walsh down and distance, and field position on every play. Walsh's view of the action often was obscured by bodies in collision, and when he stood on the sideline the sight lines were flat and it was not always easy to figure out how many yards the Cardinal needed for a first down. Sometimes Walsh, overloaded by details and decisions, would forget the down. So Shea kept him current on those things, and also whispered into his ear what to anticipate so that Walsh would continue to be a play or two ahead of himself. Shea once said he was speaking to Walsh's subconscious.

Shea, the former therapist, always talked in a soothing, almost cooing voice. Everyone needed Walsh calm, unfettered, at his best, and it was Shea's job to keep him that way. "It's third and seven," Shea would say in the same soft, supportive, interested tone a therapist might use as he asks, "How did it make you feel when your wife left you for the plumber?"

It didn't matter if things were upsetting, Shea never lost his cool. Stanford might lose the ball on a fumble, and he'd immediately be talking over the headset to Walsh about the next series, forcing Walsh away from the past, not allowing him to dwell on temporary failures. The meaning was clear. Everything was under control, everything factored in. Even the unexpected was expected. All the offensive coaches in the press box and Schuhmann down below heard the dialogue between Walsh and Shea, and they would contribute if they had something to say. Walsh could click a button and listen in to vonAppen and the defensive coaches, but he rarely talked to them.

Sometimes Shea suggested plays. At first he was reluctant, especially in the Texas A&M game when he hardly knew Walsh and was having problems mastering the Cardinal offense. But afterward Walsh told him to be assertive with his ideas, and Shea took that to heart and suggested plays whenever he could. Walsh would listen, but rarely comment. Sometimes Shea didn't even know what play Walsh had called and would have to say, "What is it, Coach?" Walsh usually got around to calling Shea's plays, although not immediately.

Over the years, Walsh had trained himself to be businesslike, almost emotionally neutral during games. He needed to be uninvolved, to achieve the distance of a critic so that he could dispassionately judge the game and his own performance. During "The Star-Spangled Banner," he would have the feeling—it was actually a physical sensation—that he was leaving the field. It was something like achieving the ideal zen state. When he first went to the 49ers, he'd had to go through a ritual to leave the field, make himself vanish, by chanting, "Get out of here. Get away from this emotion. Pull yourself out of here." After a while, the metaphors became more complex: "You're watching this game through a window. You're not here. You're just observing through a window."

It was easier to pull himself away now. He didn't have to go through an elaborate process. At the opening kickoff, he inevitably found himself in a room removed from the crowd and the noise in the stadium. He was in the soundless, timeless place generals inhabit when they send troops into battle. Staying behind the window meant that he did not become disconsolate after failure. It also meant he rarely shared in the joy of touchdowns or great plays. He couldn't allow himself to crawl through that window and join the others, even for a moment. If he did, he might not be able to return to the quiet room, and that could mean disaster. When the game ended and Walsh walked to the middle of the field and shook hands with the other coach, he could feel himself coming back to reality, breaking the glass, letting go of the coaching demeanor.

But more and more this season, Walsh was finding himself on the wrong side of the window. Maybe it was because he had been away for three years, or maybe what he saw on the field, especially with his offensive line, would not allow him to keep a neutral distance. "Frustration just freezes the brain cells," he once explained. "You can't think clearly and then you start sort of blurting out these plays, like 'Fourteen-Lead.' You start blurting that out to save your mind, so you can get time to think. I don't want to blurt that out. I want to call it just at the right time when I want to put somebody off balance. And that takes execution, and obviously we had it with the 49ers any number of years. But here it's been tough."

His frustration would spill over to his conversations with Shea. Instead of methodically calling plays—"Stay behind the window, Bill"—Walsh would bitch to Shea over the headsets. "He's had to listen to a lot of confusing profanity from me and harping and whining," Walsh explained one day. "Probably whining is the right word. I whine. I whine about the way things are going. 'I'm just so goddamned frustrated I can't believe it.' I imagine I say that all the time— 'I can't believe it. This is ridiculous.' I say things like that, because we aren't functioning offensively in our line play. It all surrounds that. I say, 'My God, don't tell me.' I feel for Terry that he has to hear it. And what happens is he probably gets conditioned to it. 'There Bill goes again. Oh, he did it again.' And all the games start to run together. I think we'll be a lot better in doing this a year from now."

Walsh's whining, his bitching, had not become public knowledge, but now he was wearing a wireless mike that would pick up everything he said. The entire nation was about to share Walsh's uncensored thoughts, his off-the-record thoughts, precisely the kinds of things a head coach and his staff don't want the general public to know.

NBC missed most of the first half because its equipment malfunctioned, but in the second half, Walsh came through loud and clear. The offense was not doing well, and there he was on camera in NBC's cleaned-up, bleeped-out version, yelling, "Ah bleep" and "Oh bleep"— just what anyone would expect a football coach to scream when his team screwed up.

Some of his monologue was more personal. Once, he had just called a play based on information Shea passed along from the press box. As Steve Stenstrom got under center—and when it was too late to make a change—Shea informed Walsh, "They're in a zone, Coach." The play obviously had been designed only for man-to-man coverage because in the next breath, Walsh yelled, "Well, goddamn it, Coach." And there was Shea in his soft, psychologist's voice, "OK, all right, all right, OK. Let's see what happens."

When Walsh called a running play on first and 17, and then realized too late his mistake, he went through the roof, berating himself. "It's humiliating for me. I should have been throwing the bleeping ball here. I'm out of my bleeping mind. Jesus Christ, Bill, you're bleeping nuts." And in the background, as usual, Shea came in, "OK, Bill. All right, all right." But Walsh talked over him. "Jesus bleeping Christ, so humiliating."

NBC picked up Walsh despairing over the outcome: "If we can get through this game, I swear to God." And NBC also picked him up criticizing Stenstrom, a major no-no in Walsh's ethic. His relationship with his quarterbacks was as personal as a man's relationship with his wife. When Stenstrom did not spot a secondary receiver who was open, Walsh could be heard complaining to Shea and, by implication, criticizing Shea, who was responsible for working with the quarterbacks: "He's not coming off his primary receiver. He's slow to do it. Well, we've got to get better at doing it. That's all."

On the other hand, when San Jose's Troy Jensen recovered a Milburn fumble and returned it ninety-five yards for a touchdown, Walsh didn't say a single word. The team had made a mistake. Those things happen. He walked along the sideline, his jaw tight, already thinking about the next sequence.

NBC had other material, just as interesting, which it did not use. The tape often caught Walsh in a self-critical mode, letting out the secret fears he controlled all other times.

"Jesus Christ, I'm going fucking crazy."

"Oh shit, I can't coach anymore. Oh shit, we had plenty of protection. It's so inept. We're trying so fucking hard. We're coaching as hard as we can. It's just not working."

Shea and Schuhmann continuously talked to Walsh, usually suggesting plays. Sometimes Shea and Schuhmann spoke at the same time, and in the middle of all that competing noise, Walsh had to think and plan and call plays. When the overlapping voices became too much, Walsh would raise a hand and say, "All right, hold on," and everything would go silent.

Once, after a botched special team's play, Walsh buttonholed Bill Singler on the sideline and complained, "We're giving them twenty, twenty-five yards when we do that. It can't be done that way anymore. You and I can visit about that."

With the exception of Fred vonAppen, none of Walsh's coaches had ever heard him on the headsets before, and some were surprised. One coach said Walsh became another person during games, letting all his emotions spill out, when in every other aspect of his life, he was careful, understated, self-governing to a fault. "He's at the ends of his personality," this coach explained. "It's sort of like tirades, but he's creative, too. He wants input to bounce ideas off. He talks the whole time on offense. One time, he said, 'You guys should tell me to shut up.' There was dead silence. No one spoke."

Another coach was more blunt about the Walsh of the headsets. "Bill goes fucking nuts. He vents. He says things like, 'I don't think I can go on coaching with pass protection like this.'" This coach thought Walsh was squandering his energy, dissipating it in useless emotion when he should have conserved it for play calling. "It's a waste of resources. Bill should be calling plays instead of venting about what went wrong. Of course, he'll rant and rave, and then he'll go ahead and score thirty-five points."

A few days after the taping, Dick Enberg, Walsh's former broadcasting partner at NBC, called to tell Walsh he would not be happy with what NBC had put together. NBC had shown him using profanity, Enberg said. Walsh felt betrayed. He was protective of his image, did not like outsiders to know he swore, although anyone who spent a minute thinking about the subject would expect a football coach, a man who spent his time in the company of male athletes, to use cuss words. Walsh refused to watch the film.

If Walsh felt betrayed by NBC, he had equal reason to feel he had betrayed himself. After all, he'd agreed to the wireless mike. It was hardly NBC's fault if it broadcast what it recorded with Walsh's permission.

But Walsh obviously knew all that, understood his own level of responsibility, and he still had given himself away during the game. When he was in battle, he couldn't always see the larger pattern, because he was part of the pattern. Although he planned to be calm, to cut a dignified figure on television, and although he thought he could control himself, he got caught up, lost in the game frenzy. At times like those, he sounded like a losing coach, although Stanford never trailed San Jose State and ended up winning easily. It was Walsh's curse not only to compete against an opponent, but also against an idealized version of football, even an idealized version of himself, one he had perfected with the 49ers.

Walsh felt sore about the tape for several days, but as he got ready for Notre Dame, NBC wasn't his biggest problem. He had a more serious one—how to visit South Bend without an offense.

C H A P T E R

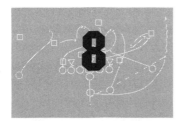

SOMETIME AFTER THE San Jose State game, Bill Walsh went into mourning. He was supposed to be getting ready for Notre Dame—focusing his thoughts, assembling his game plan—but his mind was elsewhere. To those around him, it seemed as if Walsh already had imagined losing to the Irish, had actually visualized getting humiliated in South Bend, had already seen Notre Dame's score mounting higher and higher while he stood helpless on the sideline. He walked around the Stanford football offices on Sunday and Monday in a kind of death watch, grieving over a game he hadn't even played.

He did not believe any of his offensive players could start for Notre Dame. Glyn Milburn might have been able to come in for specific plays, but even he would have trouble breaking into the Irish lineup at running back. And Walsh's doubts about himself were graver than any misgivings he had about his squad. As far as he was concerned, he hadn't proved he still could coach. Defense was winning for the Cardinal. Walsh was supposed to be an offensive whiz, and he couldn't sustain drives, couldn't rediscover the rhythm of play calling. He wasn't sure if he ever would.

Walsh usually would have completed most of his game plan by the time he went home Monday night, but now his plan was in fragments. He kept drawing up plays and throwing them out. The coaches hadn't seen him like this before. He was always focused, had an idea of exactly how to attack a defense, an insight that came to him intuitively and instantly. For Notre Dame, he was all over the place.

One of the coaches told himself that Walsh was overpreparing, trying to do too much. The reasons were obvious. Playing sixth-ranked Notre Dame in South Bend was Walsh's official coming out as a college coach. This wasn't some regional game against Oregon or San Jose State. It was going to be on national television, on NBC in fact, the network on which Walsh had announced Notre Dame home games the previous season. At that time he had spent an hour with Notre Dame head coach Lou Holtz before each of his broadcasts, and he had come to respect the man. Some people close to Walsh believed he already had conceded the game to Notre Dame because of Holtz's ability and the obvious superiority of Holtz's players. As Walsh contemplated the impending loss, he was wondering what he had done to himself by returning to football. First Holtz would have a victory against him, and then it would be somebody else, and after a while, it no longer would be a big thing to beat Bill Walsh.

Walsh had been through similar episodes, although his staff didn't know it. Even when he coached the 49ers, he would lapse into depression before a big game. Walsh came to understand that he had to feel desperate, hopeless, backed into a corner to do his best. After several days of wallowing in despair, a miracle would occur. He would kick into what he called "survival mode," a state of mind in which he performed brilliantly. "I needed it," he once said of his depression. "We won more games in that mode than when I was positive and self-assured."

By the time he struggled out of bed Tuesday morning, he had thrown himself into a state of anguish. He came to work sullen, his hands shaking. He met with his offensive coaches in the conference room, but his voice was barely a whisper. The meeting of the offensive coaches was in exact contrast to the one down the hall in Fred vonAppen's office. The defensive coaches were yelling and laughing and arguing—obviously in the right frame of mind for the game. Meanwhile, the offensive meeting sounded as if it were taking place in a library.

VonAppen stuck his head in the door of the conference room, then recoiled at the tension. Realizing he had to do something before it was too late, before the other coaches and the players caught Walsh's mood, vonAppen went in search of Al Matthews.

"Is your friend OK?" he asked.

Matthews was wondering the same thing.

"We need to do something, and you're the one to do it," vonAppen told Matthews.

When vonAppen left, Matthews shut the door to his office and sat behind his desk and lapsed into thought. His duties on the staff were modest. Just the other day, he'd walked into the conference room with a dust rag and cleaned off all the shelves holding video-tapes. Then he printed labels for each coach and pasted them in front of the shelves—one shelf for each coach. But he'd been hired to do more important things. He knew it, and so did Walsh. He was there to keep Walsh on track, to prevent him from sliding into self-doubt and immobility, to nudge him back into action. When he saw Walsh drifting away, Matthews would tell him a joke, get him to laugh, any-thing to break the downward spiral and call him back to the world.

But Matthews had never seen Walsh like this before—one of the walking dead. When Walsh left the coaches' meeting, Matthews fol-lowed him into his office. Walsh sat at the tiny table at which he drew his game plans. He was morose, listless. He had to attend his weekly press conference in a few minutes, and he slowly began to change into a Stanford T-shirt.

Matthews closed the door, but Walsh didn't look at him.

Matthews stood over him and talked to the top of his head. Matthews's voice was nervous but firm. "You may throw my ass out of here for what I'm going to say now, but you've got to snap out of it. You can't have people see you walking around with a long face."

Matthews was telling Walsh what Walsh himself would have told the players—don't quit, have pride.

Walsh looked up at Matthews, a sad smile on his pale lips. "I know, but the schedule gets so tough now."

"You've had tougher schedules before," Matthews scolded. "Just let it out on offense. Be yourself. Have fun."

Walsh walked downstairs to the Hall of Fame Room for the press conference. As he sat down behind the microphone, his mood bright-ened. He usually could pull himself together for the media, project the image that everything was fine and he was doing all right. He joked that one reporter's tape recorder looked like a Kmart special, and then he answered the usual questions, explaining that he'd gained no advan-tage over Holtz by announcing Notre Dame games because, among other things, Holtz would not allow him to observe practices.

When Walsh was finished, the reporters in the room began to inter-view Holtz over a speakerphone. Walsh rarely stuck around for the interview of the opposing coach, but by now he was enjoying being in public—it was such a relief from the private purgatory he'd endured for three days. So he sat down at one of the tables and listened to Holtz, who was going on about what a great coach Walsh was. Holtz was notorious for talking up his opponent. "I really have a lot of respect for Bill Walsh," he said. "I have told our football players this, 'He's a great coach and we aren't going to outcoach Bill Walsh.' I tell ya, you don't establish a reputation like Bill Walsh has unless you've done it on a consistent basis."

Now Holtz really began to lay it on thick. "And our players are gonna have to play hard, because if this game is won on the sideline, and there aren't as many won on the sideline as you think, it isn't gonna be won on the Notre Dame sideline."

Walsh hardly seemed to be listening. He had risen from his chair, tiptoed to the podium to stand near the speakerphone. He whispered to Gary Migdol that he would like to ask Holtz a question. Walsh was smiling. It was a mischievous smile, a playful smile, the smile of someone who had been at the bottom of the sea a few moments before, and now, for some inexplicable reason, was as high as the sky.

Migdol interrupted Holtz. "Coach, there's a person here in the room who wants to ask you a question."

Walsh put his mouth near the speakerphone. He was grinning.

"Coach, aside from football, how about those hokey commercials you do that are on TV well after midnight? Those ones about golf."

For a moment, Holtz hesitated. A golf question was so unexpected now. Then he began to answer. "Well, I've got a . . ."

Walsh could see Holtz didn't know who had asked the question, and he didn't want to embarrass him.

"Coach, this is Bill Walsh," he said, almost shouting.

Unfortunately, Holtz didn't hear him. Holtz said, "I did not go out there and say, 'Hey, I wanna tape this commercial.'"

"Lou, this is Bill."

"Matter of fact, I got a call from Bob Mann 'bout a week ago saying that they had some other videos and if I was interested in purchasing one at that time. You know, I was going out there and Bob Mann was going to explain his philosophy a little bit more, and they ended up taping it, and that's exactly how that thing came about."

Walsh was blushing. He began to ease out of the room.

Holtz paused as if expecting another question. When none came, he kept going. "I had no idea it was going to be on every night at three o'clock in the morning. I tell you what bothers me most about it. People now think I'm a good golfer and it's doggone hard to get as many strokes as I need to win."

Holtz finally wound down. Everyone in the room was laughing raucously at him.

Gary Migdol said, "Coach, for your information, Bill Walsh asked that question."

"Did he?" Holtz said.

Back in his office, Walsh told Jane Walsh to call Holtz's secretary and apologize for the practical joke. Then he drifted into the conference room, where a friend was waiting for him. "I was shaky yesterday," Walsh confessed, in a voice that still sounded shaky. He shut the door and stood with his back against the wall as if he were hiding from an enemy. He had a cough and his sinus infection had kicked in. "The offense played so badly against San Jose State," he whispered. He sat down in a chair, leaned closer to his friend. "The offensive line is too slow and the team isn't deep." He sighed. He said it would take two years to get the Cardinal playing to his standard.

"It makes a coach heartsick," he said.

A few hours later Walsh met the team in the Hall of Fame Room. When he was in front of the players, he never gave signs of despair. He became Super Bill. "Starting with Notre Dame, I'm instituting an award for the best substitute of the game," he said. "I'm calling it the Twelfth Man Award." He admitted that Stanford did not have as many talented players as Notre Dame, but that didn't mean the Cardinal couldn't win. That's where the subs came in. Every substitute was expected to study as hard as if he were a starter. His turn might come any time, maybe even in South Bend.

Walsh stared at his players. His voice boomed. "In battle, the best troops are sometimes killed early," he said. "The people who pick up their rifles and take over win the battles. It's the same in football, you have to be ready when your turn comes. There were times Matt Cavanaugh picked up a rifle and went in when Joe Montana wasn't available, and we won. We depended on the substitutes playing as well as the starters, maybe even better."

Although Walsh rarely invoked the 49ers around his team—kept the 49er experience absolutely separate—he was, at that moment, recalling one of his favorite 49er themes. In 1981, his first Super Bowl season, he had taken the 49ers into Pittsburgh to play a tough, proud Steelers team. Before the game, he lectured Montana and Ronnie Lott and Randy Cross and the rest of the 49ers in the quiet, cramped locker room, told them they were in a hostile environment and could only depend on themselves.

Then he told them about the British in Burma.

Walsh explained to the 49ers how, during World War II, the British had defeated the Japanese when it seemed impossible—they had lost their best men early in the fighting. The young 49ers went on to beat the Steelers, and after the game, the players shouted cheers like a college team. For the first time, they knew they were for real.

Now Walsh was telling the Burma story to the Cardinal. When he finished, he abruptly left the Hall of Fame Room. It was a dramatic exit. The players looked around to see where he had gone, while Terry Shea took over. As Walsh walked out the door, Shea was saying, "Notre Dame ranks eighty-sixth in the nation in defense. So they're human."

Walsh sat down on the front steps of the building, his head in his hands like *The Thinker.* He often took this pose when he was lost in thoughts of offensive game plans or when he was deciding how to motivate his team or when he was worrying. When someone came out of the room, Walsh looked up and said, "I tell them about history. I wonder if it means anything to them."

He stood up and leaned against the wall. He was still thinking about the British and the Japanese. "Some of the British would surrender, and the Japanese would kill them and scatter their body parts," he whispered, staring at his hands. "The British didn't understand this. They had a colonial mentality, believed in surrender with honor. But after a while, when the British would capture the Japanese, they killed them and scattered their body parts. They had to learn to beat the Japanese at their own game."

Standing there, Walsh may have begun to entertain a vision of Fighting Irish body parts strewn all over the field. He certainly seemed to be cheering up. He walked back inside and told Mike Wilson to cue up the videotape of a game between Notre Dame and Tennessee played the previous season in South Bend. It was the last Notre Dame game he had ever announced, and it was a galling experience for Lou Holtz. Late in the second quarter, the Irish led 31-7 and seemed to be cruising to another easy victory, but Tennessee roared back and won 35-34.

As the Stanford players watched the screen, they saw shots of the score flash before their eyes. First, Notre Dame went up 7-0. Then

14-0, and then 31-7. After that, things began to change: 31-14, then 31-21, and finally Tennessee took the lead 35-34. Walsh stood there quietly while the scores changed. In the dark room, he seemed like a sorcerer.

When the video ended and Bill Singler turned on the lights, Walsh walked onto the small stage and said, "What do most teams do when they fall way behind? They go into the tank. But Tennessee kept playing each down like it was the last down. They didn't even act like there was a score. They played every down like it was another game. That's how you have to play no matter what happens Saturday. Make each play a discrete event in your life unrelated to what went before or is going to come after. No matter what happens, we keep playing up to our standard of football."

Before each game, Walsh came up with a theme, and this was to be it against Notre Dame: Don't cave in even if you fall way behind. It was as though he had received a vision, whole and complete, of the future.

At practice that afternoon, Walsh seemed edgy. Terry Shea was working with second-string quarterback Mark Butterfield and third-stringer Chris Berg. Steve Stenstrom, who had suffered nerve damage in his chest from getting knocked all over the place by San Jose State, was standing on the sideline dressed in shorts, sneakers, and a T-shirt. He followed the action while studying his red playbook. Shea was giving Butterfield and Berg equal time. This did not please Walsh. The college mentality is to allow each player the same chance in practice, but when it came to game preparation, Walsh still thought like a professional coach. With Notre Dame four days away, there was no way he'd work out the third-string guy, no way he'd concentrate on a player who was unlikely to get near the field on Saturday. He shook his head and walked away.

Later, he turned on Fred vonAppen. The defense was dominating the offense, and Walsh couldn't get his plays to work. Everyone could see Walsh becoming frustrated; his face was red, his fingers were snapping. Finally, he yelled to vonAppen, "You control them. I can't control them. We can't get anything off."

VonAppen took a deep breath. "OK, let's work the perimeters," he shouted to his men.

Two plays later, Ron George knocked down a Stenstrom pass.

"Control them!" Walsh shouted again.

VonAppen told his players to back off.

Looking at what had happened, Al Matthews wished the offensive line would play as mean as the defense.

Steve Stenstrom didn't practice all week. He was sore all over, felt as if the entire San Jose defense had danced on his chest. He couldn't throw the ball, and this added to Walsh's mountain of worries. How was he going to beat the Irish without his Number One quarterback?

Stenstrom fully expected to play, but his opinion, so far, did not have the backing of the doctors or Walsh. Despite the elitist intellectual Stanford image, Stenstrom was the kind of guy who could go out and throw three touchdown passes after someone dropped a safe on his head. He was rosy-cheeked and relentlessly polite, and it was difficult to believe that anyone that pleasant could also be that tough. But he *was* tough, and sometimes, after he'd been blasted by a blitz and slowly staggered to his feet, his offensive linemen would feel ashamed because, though they had failed to protect him, he never complained.

Stenstrom came to Stanford from El Toro in Orange County, California, but his football roots extended to Plano, Texas, forty miles outside Dallas. His father worked for Xerox and would be shifted around the country. When Stenstrom was nine, the family settled in Plano, a mecca for football. "I loved it," Stenstrom once said. "They'd get seventeen thousand for a high school game."

Stenstrom started playing seriously in the fourth grade, full pads in eight-man peewee football. When he applied to Stanford, head coach Denny Green was impressed that he'd completed 66 percent of his passes as a senior in El Toro, but he also noticed that Stenstrom had started out in Plano. "It's like they invented football in Plano," Green said later on.

Stenstrom redshirted his freshman year at Stanford and was only third on the depth chart as a sophomore in 1991, but things changed quickly. John Lynch, the Number Two quarterback, switched to safety, and the starter, Jason Palumbis, was having problems. Stanford started out the season 1-3, and Palumbis hadn't thrown a touchdown pass.

In the fourth game, a 42-26 loss to Notre Dame, Stenstrom came off the bench at the start of the fourth quarter and guided the Cardinal sixty-nine and seventy yards for touchdowns on consecutive drives, completing eight of ten passes for 124 yards. Green, impressed, noticed that on almost every pass Stenstrom delivered the ball shoulder-high, putting his receivers in perfect position to turn upfield and gain additional yardage. Green named him the starter for the next game, a 56-6 trouncing of Cornell.

The following week, Stenstrom led Stanford to a 24-21 win over USC, taking the Cardinal to a game-winning touchdown on a drive that started on its own 35. Despite missing three plays after being kneed in the groin, Stenstrom threw the clinching touchdown pass with 1:11 remaining, breaking a streak of fifteen straight games in which Stanford could not beat Southern Cal. He won his first seven starts, becoming the first Cardinal quarterback to do that since the legendary Frankie Albert in 1940.

And now, unexpectedly, Stenstrom was being coached by Bill Walsh. It was a stroke of good fortune that still dazzled him. When he'd first heard that Walsh was coming back, Stenstrom told himself, "Oh my goodness, this is the guy who developed Montana and refined his skills and turned him into the best quarterback who's ever played the game, and now I'm to have a chance to work under him."

He had first met Walsh as a freshman. He was riding away from practice on a bike when he heard Dennis Green calling to him from a sport truck. When Stenstrom rode over, Green pointed to the driver and said, "Steve, I'd like you to meet someone." The driver was Walsh. Stenstrom gave a shy, "Nice to meet you," then pedaled madly back to his dorm room to call his parents. "I met Bill Walsh!" he shouted. "I met Bill Walsh!"

For years, Stenstrom had worshiped at the twin shrines of Walsh and Montana—of God the Father, and God the Son. But because he was a quarterback, Stenstrom was more involved with the Son. His walls were covered with Montaniana, with photos of Joe passing and Joe ducking under center and Joe running and Joe being Joe. Stenstrom's favorite was a framed photo of Montana getting ready to pass. "He has that look in his eye, so intense, so focused," Stenstrom said when describing the picture, which hung on the wall over his bed. In fact, Montana's eyes, those intense eyes, were the very last things Stenstrom saw each night before turning off the light.

It was not lost on Stenstrom that Montana had played for Notre Dame, and that Walsh had announced Notre Dame football games, and that, a year before, Stenstrom himself had his coming out against Notre Dame. Everything seemed to be converging on the game against Notre Dame. It was as if some giant spiritual apparatus had clicked in and a special destiny awaited Stenstrom in South Bend. As

he watched other quarterbacks take the snaps in practice, he told himself there was no way he'd sit on Saturday.

The Stanford team didn't stay in South Bend. Hotels were sold
out in a hundred-mile radius, and Stanford ended up at a Holiday Inn
forty miles from the Notre Dame campus. The team arrived at the
hotel late on Thursday night, and had meetings early the next morning. After lunch, the offense went out to a parking lot in front of the
Holiday Inn and performed a walk-through of various blocking patterns and pass routes, while Walsh watched from the side. Once he
interrupted Scott Schuhmann, who was running the drill, and said one
of the receivers should go out for a pass, "Here." Here was behind a
midget evergreen tree. Everyone laughed. Walsh was trying to keep
the team relaxed. He was also trying to keep himself relaxed.

After that, the team boarded buses and rode for an hour into
South Bend. A police escort led the caravan along the narrow private
streets of the town, past neat little houses, the lawns perfect emerald
green squares. As the buses turned into the campus, they passed the
Hesburgh Library with its giant mosaic of Christ on one wall. Christ's
arms are raised, and football people like to joke that this "Touchdown
Jesus" is signaling a score for the Irish.

Walsh kept the press away from the workout. This was the first
day Stenstrom would throw and Walsh wanted that kept private. If
Stenstrom couldn't do it, Walsh would have to give the start to Mark
Butterfield, who was not ready. But Stenstrom threw without pain,
long, graceful spirals down the field that Mike Cook and Justin
Armour caught with no trouble.

As the team worked out, Walsh walked around the perimeter of
Notre Dame Stadium, a sixty-three-year-old structure made of tan
brick. The Irish media guide will inform you there are more than two
million bricks in the building, not to mention four hundred tons of
steel and fifteen thousand cubic yards of concrete. The stadium seats
59,075, but twice that many would come if Notre Dame ever decided
to enlarge the seating capacity. The stands are right on top of the field,
and temporary seats are installed near the end zone. Anyone who runs
a sharp corner route at either end is likely to fall into the lap of a spectator. It was quiet on Friday as Walsh walked the field, but he knew
the mob would be loud in twenty-four hours and he wondered if his
team would unravel.

His staff had varying reactions to the stadium. The coaches were installed in a small locker room containing one flush toilet in a tiny closet. Al Matthews was the first to use it. "I peed in the same place as Knute Rockne," he proudly told the others. "It was a thrill. I mean it."

Guy Benjamin was not as taken with the old building, or with Notre Dame for that matter. He was a Stanford graduate and he was used to the large expanse of the Stanford campus, the stadium seating 85,500 with stands rising several stories, San Francisco Bay and the foothills in the distance. "I don't know what I expected, but it was just a Midwest college campus in the middle of nowhere," he complained. "The stadium looked like a place you store equipment."

After dinner, Bill Singler held the special teams meeting, which all the coaches and players attended. Singler was reading from a local publication called *The Blue and Gold*, which gave matchups in various categories. The newspaper's conclusions were remarkably balanced, even conceding Stanford the advantage over Notre Dame in coaching. But Singler was looking for an angle. The newspaper had given Notre Dame the edge over the Cardinal in special teams and Singler was trying to use that to motivate his players.

Singler waved the paper in front of the players, said they had been insulted. He reminded them that Stanford's freshman placekicker, Eric Abrams, was five for six in field goal attempts and Notre Dame's Craig Hentrich was only two for four. He did not remind the players that Abrams had experienced tightness in his chest and had trouble breathing during the week and had to be checked out by the doctors. The medical conclusion? Abrams was feeling the pressure of his first big game.

Then Singler showed game footage and exhorted his men to block well and run to the ball—all the usual things. Each time Singler told his players what to do, he would say, "OK? You know what I mean?" His tone was interrogative instead of declarative. While Singler spoke, Walsh sat near the back of the room with his head in his hands. He was breathing heavily. He angrily scribbled a note to himself: *You can't beg your players to play well.*

Singler suffered from what Walsh referred to as "Loser's Syndrome." This was no reflection on Singler himself, who was an optimistic, hardworking, energetic man. But he often had coached in losing programs, and that affected him more than he understood. The year before, his team at Pacific University went 0-9, giving Singler a two-year record of 3-14-1 as head coach. After the 1991 season Pacific

University dropped football. Singler had coached quarterbacks and wide receivers at Kansas State from 1986 through 1988. Kansas State compiled a 2-30-1 record, and went winless two of his three years. Walsh believed all this losing affected the way Singler coached. He whined during games. He screamed at officials. And he begged his players without knowing it. He had become conditioned to think like a victim.

Walsh had great faith in Singler, told himself Singler could be "converted." This was where Walsh the Mentor came in. Walsh wasn't only teaching undergraduates, he was also inculcating a coaching philosophy in the next generation of coaches. When Walsh would notice Singler lapsing into the Loser's Syndrome, he would tell himself to speak to him, that Singler was worth the effort. He would take Singler aside and remind him what he was doing and Singler would recognize his behavior, almost slap himself in the head like one of the Three Stooges, and say, "Yeah, I know. I have to work on that."

When Singler wound up his speech to special teams, Walsh headed to the front of the room and, with no warning, launched into a detailed, graphic description of a wildebeest being ripped apart by a lion. He was matter-of-fact, sounded like a zoology professor. "The wildebeest goes into shock. It stands there, submissive, its head down. It doesn't feel anything as it dies. Nature protects it."

Walsh paused a moment, let his players wonder what the hell the wildebeest had to do with them. In the back of the room, Fred von-Appen, Bill Ring, Mike Wilson, Keena Turner, and Guy Benjamin were smiling. They had heard about the wildebeest during their 49er days.

When Walsh spoke again, his mood had changed. "We have some guys here who drop their heads and go into the death throes like the wildebeest," Walsh said, his voice almost seething. "So if the game is going poorly, keep your heads up, your hands on your hips. Have pride. We will *not* go through the death throes as athletes. Ever. Not in your lives. We will not be a wildebeest."

Walsh was reminding his players to refuse to give in if they fell behind. He was also reminding himself.

Later, in the defensive meeting, the tone was considerably more aggressive. The defense wasn't a wildebeest. It wasn't even a lion. It was a tyrannosaurus rex. Keena Turner handed his linebackers two pages of "Tips and Reminders," which ended with a graphic call to arms:

This is the kind of team you put your foot in their **ASS** in the first quarter, and you keep **twisting** and **turning** your foot until their **guts** are laying on the field. And even then you don't stop **twisting** and **turning** until the last second is off the clock. The foundation of our team is **DEFENSE!!!!!**

Fred vonAppen's rhetoric was considerably cooler. He wrote on the board: 512 vs. 202. Notre Dame was averaging 512 yards on offense and Stanford was allowing only 202. From the standpoint of the Stanford defense these two numbers represented the essential conflict of the game. Could the Stanford defense, which was fast but not powerful, stand up to Notre Dame's strong running game? VonAppen reminded his players that Notre Dame was the Number One offense in the country and Stanford had the second-ranked defense. "Something has to give," he told them.

Notre Dame had two damaging runners, fullback Jerome Bettis and tailback Reggie Brooks. Bettis was six feet tall, weighed 247 pounds, and looked like an icebox with legs. Brooks was only five eight, but weighed 200 pounds and was also a power runner. The year before, when Notre Dame beat Stanford in Palo Alto, Bettis ran for 179 yards, usually right up the middle. The Stanford defense had known exactly where he would be and still could do nothing with him. This worried vonAppen. He didn't think he could stop Notre Dame's backs; he merely wanted to "manage" them. He expected Holtz to run Bettis and Brooks between the tackles, or as vonAppen said, "in the tackle box." If the Stanford defense could not stop them, everything else would open up for Notre Dame. "If you can't control the inside run, players lose their resolve," vonAppen said later that night while trying to relax with a beer. "It's as though the worst thing has been exposed about you."

On game day, Walsh went down early to the team breakfast. He looked around the room at his players and told the other coaches, "They'll play their asses off. They don't know how outgunned they are. Compare the best to the worst NFL team and the differences aren't as obvious in size and talent. I mean, the best fifteen guys on our team could fit in with theirs, but the lower level? Be serious."

Walsh was preoccupied with recruiting that morning. He had heard that a high school quarterback from Nebraska named Scott Frost was coming to see the game as a guest of Notre Dame. Walsh wanted Frost for Stanford, considered him the best quarterback prospect in the country. In Frost he saw someone with the talents of

Steve Young, whom Walsh considered the prototypical quarterback for the 1990s. Like Young, Frost was a dead-accurate passer, but he also was a fine athlete who could run like a tailback. Walsh told the coaches he hoped the offense could make some first downs for Frost's benefit.

Recruiting was a sore point for Walsh. He appreciated Stanford's high admissions standards, but he sometimes felt envious of someone like Holtz. Notre Dame also was tough to get into, but Walsh believed that Holtz could find a way to gain admittance for the one player he absolutely needed, even if the player was not up to Notre Dame's academic standards. That simply was not going to happen at Stanford.

Walsh was talking about this over coffee. He had no problem with Holtz, who, he believed, ran an honest program and insisted that his players go to class and learn. But since he'd been back at Stanford, Walsh had been the victim of what he considered dirty tricks by other coaching staffs. Rival recruiters would tell high school players, "You don't want to go to Stanford. Do you think Walsh will actually speak to you? He sits in an ivory tower." One time Walsh had been at a recruit's house, sitting in the living room with the kid's mother and father, when a coach phoned from Stanford's archrival, the University of California at Berkeley. The player said Walsh was there, and the Cal coach said, "Ask Walsh how long he's going to be at Stanford. He's not going to stay there."

"It makes me madder than hell, but there's nothing I can do about it," Walsh said as he left the breakfast table and boarded the team bus.

It was a perfect Indian summer day in South Bend. The leaves were turning and the air was warm and fresh. Walsh sat on a bridge chair in the coaches' locker room, leafing through the game plan. When Dave Tipton walked in, Walsh looked up and said, "I saw a big, good-looking kid when we got off the bus. Was that Scott Frost?"

Tipton said it wasn't.

Guy Benjamin walked in. "Those fuckers," he said of the Irish. "They invited Frost. That shows how confident they are."

The players began to walk out on the field for pregame warm-ups.

"We're really going through with this?" Dave Tipton asked.

"How did we get into this fix?" vonAppen said.

"Well, we're supporting women's field hockey with this one," Walsh replied.

*   *   *

A few minutes before kickoff, Walsh gathered his team in the visitors' locker room. The players fell to one knee with Walsh standing in their midst, his posture erect, his jaw set. "The way to beat this team is to be quicker than they are," he said, his voice confident. "They're big, slow guys. Beat them to the punch all day. They're not ready for that."

This was not mere talk on Walsh's part. He actually believed what he was saying. He knew how to beat Notre Dame. It was just a matter of getting his players to execute what he could visualize in his head. At his press conference a few days before, he had explained the key to victory, but as usual, his words were convoluted and difficult to untangle. "Well, I think they're extremely sound and well coached, and that's what Lou Holtz and his staff prefer, a sound, well-coached, fundamental football team. And as you watch them play, you are really impressed with how soundly and how fundamentally they play. And they feel that's the way you win, and I would, I think, feel exactly the same if I were in their position. They have a solid group of athletes, as fine a group as there is in college football—maybe the best, very likely the best. And they may feel that Stanford's going to have to take some chances to pull it off, and it may be true. So they just play sound football and let you take your chances, and rarely do they work."

Walsh's emphasis on the words *sound* and *fundamental* did not necessarily indicate high praise for what Notre Dame was doing. Sound and fundamental meant something like basic and uncomplicated. Notre Dame depended on having better athletes than its opponents, but its defensive ideas were conventional. Over the years, Walsh had made his reputation taking apart zone defenses exactly like Notre Dame's, and he might do that to the Irish, if only his pass protection would hold up.

Just before his players ran out for the game, Walsh reminded them that Stanford had a tradition of its own. Then he told each player and each coach to touch someone so that the whole team would feel connected. "We bond together as individuals," he intoned. "This is an experience you'll remember for the rest of your lives."

It started out as the worst kind of experience. J. J. Lasley muffed the opening kickoff, and fell on the ball at the Stanford 12-yard line. On the first play from scrimmage, Steve Stenstrom dropped straight back and looked to his right for a receiver. Unfortunately for him,

Demetrius DuBose, Notre Dame's great linebacker, was coming from the left. He was coming like a missile. He was also coming unblocked.

At some point, it must have dawned on DuBose that Stenstrom had no idea what was going on. Stenstrom was looking downfield like a man totally at peace with the world. When DuBose hit him from behind a look of sheer incomprehension crossed Stenstrom's face. That was the same moment the ball flew out of his hands and started squirting around the Stanford end zone. If a Notre Dame player fell on it, the Irish would have a touchdown. But Stanford's lineman Brian Cassidy dove on the ball and held on for dear life. The officials called a safety, and Stanford trailed two-zip after only one play.

The activity on the Stanford sideline was frenzied. Scott Schuhmann grabbed a chalkboard and frantically went over blocking schemes with his linemen. But this time the offensive line wasn't at fault. Stenstrom had blown it. On that play, Stenstrom was supposed to look for a blitz, and if one was coming, he had to call an audible. Failing that, he was expected to get the ball to what Walsh called a "hot" receiver or a "blitz beater." But Stenstrom hadn't practiced all week and was blissfully unaware of the intricacies of that play. It never once crossed his mind to consider what Demetrius DuBose might be doing at about 12:37 P.M. that afternoon.

Stanford's situation didn't immediately improve. Notre Dame got the ball and, behind the running of Reggie Brooks and Jerome Bettis, marched right down the field, with Brooks finally loping twelve yards into the end zone. From Stanford's point of view, it didn't help that no one laid a finger on Brooks. The game wasn't yet two and a half minutes old and Stanford trailed 9-0. Fred vonAppen's worst nightmare was becoming a reality—he couldn't do a thing against Notre Dame's power game.

When Notre Dame scored another touchdown at the beginning of the second quarter, the lead shot up to 16-0, and Stanford seemed finished. But no one would have known that from looking at Walsh.

We will not be a wildebeest.

Walsh kept his head up, his jaw tight. It was impossible to tell how a game was going by looking at him. Besides, he had seen things he liked. Near the end of the first quarter Stanford had reached the Irish 14 only to have the drive falter when J. J. Lasley fumbled. Walsh told himself he could move the ball against Notre Dame, that Holtz's defenders were exactly where Walsh expected them to be. No tricks. No surprises.

Walsh's confidence grew during Stanford's next series. Justin Armour broke five yards behind the coverage and Stenstrom found him with what certainly would have been a touchdown pass. Armour dropped the ball. Walsh's face remained impassive, unreadable.

Notre Dame fumbled on its next possession, and Stanford got the ball at the Irish 23 and took it in for a touchdown. The Cardinal tried for a two-point conversion, a pass from Armour to Tony Cline in the end zone, but it fell short. The half ended with Stanford again driving toward the Notre Dame goal line, but Lasley dropped two consecutive passes to disrupt Stanford's rhythm. It was Notre Dame 16, Stanford 6 when the gun went off.

Walsh was relaxed in the locker room as he drew plays on a blackboard. He resembled a math professor busily writing equations. If he had panicked the players might have thrown in the towel, but he calmly showed the team what plays had worked and said, "We'll be fine." He absolved Lasley for his fumble and drops by saying, "The last thing to do is mishandle the ball and say, 'I screwed up. I can't live like this.' Guys miss a big shot in basketball and run down and play the other end. Just make a series of first downs and the big plays will come."

By now, the cramped room was stifling. Walsh asked the players who did not usually get into the game to walk down the stairs and wait outside so the others would have air to breathe. He chatted casually with his coaches and ducked into the coaches' locker room to brush his hair. The message was clear: Everything is under control. No need to panic.

On the first play from scrimmage in the second half, Jerome Bettis took a pitch from Notre Dame quarterback Rick Mirer and ran to his left. It was one of Notre Dame's favorite plays. As Bettis began to reach full stride, his 247 pounds hurtling through the warm fall air, Stanford free safety John Lynch came up to meet him. Bettis outweighed Lynch by thirty pounds. Still, Lynch rammed his body into Bettis, and the fullback stood up as if he had been lassoed and yanked backward. Then Bettis dropped the ball, and Stanford linebacker Dave Garnett fell on it.

That was the turning point. Stanford was lucky that Lynch, a former quarterback who had been converted to free safety, was even on the field at that moment. He'd suffered a mild concussion in the first half, and Jeff Saal, one of the Stanford doctors, kept him on the bench for most of the second quarter. At one point Lynch insisted he could go back in, and Saal allowed that, but when Lynch stood around doing nothing, Saal immediately made him come out.

At halftime, Saal had to make a tough decision. Was John Lynch well enough to play? He knew it was up to him, that Walsh always deferred to the doctors. Saal admitted to himself it was a "gray-zone call." He had to factor in what Lynch meant to the Cardinal against Notre Dame. Finally, Saal decided that Lynch's head had cleared and he seemed in good shape.

The Irish remained unruffled after Lynch forced Bettis to fumble, even after Stanford scored a touchdown three plays later. It seemed so harmless at that point. Notre Dame didn't realize what this meant to the Cardinal's morale. The game had been such a major disappointment to Stanford until that moment.

Stanford still trailed 16-13, and Walsh didn't want to do anything to make the Irish change their defense. He was calling nothing big, nothing exciting, just little curl routes over the middle for five yards. To Notre Dame this kind of offense represented no threat. To Stanford it meant ball possession and a way to establish offensive rhythm. If the Cardinal had been devouring huge chunks of yardage, Notre Dame might have felt desperate, might have blitzed or altered its defense, but the Irish saw no need for that. They were content and confident.

On its last drive of the third quarter, still trailing 16-13, Stanford faced third and twelve at its own 48-yard line. Stenstrom completed a pass to Mike Cook for eleven to the Irish 41. But now it was fourth down with the Cardinal still a yard short.

The Notre Dame defenders were waving their arms and celebrating because they'd stopped the Cardinal on third down. They were ready to run off the field. But Walsh decided to go for it on fourth down, and this was a crucial moment in the game. The Notre Dame defenders had done their work, were not prepared to regroup immediately and stop Stanford again.

Ellery Roberts slammed up the left side for twenty-one yards before being brought down at the Irish 20. He ran out of the Amtrak formation, but Walsh included a clever touch. The blocking went right, but Roberts cut left, away from his protection, and this fooled the Irish. In the press box, Terry Shea almost levitated. He told himself Notre Dame's defensive coordinator would say, "Enough of this. We'll stop their ass," and would call a linebacker blitz, sending in DuBose. Stanford had a play for that very situation. Shea screamed into the headset, "Quarterback keep, fullback slide." Walsh, who did not always respond to Shea's suggestions, went with the call. He had created it in 1974 when he was with the Bengals. Boobie Clark caught a pass from that formation and went fifty yards for a touchdown against the Raiders.

The idea was for Stenstrom to fake a handoff to Milburn. While this was taking place, J. J. Lasley was to take his time snaking through the chaos of players at the line of scrimmage. Walsh assumed that whoever was covering Lasley would lose him in the crowd. In the meantime, DuBose would be charging after Stenstrom, taking himself right out of the play.

Everything worked perfectly. All the blockers ran to the right, while Stenstrom and Lasley went left. The Notre Dame defense followed the flow of the Stanford blockers, leaving Lasley so open he looked like a bystander who had wandered onto the field from the stands. Lasley caught Stenstrom's pass and scored easily, and Stanford went ahead to stay. For the first time over the headphones the communications were upbeat. "We can win this frigging game," Shea said. Stanford did, 33-16.

When the final gun went off, Walsh and Fred vonAppen embraced on the sideline. Walsh met Lou Holtz at midfield and put his arm around his shoulder, then ran into the tunnel and up the stairs into Stanford's locker room. He stood at the top of the stairs and, as each player entered, Walsh shook his hand. The team gathered around him. "We're bonded together," he told them, his voice shaking. "We'll never forget this moment." He walked away and choked back tears.

He went into the coaches' locker room, where the toilet had been overflowing since halftime. "Was that a big win?" Walsh cried out to the other coaches. "It was one of the biggest wins of my life and that includes Super Bowls."

Dave Tipton was coming out of the shower. "Do you think this will help recruiting?" Tipton asked, and then they all laughed.

Guy Benjamin said Scott Frost, the quarterback recruit, had been spotted in Notre Dame's locker room. "Let him go there," Benjamin said. "That's a great locker room to be in."

Walsh went out to meet the press. While that was going on the doctors were treating lineman Steve Hoyem, who was suffering from dehydration. Jeff Saal told Hoyem to lie on the floor of the locker room while he inserted an I.V. into his arm. The other players were taking showers and the drains became clogged, and pretty soon

Hoyem was lying in a few inches of water with adhesive tape and dirty socks floating by his head. Saal thought Hoyem was in more danger from drowning than dehydration.

Walsh came back. He walked into the coaches' locker room, which was deserted, got undressed, and took a shower. When a friend entered the room, Walsh pulled back the shower curtain, popped his wet head out, and said breathlessly, "It proves to me I can coach again. I was beginning to have my doubts. I just wasn't getting through to the team."

He ordered a case of wine for the flight home. He knotted his tie and put on his jacket and walked out to the buses in the late afternoon sun totally convinced, for the first time, that he had not made a mistake when he returned to coaching. He got on the bus. Scott Frost came walking out of the stadium. He was a tall blond boy, wearing black sneakers and jeans and a baseball cap. His shirt was not tucked into his pants. Frost's father accompanied him. He was shorter than his son and heavier. Standing there, father and son resembled a period and an exclamation point.

Frost's mother, an athletic-looking woman who'd competed in the discus in the 1968 Olympics, climbed the steps of Walsh's bus and introduced herself. Walsh got off and shook hands with her son. As if they had spotted Frost with sonar, the Stanford coaches showed up one by one—Terry Shea, Dave Tipton, Guy Benjamin, Tom Holmoe, Bill Singler. It was reminiscent of rushing for a college fraternity. When Bill Tingley, a representative of Stanford's admissions department, happened to wander by, Walsh introduced him to the Frosts and Tingley stayed a moment and made small talk.

It was against NCAA rules for the Stanford coaches to be schmoozing with Frost in South Bend, and Walsh would have to answer for it after the season.

A few hours later on an airplane flying back to San Francisco, sitting next to his wife, Geri, Walsh was replaying the game in his mind, luxuriating in the rapture of success. He excused himself and walked into the bathroom and locked the door. He took a deep breath. He leaned his hands on the sink and stared at his face in the mirror. "I'm the luckiest man alive," he said out loud. Something like a religious ecstacy came over him. "What can I do to pay back?" he heard himself whispering. "What can I do to pay back for this gift?"

CHAPTER

BILL WALSH HAD two father figures in his life—his real father, William, and Paul Brown, founder and head coach of the Cincinnati Bengals—and both let him down.

William Walsh was hard, uneducated, and he drank too much. Walsh once described him as having no conscience or sensitivity. He was the kind of man who would chase a car at high speed on the freeway if he thought he'd been cut off in his lane.

Walsh was more like his mother, Ruth, who had an artistic sensibility and a sly sense of humor. Years later, he was to say he only "felt safe" with the maternal part of his family, with his mother and grandmother, and by that he meant that he was sensitive like them, did not feel his soul would be crushed in their presence.

His mother passed down to him verbal irony, a sense of diplomacy, the ability to smooth over a crisis and avoid conflict. He'd even inherited from her an artistic temperament that led him, as a young man, to draw portraits of his friends and consider a career as a draftsman. Even now, when Walsh would hurriedly sketch a play on the greaseboard, his circles and squares were perfectly shaped, and the entire presentation was a little work of art. (Not all the coaches drew as meticulously. When Terry Shea or Scott Schuhmann diagrammed plays on the board, their circles looked like mutated eggs and their squares came off like little huts with roof damage.)

William Walsh was in charge of the paint department at a local Chrysler factory near the family's tiny house at Vermont and Gage in southwest Los Angeles, not far from where the Rodney King riots were to take place decades later. He was hardworking and ambitious, and on weekends he moonlighted by finishing and painting cars in his garage. When he was ten years old, Bill Walsh started helping out his father. He would work all day Saturday for a dollar, and at one time had every intention of growing up to be a body-fender man. He was an expert sander, and that resulted in overdeveloped forearms of the Popeye variety, which he will happily show friends if the mood is upon him.

From his father, Walsh inherited a fierce work ethic and an insane temper. As a teenager, and even when he was a young man, Walsh was a feared streetfighter. Al Matthews recalled that when they were in college, Walsh would be ready to throw punches if he thought someone had blocked his way on the sidewalk. Looking back on that phase of his life, Walsh once said, "Maybe getting into fights was a way of trying to legitimize myself, trying to convince myself that I was worth something. I needed to do that to prove I was OK and to prove to the other guys I was OK."

To this day, Walsh feels a deep shame about inheriting that part of his father, as if his temper is tangible proof of a personal original sin. He once told a friend: "I think the one thing that haunts a person is if you have one parent who's really thick, not bright at all. You wonder how much you have of that because it's hereditary. You say, 'If he's that way, where the hell do I come from?' It can be degrading, just privately. It influences how you feel about yourself, because you think, I came from him. There's got to be some of me in there, some of him in me."

Walsh's fits of rage during his reign with the 49ers were legendary. He'd blow up in front of the players, and in coaches' meetings, he'd rant and rave several times a season to keep the staff in line. Once at training camp he confronted Fred vonAppen, who had invited several guests to attend practice, and screamed, "What the hell kind of coaching is that?"

After Walsh stormed away, one of vonAppen's guests said, "You should have decked that guy."

VonAppen replied, "He's the boss and he was making a point."

When the insane rage overcame him, a red flush would scar Walsh's face, his eyes bulged, he'd scream, and in general act like a man hurtling over the edge. Before long it dawned on him what was happening, and he mentally stepped back. He could actually observe himself acting like a madman.

His rage did not displease him. If his men feared him, he could use that to his advantage. So he became theatrical. He would prolong the angry fit, would explode for effect. He was proud of his ability to instill fear. Someone who worked with him at the 49ers once said, "When Bill blew up, it wasn't like he ever apologized. It was, 'Don't question it.' He'd walk by you in the hall an hour later and it was over—he wouldn't even mention it."

One way to understand Walsh, to make a schematic of his personality, is to see him as a battleground between the conflicting personalities of his mother and father. The mother part of Walsh is the artist who sits alone in a quiet room drawing perfect plays on a yellow legal pad. From his father he inherited the raw aggression that made him want to apply his art to football. Walsh, after all, has not devoted his life to haiku or chamber music. He may look like the president of a university, but he is consumed by winning in a violent sport. To become a great coach, he had to perfect the marriage of William and Ruth in his own soul, even if their union was, in real life, not ideal.

William Walsh died in 1985 after a long struggle with Alzheimer's disease. But he had known his son's success and would wear 49er hats and call Walsh Billy. "I did a lot of nice things for him," Walsh was to say years later. "I did them because he was my father, not because there was a lot of love."

When Walsh was a junior in high school, his father decided to go into business for himself finishing and painting cars. He quit his job, sold everything, including the house, and moved the family to Central Point, Oregon, just outside Medford. Walsh, who was in the middle of the football season, went from Washington High, a school of 2,500, to one with 120 students. He was a big-city kid in the middle of the sticks, and he was sixteen and miserable.

William Walsh's business went straight down the tubes. "In those days, people were so provincial," Walsh recalled. "Anyone from California in the state of Oregon was completely rejected." Walsh's father lost everything, but, luckily, Chrysler was opening a plant in San Leandro, about thirty miles from San Francisco, and William Walsh hired on to head the paint department.

So he could finish up at his original high school, Walsh's parents sent him back to L.A. to live with his grandparents. He finished out his junior year at Washington High and was set to be the starting quarterback as a senior when his grandparents threw up their hands. Bill Walsh had become a problem. His grandparents couldn't control this kid who was too wild, drank too much, fought too much, was on the verge of getting into serious trouble.

So Walsh made his third move in less than a year, going back to the Bay Area, to Hayward where his folks had bought a home. When his father was transferred to L.A., Walsh stayed up north on his own, attending junior college in San Mateo and then San Jose State, where he played wide receiver but did not have a distinguished athletic career.

He graduated from San Jose in 1954 and, six weeks later, found himself in the army, stationed at Fort Ord in Monterey, California. He had married his college sweetheart, Geri Nardini, shortly after graduation, and because he couldn't earn enough to support her, she had to get a job. The catch was that no one wanted to hire a soldier's wife because military families were transient. Geri took a job at a bank pretending she was single. Guys would ask her out and even call her house, then hang up in confusion when Walsh answered. When she became pregnant with their first son, Steve, she had to explain that she was *getting* married.

After Walsh was released from the army in 1956, he entered a master's program at San Jose State for a teaching credential. Walsh might have been unafraid to use his fists, but when it came to speaking in public, he was petrified. He had to pass a speech test for the credential, and he flunked. The professor gently took Walsh aside, told him he appreciated his desire to teach but advised him to find another line of work because he'd never have the nerve to talk in front of people. Walsh rescheduled the test and passed—he believed they passed him because they knew he'd keep coming back no matter how long it took. Looking back now, it gives him satisfaction to know that, over the years, he's made himself into an impressive public speaker, his fee for an hour reaching $15,000.

While he was working on his master's thesis, a theoretical treatment of defensive football, he was hired as head football coach at Washington Union High School in Fremont, about twenty miles northeast of San Jose. So now, in addition to being a full-time student, he was a full-time high school teacher and coach of the football and swim teams.

Walsh's first season as football coach was 1957. His team won three, lost three, and tied two. That was quite an improvement from the previous three seasons, when Washington High's record was 1-26. In his second season, the team lost only once in ten games and, years later, Walsh still blamed his own bad play-calling for the defeat. When he thought about the one loss, a faraway look took hold of his face and he would shake his head sadly as if remembering a Super Bowl that got away.

At Washington High Walsh was already beginning to show his creativity. He used four wide receivers, sent men in motion, had his quarterback sprint out. He even used an offensive lineman as a running back. This was the same stuff he'd do on the 49ers years later. He had good players, but instead of blasting into an opponent, he was designing intricate plays. Sometimes he'd barely win a game he should have won by thirty points.

Following his third year, Marv Levy hired him as defensive backfield coach for the University of California at Berkeley. Levy needed a high school coach from the Bay Area to help with recruiting, and Walsh was handsome and vibrant and had a gift for saying the right things to high school athletes. Walsh recruited Craig Morton to Cal.

The next year Levy promoted Walsh to defensive coordinator, but eventually a player insurrection did Walsh in. A group of players was not happy with Levy and complained to Athletic Director Pete Newell, and Walsh and several other assistant coaches were pressured to leave for being too strong, tough, demanding. Cal had not done well and Walsh believed some of the assistants were scapegoated. He also came to believe that he wasn't ready for the responsibilities Levy gave him. He was not a sensitive coach. He wasn't mature enough.

In 1963, John Ralston hired him at Stanford as freshman coach and chief recruiter. Walsh stayed at Stanford for three years, but he grew restless, wanted to move ahead.

Once Walsh sat at a small table in his office reflecting on his early coaching career. "I was with John Ralston for three years, and here I was impetuously looking around. In those days, head coaches were named in their early thirties, the Darrell Royals and Bud Wilkinsons of the world. It was all a hype kind of career, like a yuppie career. It was how good-looking you were, how sharp you dressed, how glib you were, and how you recruited. It was a new wave after World War Two. America was in a state of change and young people were emerging, sometimes not with the credentials they needed.

"Now, the job at San Jose opened up and any number of my friends wanted me to be the head coach. And San Jose didn't hire me. They hired one of their line coaches, a very average guy, and the team continued to be average. But I was rejected by my school and it hurt. In fact, when I was interviewed they'd already chosen the coach, but because of the interest some people had in me, they had to give the appearance they were interviewing me. So I sat down and was interviewed and I did a very nice job, and when I was through, one of the people on the committee said, 'Amen,' like I was an evangelist. I couldn't understand why he would say that because I was talking about the program, and he said 'Amen' like I was a snake-oil salesman. They didn't want an interloper like me, although I was the logical man and I think I would have done a very nice job. So that was a major disappointment.

"But then John Rauch became the head coach of the Oakland Raiders when Al Davis became commissioner of the American Football League. At that time the AFL was in direct competition with the NFL for players. So basically John Rauch wanted me as a recruiter. I didn't think of it that way, but they were looking at this guy who could express himself well and was aggressive. So almost mistakenly I went to the Raiders.

"I was impetuously ambitious then. It took the form of overtly looking for better jobs, of overtly looking to improve myself, of overtly looking for more responsibility on the coaching staff where I was. Just pushing. Part of it might be my genetic background from my mother, might be that part of me that's got a little bit of—some people might call it charisma, others might call it bullshit. Somewhere in between.

"My athletic career had not been really what I'd hoped, although I became the starter my senior year in college and played significantly. It just wasn't right. I didn't feel that I'd given it enough. I told myself, 'I'm never going to let this happen again. If I'm going to be a coach, by God, nobody's going to stop me.'

"And that's why it took all these forms. Some of them were self-destructive. Some of them weren't in the best interest of the kids I was coaching. I wasn't mature enough for the job at Washington High School, nor was I mature enough for the Cal job. I began to mature at Stanford, but then I was hurt by the San Jose State thing and some others. At Fresno State, I came in second. At UOP [University of the Pacific] it was myself and Doug Scovil, and Doug became the coach. But that was right. Doug should have been the coach because he was a few years older."

By now, Walsh's voice had grown dreamy. He stopped speaking, stared across the room at the top of a bookcase where he had placed an old black-and-white photograph of him and Dick Vermeil and Mike White when they were assistants at Stanford. Vermeil later took the Philadelphia Eagles to the Super Bowl. White coached Cal and Illinois, and later became an assistant with the Los Angeles Raiders.

In the photo Walsh stands with his arms around the shoulders of his two buddies. He is impossibly young. He's wearing his hair, which was blond, in a crew cut and his cheeks are thin. Nowhere can you find a precursor of the white-haired legend he is to become. He has the hearty look of a lifeguard or a tennis pro at a country club.

"I was just like Mike and Dick," he said pointing to the picture. "All three of those faces were the same guy."

For a while, Walsh stayed on at Stanford to coach spring ball and help with recruiting. So he'd work all day at Stanford, get in his car, and drive to Oakland, where he worked all night with John Rauch and the Raiders.

It was then Walsh acquired the core of all his football knowledge, even though he only stayed one season. Raiders football was based on the theories of the legendary Sid Gillman, who, Walsh says, was "Star Wars compared to everyone else in football." Al Davis had taken Gillman one step further. And here was Walsh, who had never played as a professional, had never been exposed to football at this level, drinking in this knowledge.

Walsh had been used to systems that designed four pass plays for the halfback. The Raiders had twenty. The Raiders were one of the first teams to use minicamps to refine players' skills. Walsh would work late into the night with the Raiders and report to Stanford by 8:00 A.M. the next day. This was the most creative period of his life, but Geri Walsh couldn't take this new arrangement. With the Raiders, Walsh was on call every minute. He was married to football, not to her, and he realized if he wanted to preserve his family he had to get out.

So he did, and then began his most bizarre adventure ever. At that time, something called the Continental League was formed as a farm system for the NFL and AFL, and there just happened to be a team in San Jose, the Apaches. Walsh figured he could keep his hand in football and hold his marriage together by becoming the head coach of what was essentially a semipro team, mostly frustrated jocks who wanted to play a little football. He even got an increase in salary to $16,000, which was $3000 more than he made in Oakland.

The Raiders and 49ers organizations did not speak to each other in those days, but Walsh convinced both teams to let him use their cab squad players, men who practiced with the team but were not eligible to play in games. Walsh also got the Raiders to provide him with uniforms. He brought the Apaches to a 9-5 record, then lost in the league championship game. After one season, the Continental League folded, and Walsh was out of a job again. Unsure what direction his life would take, he decided to throw in the towel. He went back to San Jose State to work on a master's degree in business. He was giving up on football, planning to join the corporate world.

And then the phone rang. It was Paul Brown of the Cincinnati Bengals.

Brown, an intense, egocentric man, had been a giant in the NFL, leaving the Cleveland Browns after the 1962 season with a record of 115-49-6, seven conference titles, and three NFL championships. But by the time the Bengals started their inaugural season, 1968, he no longer was on the cutting edge of football. He hired Walsh as the receivers coach, but would not let him work with the quarterbacks. The running backs coach did that. Walsh saw this division of labor as hopelessly outmoded, and during the off-season when Brown would spend seven months in La Jolla, Walsh coached Sam Wyche and the other quarterbacks on the sly. In 1969, after his second season, the quarterbacks asked Brown to make Walsh the official quarterbacks coach and, after some hesitation, after he'd initially named someone else, Brown put Walsh in charge.

The Bengals offense took off. In Cincinnati, Walsh perfected the ball-control offense that was to bring him three Super Bowl victories with the 49ers. He concentrated on getting his quarterbacks, Virgil Carter and Kenny Anderson, to complete short passes, sometimes just five or six yards, so he could keep drives going and the opponent's offense off the field. He made his offense rehearse over and over again precise pass patterns, almost the way a choreographer rehearses for ballet. He would even show his quarterbacks and receivers where to run if the original pattern was covered. He left nothing to chance.

The Bengals went 11-3 in 1975, Walsh's last season in Cincinnati, but were knocked out of the playoffs by the Raiders in a game that proved crucial in Walsh's development as a play-caller. He was upstairs in the coaches' box running the offense when the Raiders fumbled on their own 37-yard line with time running out and the Bengals trailing by three points. If the Bengals could gain a few yards and kick a field goal, they would send the game into overtime.

But when it counted, when the game was on the line, Walsh couldn't think straight. He called a disastrous series of plays, and the Bengals never got their field goal. As Walsh remembered the game, the noise was too intense for him to concentrate, and then the plays he called had to go through several people before reaching the field. In general, the situation seemed stacked against him. But there was more to it than that. Walsh had not systematically practiced calling plays in desperate situations, largely because Brown did not believe in that kind of thing, had not even installed a two-minute offense.

Later, with the 49ers, Walsh made sure this immobility, this freezing under pressure, never afflicted him again. He'd relentlessly practice situational football—what to do with a minute to go if the Niners were on the opponent's 20-yard line; what to do if they were backed up near their own end zone; what to do at the goal line, 5-yard line, 10-yard line, 15- and 20-yard lines; what to do on third and short or third and medium, what to do on the last four plays, or in the last two minutes, or the last four minutes. He obsessively attended to every detail.

To many of his players, Walsh's practices seemed long and tedious, but Walsh's hyper-preparation won games. When Dwight Clark made "The Catch" against the Cowboys in the 1982 NFC championship game with less than a minute remaining, it may have looked like a sandlot play, may have looked as if Joe Montana was searching desperately for a receiver. In reality, it was a designed pattern the 49ers had practiced dozens of times with Clark running into the end zone, then sliding to his left while Montana lofted him the ball.

As time went by, Walsh became the Bengals' offensive coordinator, although Brown never gave him that title. Walsh would call the plays from the press box, and Brown would repeat them on the sideline to give the impression he was making the calls. Sometimes, Brown would botch the plays and he'd become offended when the players shouted, "Well, ask Bill what he means."

It became obvious in 1975, Walsh's eighth year in Cincinnati, that Brown would have to step away. He was in his late sixties and he was frail; during practices, he'd shake in the freezing cold.

Walsh assumed he would be named Brown's successor, that Brown looked upon him as a precocious son, a dear son. Walsh had never tried to show up Brown, always let him take credit for the offense, and for this reason alone, he thought, he was next in line. Before games, Brown would come to Walsh's hotel room, and they would relax together. Brown talked about his life, and Walsh listened dutifully, and then they would hug and go out to play a football game. Halfway through the 1975 season, Brown stopped visiting Walsh before games. Sportswriters were giving Walsh credit for the Bengals' success, and Brown didn't like that.

There had been other disturbing signs. In 1973, Sid Gillman became head coach of the Houston Oilers and wanted Walsh to run his offense, then take over when he retired. He requested permission to talk to Walsh, but Paul Brown turned him down without telling Walsh anything about it. Gillman called Walsh and said, "Bill, I can't do it. I feel bad, but your best bet's just to hold on and see what happens with Paul."

Walsh was sure Brown blocked him from four or five other jobs. "Paul could be downright dishonest or whatever it would take," Walsh once said. "He'd be a great guy if it was convenient. If it wasn't, he'd be himself. I had a lot of ambition. I wanted to be a head coach before I died. And he was holding me back because it was a perfect setup for him. It was as unsettling as hell because he had control of my life."

After a while, Walsh gave way to depression. This was not an unusual response for him. He's gone through mood swings his whole life. "I've always been that way," he once said. "When I'm up, I'm really effective. When I'm depressed, I'm just barely above average. Usually I have a hell of a sense of humor and, all of a sudden, it won't be there."

This manic depression was not lost on Brown, who wondered how he could trust his team to Walsh. "The fits of depression don't happen during the game or when I'm out coaching," Walsh once said. "The truth is, I wasn't his world. I was like a guy from another planet that dropped in. That was about the time of the Vietnam War, and my hair might have been a little longer than his. And I had these boots you zipped up that my wife got me for Christmas, and he saw them one day and he had a fit, he was so upset. So he was afraid that this kook would be his replacement."

Brown was not the only one who had misgivings about Walsh. Walsh's image was not right for the NFL. Most football people saw him as an intellectual who belonged in a laboratory dabbling with formulas and concepts. They doubted he was tough enough to be a head coach.

When the 1975 season ended the other Bengals coaches were sent to various all-star games to scout, but Walsh wasn't assigned to one. He sensed something was wrong, but he forced that thought out of his mind—told himself he could use the time to recover from the season and be with his family.

The phone rang at six o'clock one night, and it was a sportswriter named Dick Forbes who was close to Brown. "Bill, do you know about the story that's about to break? I want to get your reaction."

Walsh didn't even have to ask what the story was. "There it is," he said to himself, shocked by the finality of it all.

"Bill Johnson will be named head coach tomorrow," Forbes said.

Johnson had coached the running backs and was Walsh's friend, and the reporter was calling Walsh because no one else, including Brown, was in town and available to make a statement. Brown had arranged it that way. Walsh was, by default, the team spokesman, and he was in the impossible position of having to praise the man who'd beaten him out for the head job. For two days, Walsh's phone rang and television trucks parked in his driveway, and he found himself giving a nonstop series of interviews on the greatness of Bill Johnson.

He could bring himself to do that in public. In private, he experienced a complete breakdown, went through days and nights of sobbing. He had been passed over, publicly rejected, and he assumed this was death to a career.

But within forty-eight hours, Walsh received calls from five teams asking him to become their offensive coordinator. The Seahawks needed a head coach and called Walsh and said he was tops on their list. The Jets were interested.

Then, suddenly, all of that stopped. The Jets hired Lou Holtz, and the Seahawks would not return Walsh's calls, finally hiring Jack Patera. It turned out Brown would not recommend Walsh, tried to hurt him any way he could so that Walsh would be forced to remain in Cincinnati, stay in the booth calling plays. Nothing would change, except that Bill Johnson would be head coach.

To make Walsh feel better, Brown named him offensive coordinator. Brown did not tell him this, Walsh read it in the newspaper. But he was not appeased. It was like someone with the potential for a Nobel Prize being passed over for a full professorship in favor of someone who'd never even published a monograph. "If you want to win a goddamn championship, you better have the brains," Walsh said years later. "You can't win it with a dull guy as head coach, and the smart guy as the assistant. That's why we didn't win an AFC championship when Paul was the head coach, because it had to go through Paul to be done. And now it had to go through Bill."

Brown expected Walsh to stay in Cincinnati, considered him weak, malleable. Brown had forced people to cave into him his whole career by the sheer force of his will, and now he had boxed Walsh in. He thought that was the end of the matter. But he'd made a tactical mistake. Walsh's contract was almost up, but somehow Brown forgot that.

*   *   *

Walsh had gone to the Senior Bowl and run into Tommy Prothro, head coach of the Chargers. Prothro asked Walsh to be his offensive coordinator and Walsh agreed. After returning from the Senior Bowl, Walsh went to Brown's office to tell him he was leaving, but Brown was in a private meeting with Bill Johnson. Walsh took a deep breath and barged in.

"I've got to talk to both of you," Walsh said.

"It can wait," Brown said.

"No."

Walsh sat down and began to speak, but he burst into tears. Brown looked disgusted. For him, this was proof he had made the correct decision in passing over Walsh, this crybaby, this pathetic case who did not have enough character to accept his fate with dignity.

Brown assumed Walsh was crying about the job, but he was wrong. Walsh cried because he was leaving, and although Brown had betrayed him, it was Walsh who felt like the betrayer.

"Enough of that," Brown said, the way you might dismiss a hysterical child.

"Coach, I'm leaving," Walsh sobbed.

"You're not leaving," Brown shot back. "You'll never get another NFL job if you leave. I'll see to that."

Walsh was stunned. He had intended to tell Brown and Johnson how much they meant to him. He'd wanted to thank them for what they'd taught him, and reminisce about the battles they'd fought together. Instead all he said was, "Well, that remains to be seen."

"You're under contract," Brown said.

"Coach, my contract runs out tomorrow."

Afraid of what Brown might do, Walsh left without ever saying he'd talked to the Chargers. He booked a flight to San Diego, but first flew to San Jose to muddy his tracks. He was taking no chances. He flew on to San Diego, but despite his subterfuge, Brown had found out about the Chargers. Tommy Prothro and Chargers president Gene Klein met Walsh at the airport.

"Bill, I got a phone call from Paul Brown today," Klein said. "He told me you can't be trusted and that he wouldn't recommend you for anything. 'You're making the mistake of your life if you hire Bill Walsh.' That's what he told me."

There was silence. Walsh felt ill. The deal was dead.

"Bill, you know I hate to say this," Klein said, "but Paul's a sick man. Bill, you're with us. Welcome to the San Diego Chargers."

*   *   *

When Walsh received his final paycheck from the Bengals, he was paid for twenty-nine days of the last month instead of thirty. Brown cut off his pay precisely at the moment he sat in the office breaking down. Later on, Walsh received an anonymous note: *You have betrayed people who have cared for you.* The note was from Brown—Walsh knew the handwriting.

Years later, after Walsh had been head coach at Stanford in 1977 and 1978, winning the Sun and Bluebonnet bowls, and after he'd become famous as head coach of the 49ers, Brown would take pleasure in saying, "I had Walsh here. I got him from a semipro team."

CHAPTER

ON MONDAY NIGHT, the Stanford offense gathered in the Hall of Fame Room to watch the tape of the victory over Notre Dame. Everyone was excited and Terry Shea had difficulty being serious because he couldn't stop grinning. The rankings had come out and Stanford was eleventh in the AP Poll, twelfth according to CNN/*USA Today*. The team had won four in a row and stood at 4-1, Stanford's best start since 1986.

"We're not quite deserving of a top-ten ranking despite what you think of your latest victory," Shea told the players, trying to temper their and his own giddiness. "We're not quite there yet."

Bill Singler had just gone over the special teams tape and right there in living color he'd seen something that amazed him. On one kickoff, two of the Cardinal took on a Notre Dame player and kept pushing him back until finally the Notre Dame guy just quit. "You think of Notre Dame as being up here," Singler said, putting his hand above his head. "But they weren't. We had a higher standard of play. That's what Coach talked about in our meeting today, standard of play. No matter who we play we still have the same standard—Notre Dame, San Jose State, it doesn't matter. We play our game."

Upstairs in his office, Walsh was putting the finishing touches on the offensive game plan for UCLA. He'd felt a burst of creativity after Notre Dame, had completed his work in two days. At last, he'd become one with his team. He was like a novice chess player learning how the various pieces move. By now, he had learned what Glyn Milburn, Ellery Roberts, J. J. Lasley, and Steve Stenstrom could do. And it had shown in his play-calling.

He had to laugh about something Lou Holtz had come up with after the game, a creative excuse, a one-of-a-kind excuse, a doozy. Moments after the final gun, Holtz explained that his players were taking midterms and he'd failed to factor that into his preparation. The upshot was that he accidentally worked them too hard and they were too pooped to play Stanford. The hidden implication in his strange mea culpa was that Stanford, which operated on the quarter system, had started classes just four days before the game, and the Cardinal players were fresh from not having to clutter their minds with Kant and Shakespeare and Darwin.

That really got to Walsh. He got up from the table in his office and walked into the conference room to go over plays with the offensive staff. "It's sort of humorous in a way," he said, giggling. "Lou Holtz is just a brat. Very bright, outstanding coach, but he's a little spoiled brat. What in the hell—'I worked them too hard and they took midterms'? Come on, so you lost. Play the next game, win it, don't start those kinds of excuses. They're just so simple, so artificial—little superficial excuses for losing. You got beat. You should have won. Probably, you have a better team. But in this case, this happened."

Walsh paused. Shea, Schuhmann, and the others were staring at him. A moment before he had been joking. Now his mood turned serious. "But, on the other hand, in college, at the elite level, you lose a game and you're out of the national championship. In pro ball, you lose a game and you come back. In college ball, it's 'My God, we lost!' And Notre Dame, Michigan, Penn State, Miami, all those kinds of schools, they can't lose a game. And that's ridiculous."

Walsh started drawing plays on the board, and every few seconds he'd yawn, big yawns with his mouth wide open, tears flooding his eyes. Across the table, Scott Schuhmann looked as if he might nod off, and Mike Wilson seemed to be approaching a dream state. The coaches were whipped. Whatever euphoria they felt on Saturday had drained out of them. They were back to the grind of 14-hour days.

Walsh showed the others the new plays. Most relied on deception, showed Walsh at his most cunning. A play called "Full Protection" was designed to defeat the UCLA blitz—everyone had been blitzing the Cardinal, and Walsh didn't think UCLA would be any different. As UCLA edged up to the line, Walsh explained, Steve Stenstrom would yell "Full Protection." At that moment, Glyn Milburn would move forward, point to a linebacker, and call out his number, a clear indication that Milburn would block him. UCLA would assume it was a pass block, but when the ball was snapped, Milburn would take the handoff and run up the middle.

In another play, the two running backs would release deep down the field, one on each side. Meanwhile, the tight end would throw a block and fall to one knee. The defense would lose track of him. While the defense was pursuing the two running backs, the tight end would get up and run to the middle of the field, to the precise area vacated by the two defensive backs as they went dashing after the running backs. Stenstrom would hit the tight end with a pass.

Walsh was convinced deception would work against the Bruins because their defense was quick and surged to the ball. He intended to use their speed against them, to turn their chief asset into a drawback, like a judo master applying his skill to football. Walsh would trick the Bruins into flowing the wrong way, and after they had overcommitted, he'd run his play in the opposite direction. He hadn't used much deception against the Irish because the Notre Dame defense relied on strength instead of speed. Against the Irish, misdirection would not have been appropriate.

Walsh considered Bruins head coach Terry Donahue one of the best in college football, but some of his coaches didn't respect UCLA. Scott Schuhmann said UCLA had the best-looking athletes in the conference, especially at the skill positions—quarterback, receiver, running back. "They are very skilled, but they're not tough."

The Cardinal players felt the same way. When linebacker Tom Williams looked at the Bruins, he saw "a bunch of pretty boys who play football in Westwood. They wear powder blue uniforms and they never take anyone apart. They win on athletic ability."

The Bruins, who were ranked nineteenth in the country, had more serious problems than proving their machismo. Their starting quarterback, Tommy Maddox, had defected for the NFL even though he had two years of eligibility remaining, and was the first-round draft pick of the Denver Broncos. The Bruins' coaches gave his backup, Wayne Cook, a crash course in quarterbacking, but then he wrecked his knee in the season opener, and that left the job to Rob Walker, a redshirt freshman who had been running the scout teams. The Bruins were 3-1, but the previous week they had been shocked by Arizona, losing 23-3, and Walker seemed terrified.

At the Tuesday press conference, Terry Donahue fretted over the speakerphone about his quarterback, and said his best wide receiver, Sean LaChapelle, might not be able to play because of cracked ribs he sustained against Arizona. In the Hall of Fame Room, the sportswriters began to laugh. Donahue had a reputation for poor-mouthing his teams, for claiming his players were halt and lame, but then when they showed up they'd play like the New York Giants. In this case he was telling the truth. LaChapelle was to play sparingly in the first half, not at all in the second.

When Walsh was asked a few minutes later about UCLA's problems, he laughed. "I've refused to give any thought to their injuries, because we've heard that so often out of the UCLA Sports Information Department. Terry Donahue's a very wise coach, and he's a good poker player. So he's saying certain things—and I would do that myself if I could—and he's setting us up."

On Wednesday, Walsh seemed tense. The last time Stanford had beaten Notre Dame, in 1990, the Cardinal went on to lose three in a row, and Walsh worried that his team would revert to form—beating the teams it wasn't supposed to defeat, losing to inferior squads.

He walked into the Hall of Fame Room for the afternoon team meeting and said to his players, "You are in the running for the Rose Bowl." His voice was serious, the Notre Dame victory a thing of the past. "This will be your toughest game, having a great win and having to come back against a good opponent. You're going to have to grovel for this one. It's not going to be pretty." He paused a moment, remembering a similar situation with the 49ers back in 1981. The memory did not give him pleasure. "After the 49ers beat Dallas 45-14, the biggest win in our history, we had to go against Green Bay the next week and grovel for a 13-3 win. My guess is that this game with UCLA will be low-scoring. When we go down there, especially you Southern California guys, avoid big reunions after this big win, avoid second cousins, girlfriends who dropped you years ago. All this goes down the tubes if we lose to UCLA. If you see a guy suffering from euphoria, kick him in the ass."

Walsh scheduled three appointments in his office for precisely nine o'clock Friday morning. This was nothing unusual. He had a horror of saying no, and to anyone who asked for his time or a favor, he'd reply, "Sure, we'll get it done." He wanted to be obliging, intended never to come off as a bad guy, as superior or stuck on himself. On the other hand, he might forget about the appointment two minutes after he'd made it. His days were busy and would have had a less dedicated man panting like a dog.

His administrative assistant, Jane Walsh, handled his appointment book and was brilliant at turning people down politely or delaying them. She understood Walsh's desire to say yes to everyone, his tendency to forget he was committed to giving a lecture in San Francisco, or had to meet with Athletic Director Ted Leland about university policy, or was supposed to go shopping for living-room furniture with Geri. But this Friday morning three of Walsh's yeses had slipped past Jane Walsh. She was vigilant, but she wasn't superhuman, and sometimes people would buttonhole Walsh, and he would say yes before she could turn them away.

This morning one radio and two newspaper reporters were waiting for Walsh, and he could talk to only one of them. He was late—and this wasn't unusual, either. Walsh had an odd orientation to time.

Once he'd told the entire offense to come up to the football offices for a 9:00 A.M. meeting, but when the players arrived, Walsh was studying a tape of his short-yardage offense and had lost track of the moment. The players filled up the waiting room and spilled along the corridor, and sometimes they would peek into the conference room where they saw him with the VCR controls running plays backward and forward. Walsh was in a faraway world, had forgotten all about the players, and finally had to be reminded they were there.

And then there were the times he'd announce a staff meeting for one o'clock. All the coaches would assemble, and Walsh would show up an hour and a half later because he was playing tennis or watching tape or directing workmen at his new house.

With Walsh there were two kinds of time. Regular Time was what people like Jane Walsh tried to get him to conform to. He would sometimes adhere to Regular Time—always when there was a team meeting or a team bus or plane to catch—but he felt confined by Regular Time.

Then there was Football Time, which stretched endlessly in every direction, was plastic, had no beginning and no end. Football Time was where he chose to live as much as possible. It was the world of the mind, a land of pure creation in which an hour might feel like a minute. When he was in Football Time Walsh was happy. He was beyond happy. If anyone went into his office when he was in Football Time, he would glance up from what he was doing like an absent-minded professor—which in many respects he was—and he might even nod to the guest and invite him in. He was reflexively polite. The guest might say something and Walsh would nod. But he wouldn't hear. He was elsewhere, lost in the permutations of plays, running some new wrinkle from four or five different formations. It would be the job of the guest to understand that Walsh was being polite, but that he did not want to come back to Regular Time at that moment. It would be the guest's job to leave.

All the coaches, and Jane Walsh, knew when to back out of the office with a casual "I'll catch you later, Coach." They had learned to read him the way a quarterback reads a defense. If Walsh had the glassy look in his eyes, he was unavailable. Even Fred vonAppen would leave if he saw "The Look" on Walsh's face. Walsh was good-natured, but he had the power, was the source of all bounty and favor, and the coaches had to defer to him like courtiers around a king. Except for Guy Benjamin, most of the coaches felt uncomfortable even calling him Bill. They called him "Coach," even when he wasn't there in the room and they were merely talking about him. He'd made a point of telling coaches and players to "Call me Bill," and vonAppen would try, then revert to Coach. Around the football offices, there were many coaches, but only one Coach.

Walsh's obliviousness to time, his eagerness to say yes, led to paradoxes in his personality. He was a powerful man who loved his power, but he could be childlike, and that was one of the most attractive things about him.

Sports Information Director Gary Migdol got to see this innocence shortly after Walsh came back to Stanford. *Sports Illustrated* was doing a story about Walsh's return and needed photographs to go along with the article. The photographer decided it would be a good idea to get a shot of Walsh in the locker room of the gymnasium. The shoot was supposed to take fifteen minutes and, for some reason, Walsh had to pose near a row of lockers a few feet from the showers.

But the photo shoot took much longer than fifteen minutes. It dragged on to lunchtime. Professors and students began appearing in the gym to work out, and many headed for the showers. Walsh was posing with a frozen smile on his face while dozens of wet, naked men trooped back and forth in front of him. Walsh was still a novelty on campus at that time, and they were gawking at him. Pretty soon, steam began pouring out of the shower. Walsh looked as if he were posing in a steam bath, and the photo shoot was turning into a mess.

Migdol was horrified. If this had happened during the Denny Green years, Green would have called the thing off right on the spot. Walsh was too polite for that. After the shower episode, Migdol came to realize that Walsh depended on his subordinates to get him out of tough situations. It was up to Migdol to read Walsh's body language, to understand what Walsh would and would not like. This wasn't all bad. It meant that Migdol had responsibility and power, and as he came to exercise his authority, Walsh grew to appreciate him.

Walsh could be childlike in other ways. People who saw him only from the outside, who were recipients of the distant, formal politeness, never understood this side of him. He had been using VCRs for years to watch game tapes, but he didn't know how to operate a VCR. He would want to watch tapes in his office and he'd be unable to get the machine to work. At first he would walk over to the office of Chris Norte, who handled all the films for the team, and ask for help. After a while, Walsh would just stand in Norte's doorway with an impish grin on his face, and he'd throw up his hands.

When Walsh took over the Stanford job, he installed a VCR in his house, but couldn't get it to work. So Norte went to his home and showed him how to do it. Then Walsh lost the remote control.

But the ultimate VCR experience occurred the previous summer when Walsh was at his vacation home near Lake Tahoe and decided one day he wanted to watch tapes to prepare for the season. He'd bought a brand-new VCR and, of course, couldn't get it to work. So he called down to Norte's office and found out he was on Marine Corps Reserve active duty in Reno. Well, that was no problem. Tahoe was a hop, skip, and a jump from Reno, so Walsh figured he'd just give Norte a jingle, tell him to drop what he was doing, and come over and set up the VCR. He called the marines and said he was Bill Walsh and could he please speak to Chris Norte. When the sergeant finally tracked Norte down, he said, "Bill Walsh is on the phone. Who the hell are you?"

Norte explained to Walsh that he couldn't just drop everything and drive to Tahoe; the marines wouldn't like that. So Walsh phoned down to Jane Walsh, who was in the office, thank God, and she told him not to panic, that there must be a way to work things out. She went to the office of defensive line coach Dave Tipton, studied the wires on his VCR, called Walsh back and began to talk him through the steps of setting up his machine. "Can you put it in *In?*" she'd ask, and when he'd managed that, she'd say, "Do you have a plug in *Out?*"

After a half-hour, they accomplished their mission.

*   *   *

Walsh lost his keys all the time. Before he came to Stanford he kept a small office in Menlo Park, and he lost the key to that office seven times.

When he came to Stanford he had a fail-safe idea for how to keep an extra key handy in case he ever lost the one to his new office. A framed photo hung on the wall between his office and Jane Walsh's, and he'd just hide a key behind the frame. But that didn't work because of another eccentricity in his personality. He was obsessed that pictures hang straight. When he was with the 49ers a story circulated that he had once fired a custodian after he walked through the hallway and noticed the pictures dangling at various angles. Someone who was with the organization at that time said Walsh didn't exactly fire the guy because of the pictures. "There were other things going on, but it's true, shortly after that the guy didn't work there anymore."

At Stanford, Walsh had walked around the halls of the Football Department tipping the pictures to make them hang correctly, and then he had a brainstorm. He'd get the head maintenance man to bolt them to the wall so they'd never move. So when he went to hide his key behind the photo it was bolted to the wall and his plan was foiled.

He also would lose his wallet on a regular basis. Once he lost it twice in one week. After the first loss, Jane Walsh canceled all his credit cards and gave him a few more she held in reserve for just such an occurrence. A day or so later she asked for one of the cards, and Walsh looked away.

"Don't tell me," she said.

He also lost hairbrushes and contact lenses. At times he'd walk into Jane Walsh's office blinking furiously. "I have a left eye," he'd say. "I need a right eye."

This innocence in Walsh, these qualities bordering on goofiness, had nothing to do with his football persona. He might be harebrained about appointments, but he never vacillated when it came to the game. On the 49ers he would trade players or cut them if he thought their time had come. Any number of great players left in anger—Keith Fahnhorst, Ray Wersching, Wendell Tyler, and John Ayers—only to grow close to Walsh later on. He would sacrifice popularity for success and deal with the fallout later on.

He never passed blame to coaches. If his team lost, it was his fault and that was the end of it. When the 49ers met Minnesota in the playoffs after the 1987 season, Walsh was on the phone continually to George Seifert, who was his defensive coordinator at the time, asking him to change to a zone defense because the 49ers could not stop the Vikings' Anthony Carter man-on-man. Seifert refused, and the 49ers lost. But Walsh never criticized Seifert publicly, even though that game was to change his relationship with Eddie DeBartolo, Jr., and eventually cause him to leave the team. Rodney Knox, who heads public relations for the 49ers, once described Walsh's worldview.

"Bill's got the largest screen they make. He's got the big picture, huge vision. He's got huge shoulders. When things go great, it makes him larger than life. But he'll put himself on the front line. He won't spread the negatives. If things go poorly he'll take the round right in the gut. You have to respect that."

Walsh could be indirect and calculating, and when he was with the 49ers, reporters often called him Machiavellian. He once wrote a book with Glenn Dickey of the *San Francisco Chronicle* called *Building a Champion* about his years with the 49ers. One day a friend pointed out that Walsh hardly ever criticized anyone in that book, even his enemies. This seemed odd.

"It's true, I was less than direct, maybe phony," Walsh said. "One of the things I find myself doing is maneuvering all the time. So if I write a book and know someone will read it, I may have to do business with him later. In a sense, I'm writing a book and I'm still doing business. 'Manipulate' is too strong a word for what I do. 'Maneuver' is closer to it. I'm not sure how much you can accomplish by being so direct that a person is upset or offended or intimidated. So bottom line for me is getting things done, not creating a bunch of firefights or little brush wars. I don't want an enemy in going about my daily work or my career. One hundred friends can't fight off an enemy. He's always there trying to hurt you."

Walsh paused here, searching for a way to illustrate his point. "Let's just say I have a quarrel with George Young [general manager of the New York Giants], and when I hang up I'm not happy. I'll find a way to call him back, lighten up the conversation to make sure that next time I call we can do business. If I'm really angry, I try to plot out how I'm going to handle it, what I'm going to say to get the point across and yet not let the other guy respond in a way that would create confrontation.

"I suffer more doing those things than most people. If I were Bobb

McKittrick [offensive line coach of the 49ers], well, life's real easy for Bobb because he thinks he's always telling the truth. He thinks, 'As long as I tell you the truth, my conscience is clear.' I say there are different forms of truth. Rarely are things all truthful or all non-truthful. So while Bobb thinks he's just going about his life, he's leaving a lot of wrecks behind. People have to clean up around him for what he's said or done, and yet his conscience is clear."

Walsh leaned back in his chair, lacing his fingers together in his lap. "So my point is, I give more time to people, their sensitivities, than I should. I struggle more with it. Sometimes I wish I were more direct. I'd get things over with. I triple the effort I have to make to get something done, and I get mad at myself for doing it. I take on too many things. I say, 'OK, I'll see him.' Pretty soon, I get a pile stacked up. I say, 'What the hell am I doing to myself?' I give myself an awful lot of added anxiety and stress. On the other hand, over the long haul, it's more effective to cultivate people like that."

Sometimes Walsh could be direct and indirect at the same moment. One time, Russ Francis was talking to a reporter while the other 49er players were running out to practice. Francis was the most independent member of the 49ers during his time there; he had no use for authority or team protocol. Walsh observed Francis and then calmly called over Rodney Knox of the public relations staff. Walsh's tone was as pleasant as if he were inviting Knox to drop by the house for a martini. Knox walked toward Walsh pleased that he had been singled out.

But as Knox approached, Walsh began screaming at the top of his lungs. "Our fucking players don't talk to media before practice. You tell that reporter to get the hell out of here."

As he thought about what had happened, Knox understood that Walsh wasn't the least bit angry at him. How could he be? Knox hadn't been with the reporter. Walsh was ticked off at Francis and used Knox as an instrument to convey that anger—was, in fact, getting across his point without having to risk a confrontation with one of his stars. The entire team was an audience to the performance, and Francis never again allowed an interview to get in the way of practice.

Walsh also could play mind games with players. One time, running back Wendell Tyler stormed into Rodney Knox's office in the PR department and threw his helmet on the desk. Tyler was just coming off the Injured Reserve list, and Walsh had just told him, "Wendell, you'll be on the junior varsity this week."

"I've never been JV in my life," Tyler complained. "I've always been a star." That week, Tyler played a terrific game.

Sometimes Walsh would send memos to all the 49er coaches and secretaries saying their offices had to be tidy. He might never follow up with an inspection. But that wasn't the point. He wanted to keep everyone edgy.

Walsh would maneuver with his coaches at Stanford. He often would sit in the conference room and suggest they try various techniques in practice, and he'd usually explain that he learned them from Paul Brown. This wasn't necessarily true. He once confessed to a friend that, "Sometimes I refer to Paul Brown because I don't want to keep referring to myself. To justify something I do, I relate it to Paul, and sometimes it is him and sometimes it isn't. It might even be me. I need a reference point to give it credibility. Or I use Tommy Prothro or Al Davis."

Walsh knew how to be friendly with his Stanford coaches without getting close with them. He experienced toward them a sense of fellowship that comes from going to battle together, but he rarely socialized with them, kept a part of himself hidden. This was the only way he knew how to be a head coach.

"I worry that I'm not personal enough with them," he once said, "that I'm not one of the guys, and sometimes I can't tell how I'm perceived, for sure. I know it's not negative. I'm older than these guys, so it's natural I'd be a little distant. I don't know how it could be any other way. There'll always be some griping, that's just part of it. But from the standpoint of being head coach there's a little veneer there, and it should be, is almost expected to be, so that you can make impersonal decisions. You have the authority. If you get friendly and familiar, the familiarity breeds a real comfortable atmosphere, almost contempt, and when everybody gets comfortable, they accept whatever happens as fate."

Walsh's reserve contained a physical component. He was not a man you would touch. It would take courage bordering on recklessness to smack him on the back or put an arm around his shoulder. It's not that he ever recoiled, or that he asked people to lay off. The protocol was simply understood. Forty-Niner president Carmen Policy felt this distance. "After we'd win a Super Bowl, I'd hug Bill because that's what you do. But I didn't feel comfortable. I knew he didn't want me to."

*   *   *

The team was delayed getting into Pasadena for the UCLA game, so Walsh called off the afternoon meetings and let the players relax in their rooms. Before dinner, the team rode in buses through the quiet elegant streets of Pasadena to the Rose Bowl, where Walsh hoped to make a return visit on January 1. Walsh wanted the team to go through an easy practice, mostly to get used to the silent stadium and its field, which was as smooth as a putting green. A fine mist filtered through the lights.

The players dressed in one of the locker rooms, while Walsh and Fred vonAppen sat in camp chairs reminiscing about the time they had ridden from Berkeley to Palo Alto after beating the University of California 30-10 in 1978's Big Game. The coaches all rode on one bus, drinking wine out of glasses. Pretty soon, some were drinking directly from the bottles. When the bus arrived in Palo Alto, the coaches drove to Walsh's house to continue the celebration. The house was noisy and happy, and the coaches were dancing with their wives when the phone rang at about ten o'clock. Walsh took the call. Someone was on the line inviting him and his team to a bowl game. This made Walsh happy. He walked into the living room and told everyone Stanford was going to a bowl game. Everyone wanted to know which one. Walsh could understand their curiosity, and he certainly wanted to oblige them, but with all the celebrating and wine, well, the name of the bowl had completely slipped his mind. He had to wait until the next day to find out.

VonAppen was laughing at the memory as he finished dressing, and Walsh was laughing, too. Ever since defeating Notre Dame they had felt playful.

After practice, players and coaches ate dinner and went into the evening meeting, which began with a highlight film of the Notre Dame game. When the film came on, Walsh leaned contentedly against the wall. The film showed the Stanford players beating hell out of the Irish: Nate Olsen throwing bone-crushing blocks for Ellery Roberts, Glyn Milburn running like a madman, and John Lynch hitting people—Lynch tackling Reggie Brooks, Lynch blasting Jerome Bettis at the start of the third quarter and causing the fumble that changed everything. The players shrieked and pointed at the screen, while Lynch sat shyly squirming in his seat, unused to all this attention. As background, the song "Bad to the Bone" by George Thorogood and the Destroyers pulsated through the room, and each time

Lynch leveled someone the players would hear, "Buh-buh-buh-bad. Bad to the bone."

Whenever the camera picked up Holtz pacing the sideline, the players would point and yell with derision, "Lou! Lou!"

The UCLA game turned out to be a joy for the Cardinal defense and a misery for the offense. Stanford defenders sacked Rob Walker six times and they couldn't remember when they'd had so much fun. They felt frustrated with the offense, though, which played its worst game since the opener against Texas A&M. This was difficult for all of them to swallow. Stanford expected to challenge Washington for the conference championship, but how could Stanford become a legitimate contender without an offense?

The Cardinal marched seventy-one yards on its first drive but settled for a field goal by Eric Abrams, and then had to punt on its next four possessions. The Cardinal's only touchdown of the first half came on a seventy-five-yard punt return by Glyn Milburn, the longest of his career. During one streak, UCLA held Stanford to just two first downs in twenty-seven minutes. Stanford scored its only offensive touchdown early in the third quarter when Steve Stenstrom hit Mike Cook with a seven-yard pass. But even that score had been set up by the defense— Coy Gibbs intercepted Walker, giving Stanford the ball at the Bruins 22. Stanford's final points came late in the game when Ron George sacked Walker, who fumbled. The Bruins' Vaughn Parker recovered in the end zone for a safety. Final score: Stanford 19, UCLA 7.

Afterward, Walsh, who had been raging over the headsets throughout the game—the coaches had never heard him like that— looked ill. He thought his offense had come together against the Irish, and now he saw that that was an illusion. How could he feel confident when his offense had scored one touchdown and managed only one long drive in the entire game? Stenstrom had been sacked another three times, bringing the season total to twenty-one, and for the first time, Walsh publicly assigned part of the blame to him. "Our timing was awful in our passing game. Stenstrom would hold the ball and hold the ball waiting for someone to get open." It worried Walsh that Stenstrom did not spot second and third receivers, a requirement for his quarterbacks as they scanned the field in a one-two-three progression.

After the game, Walsh admitted to himself that the defense was responsible for the Cardinal's 5-1 record. "It feels like I'm just along for the ride," he confided. When Gary Migdol came to get Walsh for the postgame press conference, Walsh told him, "What am I supposed to say, 'We blitzed them at the right time'?" Then he pointed to Fred vonAppen. "You should bring in that man over there."

A few months later, Walsh was able to look back on the UCLA game with tranquility. "After the victory against Notre Dame I thought we had jelled," he said of his offense. "We played so well in the second half of that game that I thought it would carry over. But we weren't improving, and it was disconcerting. We failed to block effectively, it was that simple. Steve was unsure of his pass protection throughout most of the year. Especially at that stage, he couldn't be sure what to expect. Although we beat UCLA, we still struggled. We did demonstrate character. We demonstrated that we were certainly intense enough in the way we played. I mean, there wasn't any problem with that. And we deserved to win. But there was that ominous feeling that we weren't blocking people. Then, of course, it caught up with us the next week."

Bill Walsh as a wide receiver at San Jose State in 1952. (*Courtesy San Jose State University Sports Information*)

Mike White, Bill Walsh, and Dick Vermeil as assistant coaches at Stanford in 1964. According to Walsh, "All three of these faces are the same guy." (*Courtesy Bill Walsh*)

Walsh (*bottom row center*) first was Stanford's head coach in 1977 and 1978. Other members of his original staff: Dennis Green (*top row left*), George Seifert (*top row second from left*), and Fred vonAppen (*top row right*). (*Courtesy Bill Walsh*)

Walsh (*far left*) on the staff of the Cincinnati Bengals. Coach Paul Brown is in the center. (*Courtesy Bill Walsh*)

Bill Walsh announces his return to Stanford on January 16, 1992. (*Courtesy* Stanford Daily, *Rajiv Chandrasekaran*)

Walsh instructs Glyn Milburn ... (*Courtesy* Stanford Daily, *Al Green*)

... and stresses a point to Steve Stenstrom. (*Courtesy* Stanford Daily, *Vincent Ho*)

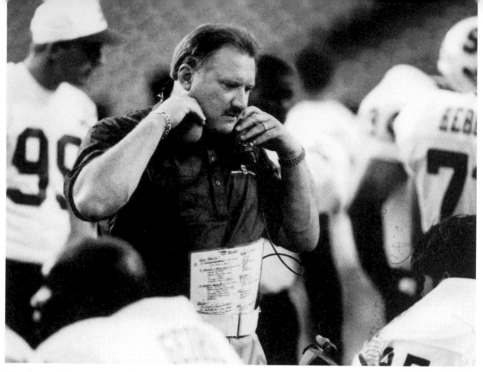

Fred vonAppen, Stanford's defensive coordinator, with a playsheet in his belt. (*Courtesy Stanford University Sports Information*)

Tom Holmoe, Stanford's defensive backs coach. (*Courtesy Stanford University Sports Information*)

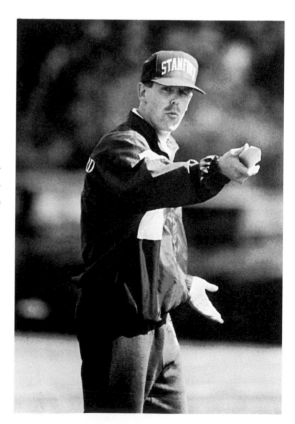

Scott Schuhmann, offensive line coach. (*Courtesy Stanford University Sports Information*)

Bill Singler, special teams coach. (*Courtesy Stanford University Sports Information*)

Al Matthews, administrative assistant. (*Courtesy Stanford University Sports Information*)

Fernando Montes, strength and fitness coach. (*Courtesy Stanford University Sports Information*)

Quarterback Steve Stenstrom on the field ... (*Courtesy Stanford University Sports Information*)

... and off. (*Courtesy Tyrone Parker*)

Defensive lineman Estevan Avila. (*Courtesy* Stanford
Daily, *Brian Dedell*)

Linebacker Ron George.
(*Courtesy* Stanford Daily,
Al Green)

The Stanford student newspaper ran this photo with the following caption: "Running back J. J. Lasley has been a consistent performer for the Cardinal on both the football and rugby fields since his arrival on campus." (*Courtesy* Stanford Daily, *Curtis Chen*)

Running back Ellery Roberts. (*Courtesy Stanford University Sports Information*)

Linebacker Dave Garnett. (*Courtesy Stanford University Sports Information*)

Safety John Lynch. (*Courtesy Stanford University Sports Information*)

(*Left*) Linebacker John Sims. (*Courtesy Stanford University Sports Information*)

(*Below*) Linebacker Tom Williams in the locker room. (*Courtesy Tyrone Parker*)

Linebackers coach Keena Turner.
(*Courtesy Tyrone Parker*)

Place kicker Eric Abrams.
(*Courtesy Stanford University
Sports Information*)

Bill Walsh forgets the name of Aaron Rembisz (#78, with head bowed) at the bonfire on the eve of the Big Game against Cal Berkeley. (*Courtesy Tyrone Parker*)

Running back Glyn Milburn shoulders a Stanford tradition before the Big Game. Under this photo, a Stanford student publication ran the caption, "Kiss my ax." (*Courtesy* Stanford Daily, *Rajiv Chandrasekaran*)

Bill Walsh in the Stanford Quad. (*Courtesy Stanford University Sports Information*)

RON GEORGE WAS the stud of the Cardinal defense, a star of the same magnitude as Glyn Milburn. But he was more flamboyant than the shy Milburn. George fed off the attention of the fans and the press and craved celebrity treatment. He wore an earring and shaved his head, and looked like a genie with magic powers.

He had transferred to Stanford in 1989, the same year Ellery Roberts and Milburn arrived, but his story was more unusual than theirs. When George was in the third grade, his family moved from Michigan to an American military base near Heidelberg, Germany, where his father served in the air force. His mother, a teacher, insisted George visit the countries he was studying in school. One weekend they drove to Rome because he was learning about the Roman Empire, and before he graduated from high school, he had gone to every European country except Czechoslovakia.

In high school he wrestled and played soccer and didn't go out for the football team until his junior year, although he never actually got on the field until he was a senior. He was accepted at Stanford, Harvard, and the Air Force Academy, and ended up going to the Academy. "It was free. I didn't want my parents to pay. Also, I was in a military community, and when you say, 'I'm going to the Air Force Academy,' everyone goes 'Oooh!' The oooh factor was a big part of it. And I was still going to get a chance to play sports. At the Academy it was mandatory. So it just seemed like the place to go."

As it turned out, it wasn't. The way George saw it, he had three full-time jobs—cadet, student, football player. There wasn't enough time to do any one thing well, and after his freshman year, he wanted out. So he applied to Harvard again and was accepted, was even assigned a dorm room, but before he went his father suggested they take a trip to Palo Alto just to look around. They saw the Stanford campus with the Spanish archways, the red-tiled roofs, the green hills in the background, and George's father casually said, "Why don't you go over and talk to the football team, see what they have to offer?"

Denny Green was the coach at the time, and he was a persuasive man. Within an hour, Green sold George on Stanford. George agreed to enroll, although he was a walk-on, didn't even have a scholarship. He had no idea how to attack a tackling dummy. His first time at a Stanford practice, he hit the dummy with his head. But George was an instinctive genius at creaming quarterbacks, and after sitting out a year because of NCAA regulations, he led the conference in quarterback sacks and tackles for loss in 1990.

George's volume was pumped to the max. He would scream most of the time he was on the field, needing to work himself up if he was going to play well, and that meant he had to be on fire all the time. "For those sixty minutes on Saturday, for those eleven games, I get to act out a side of me that at no other time can ever rise to the forefront," George once explained. "I get to be a wild man. I can be mean. I can spit. It's the freest, funnest time I have all year long. I spend nine months for eleven sixty-minute Saturdays."

George already had paid a serious price for his fun. Neither of his ring fingers worked anymore. The ring finger on his left hand was permanently bent. He injured it in 1990 and refused to have it operated on until the season ended. The right ring finger was swollen to twice normal size and one of the knuckles looked like a walnut.

He wrote an essay for an English class about his hurt fingers, about the long- and short-term implications of sacrificing parts of his body to football. He reached the conclusion that "It is inconsequential at the moment. I can't see past Saturday."

George may have acted like a madman during games, but he was a recluse away from the football field, living by himself in a two-bedroom house with a cat. He tried to keep football away from his private life, and in more than three years had only allowed five of his teammates to visit him. He was a homebody who craved neatness. For Christmas, his mother once gave him metal covers for the burners on his stove. This was a present he appreciated. His mother also threw in oven mitts and a dish towel. It was as though, most of the time, he had to be as ordinary as possible, keep his fire tamped down, in order to burn brightly during games. On Saturdays, he wanted to make the play and get the applause. If Stanford won but he didn't make a tackle, he'd feel cheated.

He did not believe that he fit in well at Stanford. He was reared in the military and he found Stanford too liberal, its rules vague. Some of the other players felt the same way and lived by themselves or in fraternities with other athletes. If it weren't for football, George believed he would have transferred again, but in football, he found everything he needed, a military-style hierarchy in which everyone from Walsh to the assistant coaches to the players and the team managers and trainers knew exactly who they were and where they fit in.

Although he was a good student, he would sacrifice studies if it meant getting a good night's sleep so he could be fresh for the next day's practice. His friends came almost exclusively from the football team, and this made his situation paradoxical. Stanford encouraged its players to be part of the campus at large, and that was exactly what George did not want. He lived his college life in a parenthetical mode.

Among his closest friends were Dave Garnett, who played the other outside linebacker position, inside backer Tom Williams, and defensive end Estevan Avila. Garnett was quiet and studious and kept a daily journal of his life. He was an omnivorous reader of fiction who on the field was as fierce as George, and in his way even more emotional. Until this season, Garnett had thrown up before every game, and even now when the offense was on the field he never took off his helmet. He could speak philosophically about football. "It's very simple because it's a game. And in any game there's a bottom line, and that's to win. It's a simple format, but you've got to make the simple very complicated so that you can get back to the simple."

Linebacker Tom Williams did not enjoy as much notoriety as George or Garnett, but they would defer to him when he wanted to speak, would fall silent when he walked into the huddle to call the play. He had the strongest will of the three. He was from Texas and had spent part of his junior year at a Stanford program in Florence, Italy, and worked three summers at a salmon cannery in Alaska. "The work was mindless—long hours, eighteen, nineteen, twenty hours a day—but I got a taste of the Last Frontier. It was a priceless experience."

Estevan Avila looked like a bouncer in a bar but was intelligent and soft-spoken. He came from a small town a few hours north of San

Francisco called Sebastopol where his father was sheriff. He never thought he could afford college until he blossomed as a football player his senior year of high school and was offered athletic scholarships.

All four of these players—George, Garnett, Williams, and Avila— were fiercely loyal to each other. All had played for at least two different head coaches, and Williams and Avila had played for three—Jack Elway, Dennis Green, and Walsh. Their loyalties extended to their teammates, not necessarily to the coaching staff or the school.

Walsh encouraged this player-to-player bonding, saw it as essential to the proper functioning of a football team. He was a student of the Civil War and liked to ponder the strategy of the great battles and the psychology of the soldiers. One night at dinner, he explained to a visitor the concept of loyalty in the Civil War.

"They were fighting for great issues, slavery and the right of the South to secede—monumental issues. But what did these kids know? Many of them were sixteen, seventeen years old. They'd come from farms, they were plowboys. They didn't understand the issues, all they knew was, 'We are here right now.' What they felt was an incredible loyalty not to let down the men in their group, and they would perform great acts of heroism because of that.

"It's the same thing on a football team. Fight for USC? What kind of USC? There's some pageantry and they wear those colors, but really what the players are feeling is loyalty to each other. That's what I'm trying to build on this team. You put all of us together and build a wall around us, you lock us in and tell us we have to break through that wall." Walsh pointed to a blank white wall in the dining room. "In a week we'll break through that wall together. No one will want to let anybody down. On a football team, you're bonded by trying to win games. Teams that come together win, and teams that don't, lose."

Walsh's talent was in recognizing that he had inherited a veteran team, especially on defense, and in leaving it alone. George, Garnett, Williams, and Avila may secretly have felt guilty for putting their teammates before the coaches or even the concept of the team, but Walsh would have applauded them.

Ron George was living proof of Walsh's philosophy. "There's starting to be two different cores of the team," he once explained. "Thirty of us were Denny Green's kids. The football player I am now is because of Denny Green, not because of Bill Walsh. The players that are really making things happen right now are still Green's bunch. When we're on the field as a defense, we put our hands together and we're eleven guys. And the coaches, they're on the sideline and they don't matter anymore.

"When Coach Green was here, we had to destroy everything Stanford was and build a new spirit, attitude, belief, because Stanford was so low. And now all these new players are building on that. This is the only way it could have happened. We built the core, the base, and now, we build the Taj Mahal on top. That's what Coach Walsh is doing. When you're the caliber coach that Bill Walsh is, I don't think you want to come in and have to train ninety guys to have a winning attitude. You just teach them how to win.

"Denny Green drives his players and he drives himself. Bill Walsh is a technician and he's a refiner. He takes that rough diamond, and he cuts it into what you put on your finger, and it's the Rose Bowl ring or the Super Bowl ring. Denny Green was the only man who could have brought us to this point, and Bill Walsh is the only man who can take us to the next level. I don't think one can do both."

Walsh may have been a refiner, may have been constructing the Taj Mahal in the Stanford quad, but he didn't look as if he knew sheetrock from plumbing when he met the team at three o'clock on Tuesday. Stanford's record was 2-0 in the Pac-10, the Cardinal's best start since 1977, Walsh's first year as head coach. But Arizona worried him. The Wildcats' defense was fast and mobile like Texas A&M's, and Walsh was pretty sure it would outmaneuver his large, slow offensive line. Arizona had given up only four touchdowns all year and held opponents to 10.2 points per game. This was bad news for an offense that had trouble scoring.

A few weeks earlier, Arizona almost beat Miami, which was widely regarded as the best team in the country, finally losing 8-7. Miami managed just two yards rushing against the Arizona defense, or 3.3 inches per running play. Even though Arizona's record was an unimpressive 2-2-1, Walsh considered the Wildcats a threat. To make matters worse, Glyn Milburn had bruised his shoulder against UCLA and was having trouble running in practice, and Ron George had a deep hamstring pull. Walsh told his coaches the team was due for a fall.

He stepped onto the stage at the front of the Hall of Fame Room and launched into a long, bitter speech about the Arizona players. His voice was loud and contemptuous. "This is out of the college arena," he said, his left hand on his hip. "They hose off their players and clean them up and bring them in. It's a hatchet fight and you guys know it.

Eight of them will be in front of the camera at once celebrating after each play, trying to claim they made the tackle. They'll be doing back flips. We leave college football for three hours when we play these guys. We're not backing down to them. You've got to hit them before they hit you. You want this experience once in your lives, this is it."

He made another dramatic exit after that, stalking out of the room as if he was about to blow his cork, but a few minutes later, in the courtyard, he was laughing with a friend, claiming he was building up a theme the same as he'd done for San Jose State.

"I took it too far. I said, 'This is not a college game—they have thirty-two junior college transfers,' where, in reality, they've got sixteen. [The Arizona media guide listed twenty-one junior college transfers.] And I just said, 'This is a mercenary group that's come in to play you. If you've ever wanted to be truly tested, this is the ultimate, because they're coming up here with one thing in mind, and that's to embarrass you, humiliate you, and stand over you and point their fingers.'"

Walsh sat down on the steps and crossed his legs. "I got real carried away. One of the players smiled, and then I had to chuckle. I couldn't help myself. It might have wrecked the full scenario. It's like two people acting something out that gets so bizarre that they just laugh. 'This is the stupidest script I've ever seen.' Usually, I don't let it get to the point where it becomes, 'Wait a minute, Coach!' But you need a reason to play a game above and beyond the fact that it's on the schedule. Some games don't have a deep tradition. Arizona's one. San Jose State's another. They're not USC, UCLA, so you need a real strong symbol to hook onto."

A few minutes later, Walsh headed back into the room. In the courtyard he'd been giggling. Now he was frowning for effect. Walsh the thespian. Terry Shea had just gone over the schedule for the next few days, but now he sat down, and Walsh began to explain the new plays, showing them on an overhead projector. Some of the plays were drawn with incorrect blocking schemes. Once, Steve Stenstrom interrupted Walsh to point out that one play was mislabled.

Walsh listened quietly, his head listing to one side, which usually meant he was weary. "You're right," he told Stenstrom. "I don't know what I was thinking of."

It was curious to see Walsh this distracted. A few minutes later, he interrupted his presentation to complain about the number of running plays. "Scott and Bill," he called out to Schuhmann and Ring, who were standing in the back of the room, "after practice, I want you to eliminate one running play."

When he'd finished and the team began to walk toward practice, Walsh lingered behind in the room, quietly whistling "Someone to Watch Over Me."

The next day, at the staff meeting, Walsh talked about relations among the coaches. It was an awkward moment for him. He sat in his usual place at the head of the table in the conference room and he was smiling, but the smile was strained, as if someone had painted it on his face.

The staff had been working together for half a season, and all the coaches were tired. They had even begun to bicker and talk behind each other's backs—nothing serious, just the kind of thing that occurs among a small group of people who see each other every day and begin to get on each other's nerves. Some of the coaches would criticize Terry Shea for taking too long to learn the offense. Walsh himself was fretting about Fred vonAppen again, that old worry about a reckless defense that infiltrated Walsh's peace of mind when he was tired.

Walsh was also concerned that his coaches might complain to their friends on other staffs. The coaching fraternity is small, and men at different schools often have worked together and are friends. Pretty soon, word could get around that the Stanford staff was in chaos.

"There are plenty of people who would like that," Walsh told the coaches.

Walsh talked to them about loyalty. "We owe that to one another," he said, his eyes scanning both sides of the long table. "I want to remind you that you're a well-paid staff. You work fewer hours than most college coaches, and you live in a beautiful part of the world."

He sat up in his chair, leaned his elbows on the table. "I want you to know you're doing a great job and I'm happy with your work."

Afterward, Fred vonAppen said, "That speech wasn't for an old fart like me. The young guys need it." Still, Al Matthews pointed out that vonAppen had seemed grumpy before the meeting, but after it he walked around the room patting the other coaches on the back. When he returned to his office, he turned up the classical music louder than usual.

Later, Walsh took a visitor into his office to talk about the staff meeting. He sat at the table and sighed. "I get gloomy sometimes and they don't know what it means. Each coach assumes I'm thinking about him. Of course, sometimes I am. But they're doing a good job and I wanted to reassure them."

On Wednesday, Joe Montana visited. Walsh closed his office door, and the two talked for almost an hour. Montana was worried about his future now that the 49ers had made the transition to Steve Young as their starting quarterback, and he had come to Walsh for advice. When he played for Walsh, Montana sometimes would complain that Walsh did not praise him enough, and after a while Montana learned to live without Walsh's praise, telling himself that Walsh had higher standards for quarterbacks.

After Walsh returned to Stanford, Montana began to grow closer to him. In the spring, he had come to campus and thrown passes for the quarterbacks, demonstrating proper technique, and he made a videotape for Walsh. While recuperating from elbow surgery, he would drive to the practice field and watch anonymously from his car.

Walsh was concerned about what Montana would do after he retired. He hoped he'd banked his fortune and could afford to go into coaching like Keena Turner. Montana sometimes would tell Walsh he wanted to run a winery in the Napa Valley, and Walsh thought that was a bucolic fantasy, lovely but unrealistic. He saw Montana as a natural coach. "He's not a broadcaster. He's not a businessman. He's not an entertainer. He needs something of substance. I'm glad to see him coming over and watching us. I'd like to see more of him. He's a tough guy to pin down. We talked about playing nine holes of golf. He's a marvelous golfer and I'm terrible, but we could go out and just sit and talk. Joe doesn't run as deep as some of the guys, Harris Barton or Mike Walter. But there is a sincerity underneath all of it, there is a good guy under there. He's a warrior, and he's a gladiator, that's what he is."

Saturday morning, Walsh quietly watched pregame warm-ups, his hand under his chin like someone sizing up a Picasso. The Cardinal ranked eighth in the nation—the last time a Stanford team ranked as high as eighth was following the 1970 season. The Cardinal was in the race for the Rose Bowl, and although that pleased Walsh, now he felt the pressure to keep winning.

After the warm-up he gathered the team in the locker room. Fernando Montes shut the front door, blocking out the sun, and in the hush of the semidarkness, Walsh told all the players to fall to one knee.

He crouched to a knee as well, and he touched kicker Eric Abrams on the shoulder, and every player touched another player. Walsh closed his eyes and remained silent for many seconds. He had been doing this ever since he could remember, bracketing off the game from ordinary life, getting his team into the mood by imposing a long moment of quiet. When he thought enough time had passed he led the team in the Lord's Prayer.

He would do the same thing after the game in reverse order. The team would enter the locker room, and the players and coaches would take a knee and Walsh again would lead them in prayer. Then they would remain silent for about twenty seconds—it could have been longer. The silence symbolized the transition back to ordinary life—schoolwork, girlfriends, healing from the game.

Walsh did not see the prayer itself as spiritual. It was a necessary ritual, a chance to let the players meditate on the enormity of the experience that awaited them or that they'd just completed. He once talked in his office about the praying:

"Virtually every team does it, even the pros. The 49ers did it. I used to ask different people to speak after practice on Thanksgiving Day, and some guys would say eloquent things from the heart about the meaning of Thanksgiving. And you'd hope, you'd wish that the players would reflect on that as one of the treasures of their lives. I've asked Harris Barton to say a prayer or John Frank, both happen to be Jewish. I've asked other people to say prayers outside the strictly Christian little gathering.

"I hope to keep it within normal expression, rather than take it a step further into Christian dialogue, giving yourself to the Lord. There are some that let this thing get out of context. It's where you get the very vocal person, let's say of the Christian faith, who wants to make this a vehicle to have people give their lives to the Lord instead of play football. I can remember Bubba Paris after we'd just busted our ass—guys were broken, bleeding, hurting—we finally came back in 1988 and won the division and the championship and I can't remember what game it might have been, but Bubba had to tell the press that the Lord just did that, won the game for us."

Walsh got up from his chair and began pacing behind his desk. "The Lord did it? I mean, maybe He did, to each person, He anointed every player or something. But why would He do it for us and not for the other team? What kind of a Lord is that? A lot of guys were really disgusted with Bubba for that, not mad, just, 'Yuck, get away, you jerk.'

Because these guys had really worked and humped and come back, and now suddenly, the Lord stepped in and did it? In other words, if they hadn't sacrificed, it was going to happen anyway.

"That's offensive as heck to me. Whoever He is—or She is—He must have higher goals than deciding who's going to win a football game, because there are about thirty million starving to death within ten hours on an airplane ride. So He comes over to the stadium and helps. Jeez, it's ridiculous."

After the team finished praying, Walsh told Seth Dittman to stand up. He would be playing left tackle today because the previous starter, Jeff Bailey, had come down with mononucleosis. Dittman, a rarely used junior, was the fourth left tackle in seven games. He was enormous, six seven, 280 pounds, and wore the beginnings of a beard. As he stood in the middle of the locker room his teammates applauded him and told him he'd do a good job. He blinked and looked away.

Walsh gave the team another pep talk emphasizing Arizona's low-life character, in case his "theme" hadn't taken the first time around. "We don't want to get in their game," he said, standing in the middle of the players. "They'll be jabbing at you, talking. We don't want any communication with them. Just knock them on their ass. That's how you do it. Keep the heat on and they'll finally crack."

Walsh felt good about what he had said, but when both teams ran out on the field he took his position on the sideline and stared across at the Arizona squad. It looked awfully impressive. He told himself his team couldn't match up.

Ellery Roberts felt edgy, too, but he wasn't sure why. From the time he woke up, the day seemed to be going in fast motion. He'd gone to breakfast and boarded the bus and arrived on campus—all too fast, everything out of his control. It was as if he were living a dream. And now he was on the sideline with the game about to begin, and he didn't feel ready.

Early in the second quarter, Stanford led 6–0 after Eric Abrams converted two field goals. After the second field goal, Ron George whispered to David Garnett, "That's it. We scored our six points." He was right.

George's gloomy prediction might have been based on the condition of Steve Stenstrom, who suffered his weekly knockout with about three minutes left in the first quarter. This knockout was more frightening than usual. As he was being sacked, Stenstrom's helmet hit someone's knee. He lay on the ground unconscious for several minutes, his left leg tucked under his right.

After a while, Stenstrom's father, who was wearing a Stenstrom jersey complete with the number 18, emerged from the stands, walked onto the field, and kneeled over his fallen son. An ambulance drove up to the Stanford bench, and some men carried a stretcher to where Stenstrom lay. Finally, Stenstrom got up and staggered off the field with two trainers propping him up.

Then backup quarterback Mark Butterfield came in. Butterfield was blond and handsome and resembled actor Jeff Bridges. He had a stronger arm than Stenstrom. In fact, his arm was a rocket. But he was slow to learn Walsh's offense, and sometimes in quarterback meetings he would sit silently when Terry Shea asked what to do on a specific play. Eventually he would answer, and usually he would be correct, but that time lag was troublesome to him and the coaches, because on a football field the opposition wasn't about to give him the chance to recall plays.

Butterfield was six four and looked impressive when he stood in the pocket. Walsh had wanted to get him more work in games, but with the offense stuttering, it just never seemed that he could take out Stenstrom. And now Butterfield was on his own against one of the best defenses in the country.

He was tested quickly. In the second quarter, Butterfield faced third and eight from Stanford's 13-yard line. He dropped back to pass. He held the ball over his head as he stared down the field. He looked good, poised to throw. Unfortunately, he wasn't poised enough to notice Arizona defensive end Tedy Bruschi barreling in from the side. As Butterfield stood there blissfully unaware of the pressure, Bruschi flicked the ball out of his hand and fell on it at Stanford's 1-yard line.

The Cardinal defense couldn't hold Arizona, which scored a touchdown on the very next play. Ater kicking the extra point, the Wildcats led 7-6. On the sideline, Dave Garnett told himself, "That's it." He knew the game was over.

Butterfield didn't have any outright disasters after that, but he was in constant trouble, partly because the new left tackle, Seth Dittman, was green and let blitzers past like businessmen hurrying through a revolving door. Following one unsuccessful series, Terry Shea wanted to speak to Butterfield on the phone. This was not unusual. Offensive coordinators speak to quarterbacks every time the offense leaves the field. But Butterfield had wandered away. He was not used to coaches speaking to him during games. Shea scanned the sideline with his binoculars. No Butter-field. He yelled into the phone, "Would somebody get me Mark!"

Finally someone had the presence of mind to grab Butterfield and lead him to the phone, and there he heard Shea uncharacteristically shouting, "Mark, you've got to come to the phone so we can talk." Shea went over a few plays with Butterfield, nothing exotic. He wanted to make sure his quarterback knew the basic formations and blocking schemes.

Arizona scored a touchdown on its next possession on a forty-five-yard run by Chuck Levy, and led 14-6 at the half. Stanford's defense had come into the game ranked fifth in the nation, second against the run, but Arizona running backs were ripping off huge gains. "You've got to be shitting me," Fred vonAppen shouted at the defense. "Shove it up their ass."

In the third quarter, Arizona scored on a thirty-three-yard run by Billy Johnson, and later, Stenstrom, who had returned to start the sec-ond half, was knocked out of the game two more times by defenders who ran past the offensive line as if it didn't exist. The final score was 21-6, and Stanford's statistics were gruesome. The Cardinal's rushing yardage amounted to minus 33, the lowest total since the school started keeping records in 1955. The offensive line allowed eight sacks, and Glyn Milburn, slowed by an injured shoulder, gained six yards and dropped out of the race for the Heisman Trophy.

The Cardinal players made The Walk back to their locker room and sat in front of their cubicles without saying a word. Running back J. J. Lasley was struck by the silence. His friends Dave Garnett and Darrien Gordon sat near him staring at the floor. "This probably means we're not going to the Rose Bowl," Lasley whispered to himself.

Down the row of lockers Ron George was asking himself if he could derive a lesson from this brutal loss. At first he was too bitter to think straight, but suddenly it occurred to him. The players on defense had been telling each other they could win games on their own. When George thought about the Cardinal it was the defense that "made the music." The offensive players were "lesser instruments." Against Ari-zona, it had become obvious that the defense couldn't do it alone. "I have to give up my selfish attitude," George thought as he slowly made his way to the shower. "Control what you can," he told himself. "You must release some of the responsibility."

*   *   *

After meeting the press, Walsh made The Walk back to the gymnasium and was mobbed as usual. He felt low. His team had been exposed, even the defense, which allowed 256 rushing yards. The toughest part of the schedule loomed ahead of him.

Then he noticed in the mob of well-wishers an older woman who waited for him after each home game. She was waving to him. Seeing her friendly face cheered Walsh. He went over to her and stuck out his hand.

"Remember me?" she asked.

"Sure I do," Walsh said.

She came closer to Walsh, so that her mouth almost touched his ear. Walsh didn't pull back

"Mr. Walsh," she suddenly shouted, "how come you didn't throw to Justin Armour more? And how come Ellery didn't get the ball more?"

Walsh recoiled.

"Thank you," he managed to get out, and he left. But he was fried. "Here's this woman," he told Al Matthews as they hurried past hundreds of tailgaters. "She's got to be sixty-five years old. She just came right up and asked me those questions. Somehow I lost my feeling for her when she did that."

When Walsh walked into the coaches' locker room, his assistants weren't exactly breaking out the champagne.

"I told them there's no margin for error," vonAppen said.

"We're not that good," Keena Turner mumbled.

"Well, we're back to reality," Walsh said. "We're going to have more games like this."

"It came down to our defense against theirs," vonAppen told Walsh. "Neither offense had done much, and their defense won. Arizona laid bare our weaknesses."

The conversation went on like that for several minutes while the coaches sat in front of their lockers, too upset to shower and go home.

Walsh dropped out of the conversation. He had more pressing problems. A few days before, he'd invited a group of former 49ers to a postgame party in one of Stanford's picnic groves. At the time it seemed like a heck of an idea. The letter of invitation said:

Our victories over the Irish and the Bruins were sweet, but the Cardinal now prepares for its next crucial Pac-10 battle against the Wildcats of Arizona— and we're excited that you are going to be our guests! Coach Walsh is preparing an exciting game plan for you. We hope you are looking forward to your Saturday with Stanford Football.

The guests included Dwight Clark, Eddie DeBartolo, Jr., Joe Montana, and Carmen Policy, and they were supposed to celebrate the victory over Arizona with Walsh. But there wasn't any victory to celebrate, and the whole idea now seemed ludicrous.

Walsh got up slowly from his chair. His skin was pale. "Now I have to go to a cocktail party," he whispered. He might have been talking to himself, although he addressed his remarks to the refrigerator. He started to walk out of the locker room, but stopped when he reached the door. He stood there, head down, steeling himself. He walked to the grove and sat down on a bench with Montana and talked quietly. He stayed at the picnic for ten minutes, leaving before most of the guests arrived.

The offensive coaches got together late the next morning to go over the Arizona game tape. Walsh was in a state approaching despair. Once again his offense couldn't cope with a quick team, and now his defense had failed as well. Two weeks ago, he'd felt sublime after the comeback victory in South Bend, and now, to use Fred vonAppen's phraseology, the team was "lower than whale shit." Walsh still had faint hopes of going to the Rose Bowl, but Stanford would have to beat Washington, which seemed unlikely.

Walsh was still brooding when someone turned off the lights in the conference room. Walsh clicked the remote control and started the film. It wasn't long before he noticed two Arizona defenders run past a Cardinal offensive lineman. The lineman never touched them, just waved them through like a cop directing traffic. Walsh's jaw dropped. He ran the play again. He sat there without saying a word. He never had seen anything quite like that before. "Jeez-us Christ," he whispered under his breath. He sat there for another second. Then he stood up.

"I'll be right back," he told the others.

He walked out of the conference room, went through the main door of the football offices into the hallway, walked down the hallway, pushed open another door, and dashed down an outside staircase to the parking lot.

"Jeez-us Christ," he repeated to himself.

He got into his car and started the engine. He steered his car onto Campus Drive and found himself leaving campus. As he drove, he kept seeing the two defenders storming past the poor overmatched lineman, and before he knew it he'd parked his car in front of an ice cream parlor. He killed the engine, got out of the car, and walked inside. He studied the menu, then ordered the biggest, richest, gooeyest chocolate sundae in the place. He ordered it to go.

He walked back to his car, slid behind the wheel, and turned on the radio. The Everly Brothers were singing. That made Walsh happy. He liked Don and Phil. He heard "Wake Up Little Susie," and "Cathy's Clown." Then "Bye Bye, Love" came on the radio. Walsh turned up the volume.

Bye bye, love

Bye bye, happiness

Hello loneliness

I think I'm gonna cry.

He sang along and tapped his foot and ingested chocolate sundae, while shoppers, surprised to see Bill Walsh alone on a Sunday morning pigging out on ice cream, walked past his car and waved.

Walsh waved back.

His bad mood began to lift. He drove back to campus, climbed upstairs to the football offices, and walked into the conference room. Terry Shea, Scott Schuhmann, and the others were waiting for him like men who had gone into suspended animation. The VCR was on Pause.

Walsh smiled at them. "Okay, let's go," he said, and he pushed the Play button.

That was the last time Walsh viewed tape of the previous day's game with his coaches. He found it too painful to see the mistakes, didn't want to blow up in front of his staff. After that, he watched alone in his office with the door closed.

CHAPTER

12

OFFENSIVE LINE COACH Scott Schuhmann did not know his fate had been sealed after the Arizona game, and neither perhaps did Walsh. If Schuhmann had thought about it, and he probably did, he would have understood that he was in trouble. One of the coaches reflected on Schuhmann, "He's a good coach, great guy. But he's not picking up Bill's system. Under Denny, it was simplified. He must know he's vulnerable."

Sometime between the end of the Arizona game on Saturday and the team meeting at three o'clock Monday, Walsh began thinking about changing offensive line coaches at the end of the season. Schuhmann would not know anything about this for more than two months, and as he entered the meeting in the Hall of Fame Room for Walsh's first remarks about next Saturday's game at Oregon State, he looked relaxed. That may have had something to do with Walsh's demeanor, which was gay. He was joking with a few players and, as the meeting began, no one could have guessed that a significant part of the Cardinal's coaching equation soon would change.

Walsh began in a matter-of-fact tone. If he was displeased he didn't show it, at least not right away.

"We just lost a ball game," he told the players. "I don't like the way we lost it, but we lost. We have lots of directions we can go. This team embarrassed the hell out of us in front of our students, and we've got to get it behind us. We're five and two, so all the great things we wanted to do we can still accomplish in the next five weeks. But we can go up to Corvallis and have real problems. The weather can be bad. They can see a chance to beat someone nationally ranked."

Walsh paused and wiped a hand across his face. It had galled him to make that last remark about Oregon State giving them problems. Oregon State was the worst team in the Pac-10, for heaven's sake, the Northwestern of the conference. Even its nickname was goofy, the Beavers. And here was Walsh sweating out a win over a team with a record of one win, one tie, and five losses. Oregon State's defense was a joke; it had given up thirty-five or more points six times, forty or more in four games. And yet Walsh had visions of the Beavers lining up eight men on the line of scrimmage, flowing over and around his offensive line, and knocking the hell out of Steve Stenstrom.

Walsh took a deep breath, then tried to put things in perspective. "There may be one or two top-ranked teams that will go undefeated. Usually they don't play anybody. We have tough games week after week. We have a great, great program, but we lost. The offense has to start producing. We can't go sputtering along."

In spite of his efforts to act calm, Walsh was beginning to work himself up. His face had assumed the light shade of scarlet that indicated he was about to erupt. "I know one offensive lineman who lost $250,000 in the Arizona game," he shouted. "He played so goddamn bad, he went from a first- or second-round draft choice to an eighth or a ninth. It was a quarter-of-a-million-dollar game for him. Lots of NFL scouts were there and they saw."

He walked to the back of the stage, returned to the front. He put his left hand in his pants pocket. He stared into the room searching out the offensive linemen. "I'm really sick of this offensive line. I'm disgusted. I wouldn't say this if you weren't good athletes. At the beginning of the season I said you were the strength of this ball club. You're the weakness. We can't throw the ball. You're getting the quarterback's eyes knocked out. There's too much at stake. We have four of the best teams in the country lined up waiting for us. I'm totally frustrated with that unit, and it wasn't just them—it was a sorry offensive effort. We don't want to finish this season thinking it was the offense that let us down."

The room was deathly quiet. The offensive linemen sat staring at the floor. Walsh had never attacked his players before, but even at that moment, when he seemed to be making a frontal assault on the linemen, his message contained a subtext that had nothing to do with them. Walsh's method always had been to criticize a coach in front of the players so that the players would feel responsible for letting down the coach, and then try harder. When he was with the 49ers, Walsh sometimes would prepare a coach for what was going to happen: "I'm going to get you today."

Now the situation was reversed. Walsh wanted to motivate Scott Schuhmann to get more out of his players, and he was getting the message across through the players, believing that Schuhmann was savvy enough to know what was going on.

The attack became almost brutal when Walsh criticized center Glen Cavanaugh for going the wrong way on several plays, then added, "I don't know, maybe you were told to do it."

This was a direct assault on the coach in front of the entire team. If Cavanaugh had been taught to do the wrong thing, Schuhmann had done the teaching.

Schuhmann sat quietly near the back of the room. He was a slightly round, friendly, fun-loving man who had confidence in his opinions and was outspoken during staff meetings. At least, he had started out that way. But lately his demeanor had changed, and this was not lost on the other coaches, who were aware that in some atavistic, primal way he was being singled out, separated from the rest of them, sacrificed. As the pressure on the offensive line mounted, as the line failed week after week, Schuhmann became tentative in staff meetings. Instead of forcefully making his points, he would speak in questions. "I'm just asking," he'd say after suggesting something. Or he'd go to the board, draw a play, explain it, and then say, "You know what I mean?" as if he had lost confidence in his ability to talk football.

Walsh, aware of every nuance of his coaches' behavior, saw the change in Schuhmann and told a friend, "Scott's under so much pressure. I grieve for him, but there's nothing I can do."

Actually, there was something Walsh could do. He could have become actively involved in coaching the offensive line—and for several weeks he had thought about doing just that. As he ruminated about the line, he could make a case to himself that Schuhmann deserved help. To begin with, Schuhmann was coaching five positions, more than any other staff member. Keena Turner, for example, was responsible only for the outside linebackers. Fred vonAppen handled the inside linebackers, and that had proven to be a sane, manageable way to divvy up the task. But Schuhmann was on his own, and it was almost impossible for him to see everything at once. The year before Schuhmann had had an assistant, and somehow, when he took over the team, Walsh lost track of that, assumed Schuhmann alone could handle the entire offensive line. Walsh blamed himself for leaving Schuhmann unprotected, told himself he had been away from coaching for three years and had let a few things slide at the beginning. Another gross error had been Walsh's failure to insert Chris Dalman, his best offensive lineman, at left tackle. If Walsh had done that, the line would have stabilized and Steve Stenstrom could have avoided half a dozen concussions.

Several times, Walsh had decided to get involved in the hands-on coaching of the offensive line, and each time he backed off. This vacillating disturbed him. Fifteen years ago, he would have grabbed the offensive line and shaken it up, but now he wasn't sure about his stamina. If he gave too much energy to Schuhmann he might drain himself for the game plan, lose his effectiveness on the sidelines during games when he had to be brilliant.

Finally he decided not to help Schuhmann. He told a friend, "At sixty, I just don't have the vitality to go over and be a line coach. I want to be the head coach."

Whenever he thought about the offensive line, Walsh felt ill. His play-calling was forever being disrupted because the line couldn't protect. "I'm humiliated," Walsh said. "That defensive coordinator from Arizona thought he really did a job on me. And I don't blame him. I ought to drop him a note and say, 'Nice job.'"

Walsh had no quarrel with Schuhmann's ability, and he respected his knowledge, even if his unit was a disappointment. Schuhmann had been Denny Green's offensive coordinator at Northwestern, and in 1988 he worked for the Canadian League Champion Winnipeg Blue Bombers. What worried Walsh was that Schuhmann had spent the last three seasons under Denny Green teaching the linemen to block straight ahead for big, powerful running backs. Walsh's system was infinitely more complex. While he believed Schuhmann would eventually adapt, he could name several line coaches who could come in right now and implement Walsh's system.

After Walsh left the 49ers, one of the assistant coaches got fired for scalping tickets. A situation like that would have been a no-brainer for Walsh. "He was making thousands of dollars every week. The minute I'd have learned of that one, he'd be gone." But Schuhmann was a moral, hard-working coach who was in his office at 7:30 every morning looking at film. Walsh simply believed he needed to make a change to someone he knew, preferably a contemporary.

Walsh had confided to several people his inclination to change offensive line coaches at the end of the season. Walsh was not a gossip, far from it, but he believed if he said the words "I may have to change coaches," actually got the thought out there, he wouldn't lose his nerve at the last minute. Talking about the coaching change was a fail-safe against backing down.

Walsh already had two coaches in mind for next season. His old friend Mike White was with the Raiders, and there was Monte Clark, generally regarded as one of the best offensive line coaches in the history of the sport. Clark was fifty-five, a big, gruff man who loved to argue football and was a brilliant teacher. He'd been head coach of the 49ers and Lions, and in the early 1970s he put together the offensive line for Don Shula when the Miami Dolphins were the best team in the league.

As Walsh thought about Schuhmann he realized he was caught between his compassion for the man and his duty to the team. Schuhmann was forty-seven and Walsh did not want to disrupt his life. He had a home near the ocean; his wife, Berni, taught in a local elementary school; he had two children, thirteen and eight. It troubled Walsh when he'd heard secondhand that Berni Schuhmann told the wife of Stanford Athletic Director Ted Leland, "They'll probably fire my husband after the season."

Although Walsh kept up outward appearances, was charming at his weekly press conference, he confided to friends that he was afraid of losing his remaining five games. This was unrealistic considering that Oregon State was likely to be a pushover, but Walsh was in another downward spiral, and from where he sat, everything added up to disaster.

At times like these, he was sensitive to the slightest criticism. Jane Walsh would try to keep negative mail away from him, but once in a while he'd get his hands on a letter questioning his ability, implying he was washed up, and he would steam.

One well-meaning alum faxed a note suggesting several changes, two concerning quarterbacks—use more of Mark Butterfield and tell the quarterbacks to roll out instead of dropping back in the pocket. Walsh was apoplectic when he read that. Someone was telling *him* how to coach quarterbacks. With Terry Shea, he studied every syllable of the letter as if it were a bomb threat. Then he sat down at his desk and dashed off a searing reply, reminding the guy he had won three

Super Bowls, developed Joe Montana and Steve Young, and didn't need any advice. He stormed into Jane Walsh's office, threw the note on her desk, told her to type and mail it right away.

Jane Walsh typed the letter but hid it under a stack of papers. A few hours later, Walsh had cooled down. He ripped up the letter and sent a handwritten note thanking the alum for his advice. The man sent a donation to the Buck Club, one of Stanford's booster groups.

In the next few days, Walsh seemed almost paranoid about criticism. When he lost a game it felt like a judgment against him as a person. He said to a friend, "After we lost to Arizona, there were some changes in people's responses to me, you know, the alums. One of them whom I've known for years, who's a terrible gossip, was out at practice and just started talking about Denny Green and how he built this program. What he wanted to say was, 'We sure as hell wish we had Denny Green back.' And I just let him talk and I said, 'Denny did a great job.'"

Walsh's voice was breathless, a whisper. "It's almost like I'm letting the program down because we lost that game, and Denny wouldn't have lost it. So I'm offended, but I'm just not responding, and he said a few other things, so I can read right between his lines. And he leaves. I thought, by God, I'm going to call him and just put it straight to him. And I said, 'Wait a minute. That's just what they said about me when George Seifert took over—if Bill was here we wouldn't have lost that game.' So I quieted down. The way I deal with that guy now is just stay clear of him."

The team flew to Oregon on Friday and worked out in Eugene at the University of Oregon's field—the Cardinal would bus to the Oregon State campus in Corvallis early the next morning. At the evening meeting, Walsh corrected Scott Schuhmann in front of the offensive linemen. He never had done this before. Schuhmann was going over plays on a greaseboard while Walsh, who rarely attended position meetings, sat in the back of the room. Walsh suddenly got up from his chair, walked to the board and re-diagrammed a play. If Schuhmann felt threatened, he didn't show it. "Thanks, Coach," he said.

Later, at the meeting of special teams, Schuhmann reminded the players on the return teams to catch the ball and hold onto it because strange things happened on artificial turf. This was a valuable reminder, but Walsh treated it as if it was the most radical insight since the introduction of the forward pass.

"Great point," he told Schuhmann in front of everyone. "It hadn't occurred to me."

Walsh would do things like that. He'd criticize a coach and then overcompensate with praise because he felt guilty. At that point, Schuhmann wasn't concerned with Walsh's motivation. He was grinning like a kid.

Walsh explained his concerns about Oregon State to the team. He pointed out that the Beavers had rushed for 236 yards a game and they ranked fifteenth nationally in per-game running yardage. Their quarterback, Mark Olford, a chunky little guy who had trouble seeing over the line of scrimmage, ran an efficient option offense. Olford himself had already run for more than 400 yards, and if he couldn't get clear, he would flip the ball to his running backs. By contrast, Stanford ranked eighty-ninth in rushing, averaging less than 120 yards a game.

The other side of this equation, of course, was that the Beavers could barely throw, hardly seemed to have heard of a passing game. They currently ranked 107th in the country and averaged under 49 passing yards a game. They had thrown only 65 passes all season, which lent something of a Stone Age flavor to their football.

Walsh didn't take much consolation from that. "They can score a touchdown and not even know how they did it," he told his players. "They get a good punt return and two runs by their option quarterback and anything can happen. It's the kind of game that can turn on a couple of crazy plays. We're behind, and the officials take over, and we watch it drift away from us."

This wasn't empty rhetoric. Although he was the most premeditative of coaches, preparing for every conceivable situation, Walsh was painfully aware of the role of chance in football. It was more than an awareness. It was a philosophical position straight out of Euripides—a certain amount of gratuitous, absurd evil would befall his team in the form of awful calls by the officials, and his only reasonable response was imperviousness.

He once told a friend, "In the Civil War, before warfare became so computerized, it was eighty percent chance, twenty percent tactics. But you still had to use tactics. In football there's a chance factor, maybe thirty percent. Your creation can blow up on you simply by chance. The better you are, the less chance. We are a high-chance team. Anything can go wrong. The Oregon State quarterback could slip through the line, and one of our guys falls to the turf, and the quarterback goes by us for fifty yards. That could win the game seven to nothing. Very, very scary. And the officials at this level—I equate them to chance. It's good luck or bad luck if the guy throws a flag, has very little to do with the game."

Walsh threw an imaginary flag. "Well, I'll be damned, a flag!"

Early the next morning, the team rode on buses through miles of misty fields to Corvallis. The players entered their locker room, which was across the street from the stadium, by descending a staircase into a cramped, dungeonlike basement with exposed overhead pipes. During the week it might have been the boiler room. The coaches' locker room doubled as a small meeting area barely large enough for the offensive team. Fred vonAppen would have to conduct his pregame and halftime defensive meetings in the showers, underneath the spigots, while he reminded his players of the points he'd typed on the OSU tip sheet:

We must overcome mediocre practice and a slow rebound from last week's defeat to best the Beavers in Corvallis—not an easy task. Remember, these pricks are 15th in the country and 1st in the Pac-10 in Rushing Offense—you better be ready.

VonAppen finished the sheet with this bit of wisdom, typed in boldface: **An error is not a mistake until you refuse to correct it!**

Walsh walked around the locker room, staring at the ratty old cubicles and the dismal meeting facilities like someone fingering grease-stained suits in a Salvation Army store. "Oregon State doesn't belong in the Pac-10," he complained. "They should play with Boise State, but they can't give up the millions of dollars that come from the Pac-10. Obviously, they don't put it back into football." He paused. "I know the Oregon schools have had trouble competing since Arizona and Arizona State joined the conference. They've lost a lot of good recruits. But that doesn't mean I have any pity for them when I walk onto the field."

Walsh was interrupted by two officials who came in for pregame instructions. He shook their hands and said, "I'm Bill Walsh," as if they didn't know. The officials asked if Walsh would be running any unusual plays. This was a standard question and put the officials on alert to make sure the play was run properly. "A pass to the flat," Walsh said. It was hardly exotic, and it indicated how basic his attack was for Oregon State—simple runs and short passes. He didn't trust his offense with much else.

*   *   *

Terry Shea, Mike Wilson, Al Matthews, Guy Benjamin, Keena Turner, and Tom Holmoe squeezed into a small press box at the top of Parker Stadium, a structure that Shea had referred to as rustic. A statue of a beaver stood at the entrance to the stadium. When Glyn Milburn, his shoulder fully healed, fielded a punt two minutes into the game and glided left, found blocking, and went seventy-nine yards for a touchdown, Al Matthews jumped out of his seat and barely missed hitting his head on the ceiling. For a moment it looked as if this game would be a walkover, but on the next series Steve Stenstrom was sacked the first of three times in the game and a drive fizzled, and later in the quarter, with the Cardinal at the Oregon State 26, J. J. Lasley fumbled and Stanford lost the ball. Terry Shea mumbled, "That's the easiest handoff in the book."

Shea had barely gotten those words out when the Beavers scored a touchdown on a seventy-two-yard run by left guard Fletcher Keister on a play known as the Fumblerooskie, not that Shea or anyone else in the press box knew what had happened—at least, not right away. What they saw was quarterback Mark Olford hand off the ball to one of his running backs, who ran to the left where he was easily tackled by linebacker Tom Williams. But in this case appearance had nothing to do with reality, because the handoff to the running back never happened. Olford actually took the snap from center and laid the ball on the ground, then faked the handoff to the back. Keister picked up the ball, ran around the right end, and steamed into the end zone without anyone laying a hand on him. It was a sucker play, like the villain in professional wrestling turning his back to the referee, pulling a blackjack out of his pants, and smashing his opponent in the face.

When Williams realized the man he tackled wasn't the ball carrier, he stood up in a state of confusion, stared downfield, and saw Keister running free. Then Williams began to laugh. What else could he do? The whole thing seemed comical to him, even if it meant the Beavers were about to tie the score.

Up in the coaches' box, defensive secondary coach Tom Holmoe didn't see the humor. He slammed down a phone, punched a table, and threw a pencil against the window. No one else noticed what he was doing because going nuts in the press box was normal behavior for Holmoe.

You wouldn't have known he was a wild man to look at him. He was thirty-one but still had the smooth skin of a preadolescent. He was blond and so fair-skinned that he looked like an angel from a medieval painting. He wore a mustache that seemed out of place on his young face and gave him the appearance of someone trying to look older so bartenders wouldn't card him. At most times, he was as mild-mannered as a mortician, and instead of swearing he would say "Jeez." He said *Jeez* so often that the players began to wish he had another swear word—anything would do, darn, the dickens, shoot. Tom Williams became so bored with Jeez that he said if he could leave Holmoe anything in his Last Will and Testament, it would be a lexicon of curse words to lend a little spice to his speech.

Holmoe played defensive back on three of the 49ers' Super Bowl teams. He was known as a hard worker and a vicious hitter. For most of his time on the 49ers, he was in awe of Ronnie Lott and Joe Montana. His point of view, in fact, was exactly the same as a fan might have if he were allowed to linger in the 49er locker room. Holmoe never hung out with Lott, but observed him and admired him, and Montana, well, he worshiped Montana.

Before coming to Stanford, Holmoe had been a graduate assistant for two years at Brigham Young. He was working on a master's degree in athletic administration, writing a thesis on the role of team captains, and he wanted to ask Joe Montana what he thought of being a captain on the 49ers. He got Montana's phone number from Keena Turner. It took Holmoe a few days to work up the nerve to phone Montana, but when he finally did, he immediately apologized for bothering him. Then Holmoe talked so fast Montana had trouble understanding his words. Every few seconds, Holmoe said, "This won't take long, Joe. I'll be done in a minute." After a while, Holmoe finally understood that Montana was happy to talk, was in no hurry. When he recalled that incident, Holmoe was amused by his shyness. But in staff meetings he never seemed shy, and the veteran coaches agreed that someday he would be a head coach.

At first, no one was prepared for the transformation that took place in him once he took his seat in the press box and the game got under way. He would leap out of his chair. He would shout into the headsets, "Get me Darrien Gordon," or "Get me Seyon Albert." Never mind that he might be speaking to defensive line coach Dave Tipton, who was a senior member of the staff and had played for six years in the NFL as a defensive lineman and could have torn Holmoe apart. No one got angry at Holmoe during games. The coaches in the press box would wink at each other and smile when Holmoe went berserk. He often yelled at officials—"You can't call it from there"—or players—"Get him! Get him! Get him!"—though he was separated from them by several hundred feet and a thick pane of glass.

When the Beavers pulled the Fumblerooskie, Holmoe achieved a personal record for spontaneous combustion. Aside from slamming down the phone and punching the desk and throwing the pencil, he shouted "Jeez" louder than he had ever shouted it before.

Then he said "Jeez" again.

And then, because it was a special occasion, he added, "God dang it."

Keena Turner was trying to get ready for the next play, and although he and Holmoe were close friends, Holmoe was interfering with his concentration. "Be quiet, Tom," he said. Holmoe didn't hear him, so Turner said it louder, and pretty soon, they were glaring at each other nose-to-nose.

Al Matthews giggled.

Ellery Roberts put the Cardinal ahead in the second quarter with a two-yard touchdown run, but the Beavers came back a few minutes later with their own touchdown drive, kept alive by a fake punt—the Beavers may not have been good, but they were clever. Holmoe saw the fake developing and began going crazy in the press box, calling people on the phones, shouting into the headsets, "It's a fake! It's a fake!" After Oregon State fullback J. D. Stewart gained seven yards on the play, Holmoe shouted into the phone, "Damn it, if you'd only listen to me."

Just before halftime, Stanford's freshman kicker Eric Abrams put the Cardinal ahead 17-14 with a forty-nine-yard field goal. At the gun, the Cardinal players ran into the locker room with mixed emotions. Sure, they were ahead, but they were having trouble handling this pathetic bunch. How would they do in the next few weeks against first-ranked Washington, Number 15 USC, and Number 13 Washington State? No one was happy. The offensive linemen believed they were pushing Oregon State off the line of scrimmage, setting up the running game, but Walsh, for whatever reason—it might have been his need for aesthetic satisfaction—had started calling pass plays, which screwed up everything.

The defense wasn't pleased either. Fred vonAppen was throwing several different defensive schemes at Oregon State, but the Beavers didn't respond, just ran their simple option play and gobbled up yardage. Estevan Avila couldn't decide whether the Beavers were a bunch of geniuses who figured everything out on the spot, or played such a simpleminded brand of football that they were impervious to the complexity in vonAppen's plan.

Glyn Milburn, usually stone silent, stormed into the locker room outraged. "They think they can beat us. They're talking trash." Terry Shea, who almost never lost his temper, yelled, "Ellery, hold onto the fucking ball!" Walsh was the only one who seemed calm—at least, he was struggling to remain calm. He was displeased because his team had trouble scoring, twice getting inside the Beaver 30 but coming away with nothing. And Walsh couldn't understand why Steve Stenstrom was throwing too soon, which caused him to miss wide-open receivers. To others, the reasons were obvious. "Steve's shell-shocked," Al Matthews whispered. "He's looking to get hit on every play."

Stanford went ahead 27-14 with six minutes left in the third quarter, and it looked as if the game was in the bag. Then a curious thing happened. The Beavers ran eighteen straight running plays, finally scoring a touchdown early in the fourth quarter. After the extra point, Stanford led only 27-21, and Walsh had visions of the season disintegrating on the artificial turf of dinky Parker Stadium in Corvallis.

The Beavers got the ball for the last time with 3:05 to go in the game, which gave them time to drive down the field and win. Everyone in the press box was quiet, even Holmoe. On the first play Oregon State tried the Fumblerooskie again, but Stanford was ready for it this time, and stuffed it. Offended that the Beavers thought they could fool Stanford with a rinky-dink play twice in one game, Ron George shouted into their huddle, "What do you guys think we are?"

Olford threw four passes on the final drive, bringing his total for the entire game to seven—he ended up throwing for fourteen yards. Near the end, with Oregon State trying to drive for a game-winning touchdown, Walsh noticed that Fred vonAppen didn't have a free safety playing deep just in case a receiver, by dumb luck, caught the ball and broke free. Walsh's life must have flashed before him at that moment. He ran over to vonAppen and screamed for a free safety, but vonAppen had on his headphones, and couldn't hear Walsh and wondered why he was making a fuss.

In the end, it didn't matter. Oregon State couldn't get things together, never advanced past its own 26-yard line, and Stanford got the ball back, ran out the clock, and won a close game. In the locker room Walsh told the team, "The Oregon State score is good. Washington will look at it and think Stanford is easy. They'll think they have nothing to worry about."

He was trying to put the best face on things, but he was worried that Stanford managed only 290 yards against a team ranked last in the Pac-10 in every major defensive category. He told the press that Stanford had played "sophomoric football," and he wondered publicly why the offense wasn't executing. Privately, he was concerned that Steve Stenstrom had changed several plays that could have worked. When Walsh saw Stenstrom calling an audible, he'd find himself yelling, "Don't do it!"

Walsh brooded about his team while the players and coaches showered. He was sitting in front of his cubicle, trying to relax, when he glanced across the locker room and happened to notice placekicker Eric Abrams. Walsh grinned. "Isn't he adorable?" Walsh said to a friend. "You want to hug him, just put him on your hip."

Walsh had several good reasons for finding Abrams adorable. Some had to do with football. Abrams's two field goals had provided the margin of victory, and Walsh understood that the best move he had made all season was in taking a chance on the freshman after the Texas A&M game. A few moments earlier, Walsh had said to the press, "As a matter of fact, I'm taking over working with him. Terry Shea can have the offense. I'll take the kicker."

But Walsh also meant something else when he called Abrams adorable. At five seven, Abrams looked twelve years old, had a cherry complexion, and blushed easily. He faithfully attended offensive meetings even though he didn't have to and had no idea what Walsh was talking about. He was exactly the kind of innocent, eager player Walsh had come back to college to coach.

Abrams was from San Diego and had been a placekicker at La Jolla Country Day School, where they played eight-man football. As a senior, *Parade* magazine named him National Player of the Year. Denny Green had recruited him for Stanford. Well, not exactly. Abrams recruited himself. At the urging of his parents, he began to send Green videotapes of himself kicking, and he followed up with newspaper clippings and phone calls—he was his own press service.

It would have pleased Abrams to play for Green, but now Green was gone and Walsh had appeared, and it almost felt to Abrams as if he was having a religious experience. He could barely find the vocabulary to describe his ecstasy. "Coach Walsh knows everything that's going on," Abrams once said. "He has a real presence about him, a majestic presence. When I first got here, I'd just look at him because it was so incredible that he was out on the field. I mean, just the way his hair is all shiny.

"We all wonder how long he's going to be here. We talk about stuff like we don't know what his motive is for doing it. He says this is his bliss, but we all wonder why a coach of such recognition and status and so many achievements would come back to a school like this when, maybe, he'd go somewhere like Washington where there are so many athletes and he could really utilize his stuff. But he comes here and we wonder if it's his own personal project to prove to himself how good a coach he is. We wonder stuff like that, not because we're doubting him. We just wonder why, because he really doesn't seem like he's got anything left to prove."

Sometimes Abrams had the feeling there were two Walshes, the human being who joked with the players, and the coach, the demigod, who was all-knowing, could tell if someone wasn't doing his calisthenics, even if at that moment Walsh had his back to practice. When he thought about the all-knowing coach, Abrams could almost conjure up an image of Moses. Instead of the Ten Commandments, Walsh had handed down to the Stanford Cardinal the very same game plan he'd given the 49ers.

Abrams once told a journalist, "Just to know that Coach Walsh is going to die knowing who I am is sort of an incredible thing."

Within half an hour of the victory over Oregon State, Walsh was already beginning to worry about going up to Seattle the next week to play the University of Washington. Walsh never beat Washington when he was head coach at Stanford the first time, and there was no reason things should be easier now.

Walsh got up from his chair and let out a sigh. All the other coaches were on the buses by now, and only a few players remained in the locker room. Walsh took a shower and dressed slowly, taking a long time to knot his tie because his hands shook. His team was 6-2, and that was better than he'd expected, but from the offense's standpoint it was a soft six and two, and he knew that. The last four games of the season would be as tough as anything he'd faced with the 49ers.

He picked up his briefcase, and as he got ready to leave, turned to a friend. "Can you imagine if we had lost?" he whispered.

CHAPTER

WASHINGTON WAS THE critical game of the season for the Cardinal. The Huskies were undefeated, hadn't lost in two seasons, and were shooting for their third Rose Bowl victory in a row. If Stanford could knock them off, the Cardinal would be the front-runner for the Rose Bowl. If the Cardinal lost, their Pac-10 record would fall to 3-2 and the best they could hope for would be a postseason bowl game of the second magnitude.

Walsh didn't believe he could beat Washington. This didn't imply any surrender on his part or a fatalistic unwillingness to prepare for the game. In fact, he was to work harder on the Huskies than on any team he'd faced so far. It's just that he was realistic.

In his mind, he saw exactly how his offense could take apart Washington's defense. Walsh anticipated Washington stacking as many as eight men on the line of scrimmage. At the snap of the ball they would come charging after Steve Stenstrom, giving him almost no time to get the ball away. In the meantime, the Washington cornerbacks would cover Stanford's wide receivers man-to-man. This was an easy formula to defeat. Walsh would simply tell his quarterback to throw the ball on the count of three. By this time, the Stanford wideouts would have eluded the man-to-man coverage of the Huskies' secondary. Anyway, that's how it would have worked in theory. That's how it worked in 1977—not that Walsh was able to beat Washington then, either. But in his first stint as Stanford's head coach, Walsh had James Lofton, a receiver with a sprinter's speed. His current receivers,

Mike Cook and Justin Armour, were tall and strong and could out-muscle most cornerbacks, but they couldn't outrun them. This meant Walsh had no weapon to defeat the coverage of Washington's secondary.

He considered switching cornerback Darrien Gordon to wide receiver to take advantage of his speed, and he even thought about suiting up redshirt freshman Jamie Webb, the fastest runner on the squad. He went so far as to ask Terry Shea if Webb would use up a year of eligibility if he played in one game, and when Shea said he would, Walsh scrunched up his face and dumped that plan.

He spent Sunday alone in his office watching tape of the Oregon State game and then studying Washington film, while the other offensive coaches worked in the conference room. Terry Shea was in a snit, had been in one since the minute he showed up that morning. He was working himself up to hate Washington, and because Shea was the most mild-mannered of the coaches, what he was doing seemed out of character. To begin with, he refused to refer to Washington as the Huskies or even Washington. "Seattle" was what he called the university. Not acknowledging the name represented to Shea a form of disrespect, which he would continue all week with the coaches and at player meetings. At this moment, he was complaining about Washington's uniforms. Shea noticed on the tape that one of the Huskies' defensive backs wore his pants above his knees. This was a violation of the dress code, but it was the kind of thing coaches never noticed in strategy sessions, and certainly never talked about. But Shea thought there were two sets of rules—the rules for nine of the Pac-10 teams, and a separate set for Washington and coach Don James.

"Why don't they ever call those things against Don James's teams?" Shea asked angrily, as if he were talking about flagrant face-mask violations.

"It's not in the interest of the Pac-10 for Stanford to win," Scott Schuhmann said. "When you have a kingpin, you don't want to get them knocked off. They're going for the national title."

Not all the coaches felt jealous of Washington. Mike Wilson had just finished cataloging the Huskies' defensive plays, and in the process he experienced a kind of awe. It took Wilson an hour to identify everything Washington was doing. When Bill Ring commented on how often Washington players raised their arms to celebrate, Wilson defended them. "If you can back it up, you can raise your arms," he said.

Walsh didn't make an appearance until dinnertime, and then only briefly. He wolfed down a slice of pizza, gulped a diet soda, and retired to his office without saying a word. He was in Game Plan World and on his face he had The Look.

After dinner, Mike Wilson, Scott Schuhmann, and Bill Ring sat at the conference table cutting up copies of the opponent's media guide, something they did every Sunday. The exercise may have looked like a strange holdover from kindergarten, but in reality the coaches were putting together the week's playbook, and part of the package included pasting in photos of the Washington personnel so the Cardinal players would know whom they were up against. When the wide receivers, for example, opened up their playbooks, they would see the mug shots of the Huskies' defensive backs. Pasting in the pictures helped create a composite sketch of the opponent. Guy Benjamin liked to say it was something the CIA might do during a war—come up with a composite of an enemy general, get into his head to make it easier to plan strategy against him. It was the same with the playbook. If the Cardinal players could study a photo of an opposing player they might get a feel for his character, divine a flaw they could take advantage of. They might even work up a personal hatred for him, and that would be OK, too.

Walsh did the same thing, although he did not study photos to achieve his result. He would sit in the conference room going over film of an opponent's defense, and the whole time he'd try to psych out the defensive coordinator, almost go into a trance as he tried to seep deeper and deeper into the coordinator's mind. In football-speak, Walsh was trying to learn the opponent's "tendencies," and when he was done he would gather his coaches around him and introduce the plays he'd designed for that game, for that coordinator, and explain exactly why the guy would fall for them.

Stanford playbooks were precious, top-secret items that the players were required to turn in on Saturday mornings before the game. It was Bill Ring's job to collect them, throwing the large red binders into a huge sack for safekeeping. Sometimes playbooks from other teams would be misplaced or left behind, and the coaches considered playbooks acquired in this manner an invaluable treasure. An Arizona coach left a playbook in the locker room after the Wildcats beat Stanford, and the Stanford coaching staff studied it like Scripture.

Scott Schuhmann recalled flying on a Cardinal charter the previous season; by coincidence, Oregon had used the same plane earlier in the day. Schuhmann was sitting in his seat looking for something to read, and as he searched through the seat pocket he came upon an Oregon playbook that a coach had forgotten. Schuhmann devoured the entire playbook before the team landed and Stanford used the book as a resource when the Cardinals met Oregon later that season, defeating the Ducks 33-13.

The coaches worked on the playbooks until almost eight o'clock, waiting for Walsh. The football offices were as hushed as a church. Finally Walsh came in, carrying a yellow legal pad on which he had scribbled pages of notes and plays. As he took his seat at the head of the table, he was smiling, trying to relax his coaches. "So what are we going to do about Washington? We've got to play them, got to get on the plane, can't get the measles."

To start things off, Walsh focused on a small problem, something they could manage without having to confront the larger issue—did they stand a chance of beating the Huskies? He had noticed that the Washington players would set themselves in a defense, but as the quarterback ducked under center and began to call his signals, the defense would shift into another formation at the last instant. This technique, called "stemming," would confuse the offense, especially the offensive linemen, and Walsh's linemen were plenty confused to begin with. If the defense stemmed, the quarterback was in essence calling a play against the wrong alignment, because the formation would change before he ever got his hands on the ball.

Walsh had figured out a simple way to neutralize the stemming. He would tell Steve Stenstrom to yell "Ready down" at the line of scrimmage. "Ready down" would have no meaning whatsoever, would merely be a verbal cue to get the Huskies to commit themselves to a specific defense. After Stenstrom had yelled "Ready down" and the Huskies stemmed, Stenstrom would call the play.

Everyone agreed stemming wouldn't be a problem in the game. Walsh moved on to his game plan, which was entirely different from what he had come up with against Oregon State. For the Beavers he'd been conservative, stressing runs and ball-control passing. Walsh didn't see how he could play that way against Washington, not with his running game, which ranked last in the conference. So he decided to let everything hang out. He would play balls-out, wide-open football—his best against Don James's best.

With a manic energy he hadn't demonstrated in weeks, Walsh

began drawing plays on the greaseboard while the other coaches frantically took notes. He would put down the squares and circles for a play, explaining in a breathless voice how it worked, and then he would erase it with his hand, which was quickly assuming a sky-blue tint, and go on to the next play. His mind was ahead of his hand—he almost couldn't put down the ideas fast enough—and his energy buzzed across the room to the other coaches like electricity surging through a wire.

Terry Shea was the most worked up. He encouraged Walsh to run plays at Washington's number 7, the defensive back with the high pants. Number 7 had a name, a very serviceable name, Josh Moore. But Shea refused to confer on him the dignity of a name. "Let's run plays at number 7 and make him play football," he said.

Then Shea added, "I'm getting to fucking hate him."

Walsh stormed into the Monday team meeting. He told the players it was a damn good thing they hadn't trounced Oregon State—their shaky performance would give the Huskies a false sense of security. "Washington sees that score and they can't get excited. This is the time of year a team like that gets knocked off, especially at home. They're worried about where they put their three girlfriends or whatever. We have to put up with some noise in the tunnel before the game, pointing fingers and acting tough. They do it in a crowd, not when they're alone. We haven't backed down from anybody yet. We've played teams like that before and kicked their ass."

Then Walsh diagrammed several pass plays that he intended to use in Seattle. "They cannot cover these passes," he promised, his voice booming. "I guarantee that. They haven't seen them before. We beat this team with big plays, big plays all over the field."

Walsh looked at his watch, saw it was time for practice. "Come on, men. Let's roll," he said with the manic energy of George C. Scott playing General Patton.

The Stanford Cardinal burst out of the Hall of Fame Room, and there was Walsh, at the door, putting his hand on the back of each offensive lineman, grinning, repeating over and over again, "You've really got a job to do."

On his way to practice, Walsh, who was caught up in the spirit of his own speech, told someone, "I'm really excited. These are the games I just love. When I was with Cincinnati we killed these defenses."

Walsh seemed optimistic at that moment, but with him things were never as simple as they appeared. As part of his preparation for Washington he had to get himself into the right frame of mind, and that meant pumping himself up just as he'd pumped up the team. If he was playing mind games with his players, he was also playing mind games with himself.

He was almost euphoric at his Tuesday press conference, and that led him to say reckless things, some he would come to regret. One of his themes was innocent enough. He said Washington intended to go to the Rose Bowl, while "Stanford is looking more at alternative bowls." He also said, "We're just another team being served up." It was all meant to be a put-on. Up in Seattle fans were anticipating an apocalyptic event, and Walsh was downplaying the whole thing. Maybe Don James would think Walsh wasn't up for the confrontation, although that would be impossible to imagine.

Just the day before, on a conference call with Seattle writers, Walsh had said almost the same thing. First he'd turned to Scott Schuhmann. "How do you think they'll react to this?" he whispered. Then he told the media, "I hope we play well enough to qualify for one of those secondhand bowl games." The writers couldn't figure out where Walsh was coming from. Maybe the guy was on the cusp of senility.

Later, at a team meeting, Walsh admitted he'd been striking a pose. "Don't pay a bit of attention to what I tell the newspapers. I'm trying to play games with the other teams. My response when asked if this is a big game for Stanford was, 'No, it's a big game for the Huskies. They will be Number One in the country and go to the Rose Bowl. We just want to go to an alternative bowl.' We want them to be real comfortable when they play us. It's not only for Washington I say these things. It's for other Pac-10 teams also. Berkeley reads this stuff every day."

He smiled, stretched out his arms like a preacher. "Can we beat Washington? Hell, yes. These are the guys that unravel, just like Notre Dame. They'll go into a stupor."

Something else Walsh said at the press conference had consequences that dogged him long after the season ended. Over the speakerphone, a writer from Seattle asked him to compare himself to Don James, and referred to the "saintlike aura that everybody down there seems to have you labeled with."

At first, Walsh was diplomatic. "Well, if any of the people from out of the area had been to some of my 49er press conferences, I was hardly a saint. There was a lot of give and take in those press conferences, especially in the later years, and I believe there was some personal involvement between some of the sportswriters and myself."

Then Walsh began to focus on the writer's question. "Between Don and myself, I'd like to think I'm a gentleman coach like he is. And I'd like to think that I've been a credit to coaching as much as he has. But all in all, I like to be considered on the same level as Don from an ethical standpoint." Walsh was grinning as he said that, a grin the out-of-town writers couldn't see. "I swallowed on that one," Walsh added for the benefit of the speakerphone listeners. The writers in the room laughed and snickered.

Rumors had circulated for years that Washington's program wasn't what it should be. The NCAA tracked graduation rates for football players who entered college in 1983, 1984, and 1985, and according to NCAA figures Washington had the second-lowest graduation rate of any team in the Pac-10, with 40 percent earning degrees within six years. It was to come out after the season that quarterback Billy Joe Hobert had dropped out of school after spring practice in 1992. To regain his eligibility, he took fifteen units of Swahili in nine weeks of summer school. Technically, the maneuver was within the rules, and the Washington administration defended intensive Swahili as a legitimate course. Still, such practices invited Walsh's sarcasm.

After the press conference, he was privately disturbed about his joke. "I know that was theatrical," he said. "I almost made a stupid mistake, a fool of myself. I shouldn't even have responded."

If Walsh had eased up after the press conference, a problem might never have developed, but he wouldn't leave Washington alone. Several months after the season ended, he was invited to speak at a Stanford alumni luncheon at the Sutter Club in Sacramento, where he would attack Washington.

The day began badly for him when he heard that the admissions department would likely turn down a player's application for transfer to Stanford. Walsh had cultivated a good relationship with Admissions and in principle supported their high standards. But as he drove to Sacramento, it frustrated him that head coaches at most other major universities could offer admission on their own to promising players, while at Stanford the final decision was out of the coach's hands.

What turned his attention to Washington was a series of critical articles that had run in the *Seattle Times* a month earlier. The articles pointed out that UW offered admission to more players who did not meet minimum academic requirements than any other school in the Pac-10. The articles also showed that the disparity between the graduation rate of the general student body and football players at Washington was the worst in the conference. Scott Schuhmann stuffed a stack of these articles in Walsh's mailbox, and he read them shortly before visiting Sacramento.

When Walsh got up in front of the Stanford alums, he had an evangelical spirit, a righteous reformer's temperament, and intended to speak for the good of college football.

The *Sacramento Bee* quoted him as saying, "The football players there have almost no contact with the rest of the student body. They have an athletic department compound and that's where they spend their time. When they use up their eligibility and are expected to return to society, they have none of the skills you are supposed to gain in college." Walsh was also reported to have said, "They bring in football players without any kind of preparatory courses. They just throw them in and expect them to compete."

When his comments were picked up in other newspapers, it was reported he'd called Washington "an outlaw program." This was untrue.

Walsh later insisted he was making generic comments, criticizing the system of big-time college football. He never mentioned Washington by name, referring to the Huskies from time to time as "our Pac-10 co-champions." But later, he went to a private room with three newsmen from the *Bee* and expanded on his remarks. Dan McGrath, a *Bee* columnist and former sports editor of the *San Francisco Chronicle*, later said, "My impression was we were talking about Washington."

Sports columnist R. E. Graswich recalled, "We went over parts of his speech for about twenty minutes. I said to him, 'I was stunned about your remarks about Washington. It's high time.' He nodded. 'It's the kind of thing we need to do,' he said. Half our conversation was in direct reference to his speech, so there was no mistake. At no time was it an off-the-record conversation. Walsh made the point in the post-banquet conversation. He said, 'I didn't say anything new out there. It's stuff you guys know about.'"

After the Pac-10 censured him for his lack of "collegiality" to a fellow conference coach, Walsh tried to distance himself from his remarks, saying, "I thought I was in a setting where I wouldn't have to concern myself with the media. But that's not a very good answer. Whatever the setting, it was foolish, out of line. I was wrong, let's face it."

Sometime later he said he'd been "sabotaged" by the *Bee* reporters. "I've been apologizing for things I didn't say. It's upsetting to me. I've been terribly misrepresented in the whole matter. Did I call Washington an 'outlaw program'? Of course not. Did I trash Don James? Of course not. My only reference to Don James is he's a great coach. I was taken advantage of by a writer. I spoke generically about college football and basketball, and I'll continue to do so, whether Washington likes it or not."

R. E. Graswich did not see Walsh as a victim. "Now he's presenting himself as a rube, like he'd never been interviewed before, and we wily Sacramento reporters got him to say things he didn't want to say. I mean, come on, he's only Bill Walsh."

Walsh was partly vindicated in August 1993 when the Pac-10 put the Huskies on probation and banned them from postseason play for two years for a variety of violations, including an improper $50,000 loan from a booster to quarterback Billy Joe Hobert. Don James quit after the sanctions were announced, although the Pac-10 found no academic violations.

When Walsh would travel to Seattle the next season to play the Huskies, he'd walk off the plane wearing a Groucho nose and glasses to ease the tension, and would continue to wear them during practice at Husky Stadium.

But in the last week of October 1992, months before the controversy even began, Walsh couldn't have anticipated where his distaste for Washington would eventually lead him. All he knew was that he had to find a way to score points, and when it came to that, he wasn't the least bit confident.

The Stanford team flew to Seattle early Friday afternoon. At San Francisco Airport the sun shone, but when the team arrived in Seattle it was gloomy and raining. Buses took the players directly to Husky Stadium, where the bleachers seemed to rise on each side of the field like skyscrapers. Bob Griese, who would be announcing the game for television, told Fred vonAppen that Husky Stadium looked like something put up by Hollywood that they'd take down after the game.

The artificial turf was soggy, and when Glyn Milburn or J. J. Lasley ran on it their feet set off small explosions of water. Walsh stood in the middle of the field watching, thinking. He wore a red Stanford baseball cap pulled down so tightly on his head that his ears stuck out. When the run-through ended, everyone bused to the hotel to shower, change into dry clothes, and eat dinner.

The special teams meeting began at eight o'clock. It was the usual thing, Bill Singler showing films of Washington's special teams and trying to induce his players to be disciplined and tough. Walsh usually attended, sitting quietly in the back, occasionally making a comment, but tonight he wasn't there. Neither were Terry Shea, Mike Wilson, Scott Schuhmann, Guy Benjamin, or Bill Ring. All the offensive coaches had gathered next door in a tiny meeting room with the lights turned off. Walsh thought he had spotted something in the Washington defense and he was running tape, studying play after play, showing his coaches that the Huskies' free safety always vacated the middle.

It was unusual for Walsh to study an opponent the night before a game. By this time his game plan was put to bed, the first twenty plays already scripted. He was sitting on the left side of the room. He allowed his head to lean against the wall. From time to time he would sigh. The special teams meeting ended, and the other coaches wanted to know where Walsh was. He was still in the tiny room. Mike Wilson worked the projector and Terry Shea took notes. It seemed to Walsh that he had at last discovered the fatal flaw in Washington's defense, the key to victory. For a moment, it made him smile.

Finally, he went into the general meeting of the team. The room was small, the players packed in, some almost bursting out the door. Dave Garnett and J. J. Lasley had fresh new haircuts, the hair on the back of their heads shaved to show the words NO FEAR.

Walsh's skin looked gray. "How do we handle it if things go badly?" he asked. "It's the same as we did at Notre Dame. Don't worry about the score. This is the kind of defense they stop you and stop you and, boom, you kill them."

Walsh left the meeting early, took the elevator to his room, where he drank a glass of white wine and thought about Washington's free safety. No one saw him the rest of the night.

The team bused to the stadium late the next morning, the skies black and unfriendly. Fred vonAppen, who always worried on game day, tried to distract himself by reading. He would search through the Stanford bookstore during the week for books to take on road trips. One time, he asked Al Matthews to go with him. Matthews thought that meant a quick trip to the store and then back to the office, but when they got there, vonAppen went into a trance at the sight of all those shiny colorful books. He lingered in the poetry section and then nonfiction, running his hand lovingly over the bindings, while Matthews wondered if he were nuts. VonAppen felt awe for writers and professors, and did not consider himself an intellectual although he read every spare moment he could find. It was as though he were trying to decrease a deficit, close a gap that he and no one else perceived. After two hours, he and Matthews, who bordered on the hyperactive and was now desperate to get going, left the store.

This morning vonAppen was reading *Lolita* on the bus on the way to the University of Washington. He was a big fan of Vladimir Nabokov, considered his prose almost poetry. As he read, he took out a pencil and underlined a passage: "The days of my youth, as I look back on them, seem to fly away from me in a flurry of pale repetitive scraps like those morning snowstorms of used tissue paper that a train passenger sees whirling in the wake of the observation car."

VonAppen was closing in on fifty, and he had begun to think in an abstract way about loss. By the end of the day, his sense of loss would be immediate.

The visitors locker room at Husky Stadium is divided into several smaller rooms that branch out from a meandering corridor. Two hours before the game the coaches, along with the offensive linemen, were installed in a cramped, windowless room at the very end of the corridor. While the other coaches changed into khaki pants and red Stanford shirts, Walsh sat on a folding chair at the end of a row of lockers. He was wearing the same clothes he had worn the day before, baggy cords and a rumpled blue oxford shirt. He leaned his head back against the metal locker, folded his arms across his chest, stretched his legs in front of him, and closed his eyes. He seemed to be meditating. From time to time, he would clear his throat, and briefly open his eyes and say things to Terry Shea like, "I think 22-ZN would be viable for us." Shea would barely acknowledge him, and Walsh would drift off again, occasionally popping a sour ball into his mouth. After a while, he leaned forward and put his head into his hands.

At 11:15 he began to put on his waterproof outer jacket, and the act of putting on his game clothes resonated within him, taking him down the corridor of the years. He had been a boxer in college, a light heavyweight, and he often thought of big games in terms of fighting, of standing his ground, of kicking ass.

He stood up, began to walk into the hallway, and motioned for a friend to follow. Walsh was smiling. "In boxing there's a ritual to getting dressed, a ceremony that has great meaning," he said as he balled his hands, large and red and raw, into fists. "They put the strips of tape on the wall and then they take them off and wrap your hands and put on the gloves. Second to that is the ritual of getting dressed in football."

Walsh's voice was almost a whisper. His eyes gleamed. Behind him he could hear the sound of players putting on shoulder pads and cleated shoes. "You're getting ready for combat, taking on that personality," he said. "Guys put on shoulder pads, and need help getting them on. It's like putting on armor. I remember how Jerry Rice was so meticulous about getting dressed, down to the neatly folded towel tucked into his pants which said 'Flash 80.'" Walsh paused, glanced into the locker room to see if the other coaches could hear him. He seemed almost embarrassed by what he was feeling. "When players retire they miss the ceremony of getting dressed as much as the actual playing."

Walsh walked back into the locker room and changed into khaki slacks and athletic shoes, but he hadn't finished talking. Two more times, he led the friend into the corridor, while the coaches began to notice his secret conversations. He whispered, "Even after a boxing match when I was cut, I would feel proud, sitting there getting stitched. Three times I was stitched over the left eye—twelve, four, and three stitches—all from overhand rights. Only recently I had some of the scar tissue removed."

Walsh pointed to his brow, which still bore faint scars like a badge of honor. Walsh was moved by the knowledge that he, too, was getting dressed, gearing up, taking on the personality of a warrior. It all had come to him again at age sixty, this feeling of battle, of risk, yes, even of potential loss, if it came to that. This was combat, and he was an underdog, and even that excited him.

The mere fact that Walsh was talking about boxing was astonishing. He guarded this part of his past like a guilty secret, as if his boxing were a moral flaw. Some of his old 49er players knew he had been a boxer, but they never talked about it on the record. When he and Geri decided to marry, her parents wanted to know about his career plans and, in all innocence, she told them Bill wanted to be a professional boxer. He would laugh about that privately as he got older, the idea of him being a pug. He believed he would have been just good enough to meet top-quality opposition and get his head handed to him. He had fought as a righty, although he was born a southpaw. When Gerry Cooney was near the top for a brief time, Walsh saw himself in Cooney—they were both left-handed Irishmen who had been turned around to fight right-handed in the ring. Walsh would get Cooney on the phone and discuss strategy with him and tell him he admired his big left hook.

When Walsh was in the army, stationed at Fort Ord, he boxed as an amateur, and he would spar with professionals like Bobo Olson who sometimes came down there. Walsh could remember driving up to Newman's Gym in San Francisco's Tenderloin District and offering to spar with former light-heavyweight champ Joey Maxim, but being turned down because he had the wrong style. When he ran the 49ers, he once invited lightweight champion Tony Lopez, a Sacramento fighter, to drive over to the 49ers' training camp in nearby Rocklin to address the team about being a champion.

Sometimes during Stanford practices or before games, Walsh would bounce on his feet and even throw a few punches like a boxer warming up. At those times, Al Matthews, who remembered Walsh the fighter, would smile. Walsh would lecture his players on beating the opponent to the punch and getting off first, both boxing metaphors, and his primary criticism of his offensive linemen was that they were big and slow, had the collective persona of a ponderous heavyweight who could be taken apart by a smaller, quicker, more mobile fighter.

It was easy to understand why, at this stage of his life, Walsh was taken with boxing. When he watched a fight, he could escape to a simplified, idealized world where football's complexity had been reduced to two men duking it out in a twenty-foot square. It wasn't as easy to understand why Walsh seemed ashamed of having been a boxer. This macho side to his nature provided the perfect counterpoint to his image as the chardonnay-drinking Mr. Finesse, which used to drive tough guys like Mike Ditka and Don Shula crazy. He was both a creative artist and a general, and the fact that he'd made these two personalities coexist led to his greatness as a football coach.

But Walsh had worked hard over the years to suppress any mention in the newspapers of his boxing past. He had come out of San

Jose, made himself into the greatest football coach of his era, taught himself about history and wine, formed friendships with George Schultz, Neil Simon, and Dianne Feinstein, and the image of a pug—broken noses, bleeding eyes, guys writhing on the canvas, guys mumbling and hearing bells long after they'd retired—didn't fit with the personality he had invented. When a journalist who often traveled with the Cardinal expressed a desire to write about Walsh and boxing, Walsh grew red in the face. Boxing may have reminded Walsh of that side of himself he constantly had to repress, the street-fighting kid, the side he saw as explosive and dangerous. This is only a theory, never verified by Walsh, because the curious fact is that, when asked why he didn't want people to know about his love for fighting, Walsh would unaccountably become inarticulate and shrug and turn away. He could not see the paradox in his position, that he was a man in a war game who was ashamed he'd been a fighter.

The Cardinal played well at the beginning of the game, giving players and coaches hope that they were about to pull off a bigger upset than the one in South Bend. Cornerback Darrien Gordon intercepted a pass by quarterback Mark Brunell in the Huskies' first series. Stanford's offense got the ball at the Washington 37 and quickly drove for a touchdown, scoring on a thirty-one-yard pass from Steve Stenstrom to Justin Armour. It all seemed so simple. Armour broke down the middle of the field, ran behind the coverage, and was open when Stenstrom got him the ball. After the extra point, Stanford led 7-0.

But late in the quarter, Washington's tailback Napoleon Kaufman ran back a punt sixty-five yards to the Stanford 4-yard line. The Huskies scored a touchdown three plays later, the quarter ending with the score tied at seven. Stenstrom had already been sacked three times. It was Texas A&M all over again, but worse. The Cardinal offensive line couldn't cope with the speed of the Washington defense—the big, slow heavyweight was being outmaneuvered by the smaller, more mobile fighter.

Washington scored a touchdown on its first possession of the second quarter, and on Stanford's next series, linebacker James Clifford intercepted a Stenstrom pass and chugged forty-two yards into the end zone. The Huskies had scored two touchdowns in two minutes and twenty-four seconds, and with the quarter only half over, Washington already was up 21-7, and the game was turning into a rout.

The weather wasn't helping Stanford. It rained steadily, and Stenstrom complained that he couldn't get a grip on the wet balls. The night before, Walsh had actually hoped for bad weather. Rain would add an element of chance, he said, would aid the weaker team. "If the weather's bad, they think we won't be able to handle it," he'd told the players. "They'll let down. I hope the weather's bad."

The Huskies weren't letting down. Stenstrom got knocked out of the game on Stanford's next series. He was sacked, and as he went down someone stomped his forearm, which instantly ballooned to twice its normal size. Stenstrom lay on the ground in pain and finally had to be helped off the field.

Lately, Stenstrom had not recovered as quickly from sacks, seemed less resilient. He had taken a heavy cumulative beating during the season, and after being blasted would end up lying on the ground for several minutes while the game stopped. The problem with Stenstrom was familiar to Walsh, who preferred his quarterbacks to get up and play, or else take themselves off the field. Walsh once had a quarterback with a special propensity for getting knocked out of games. He would seem to be near death, only to make a dramatic comeback a few minutes later, while the crowd cheered his courage. "He lay there inert in the fetal position," Walsh once said of him. "Suddenly, he's ready to come back in and the crowd cheers, when in reality nothing happened of consequence."

Although the half ended 21-7, Walsh's voice was calm when he addressed the offense. This was essential. He had to convey through his tone and manner that things were not out of control, that no matter what, he always had an answer. "Now it's just a matter of you showing some patience and we can pull it out," he said. "We may not win, but we have to play well. It's so important to the future of the program. Washington will get tired and, when they do, we can come back. At Notre Dame we were down by ten. Here, we're down by fourteen, but we get the ball first. They're going to have to make some mistakes, but hell, they're going to."

After going over several plays, Walsh sent one of the managers to get the defense from the back rooms. A few of the defensive players filtered into the meeting area, and one of them, Vince Otoupal, started to exhort the others not to give up. Otoupal often worked himself up by chanting things that had been discussed in the defensive meetings, and the other players appreciated this. The problem was that Walsh wanted to address the players at this moment, and it seemed that every time Walsh got ready to speak, Otoupal would walk in front of him and interrupt. Walsh would say, "OK, men, let's come together," and Otoupal would burst out with "It's not over" or "Let's not take this shit."

To make matters worse, the defense was slow to appear, even though it was almost time to take the field. Walsh had to wait and wait. At a certain point, he erupted.

With his face as red as a Cardinal jersey, he told all the players to take a knee. "There's a couple of fucking ways to go," he screamed. "You can lay down and let someone kick the crap out of you. You can throw it away for Denny Green and everyone else who was here the last four years. I can see some of you, the way you're acting, you're ready to belly up. I want you to bust your ass. Don't let this program go into the tank. I've seen some of you hang your heads out there like the wildebeest. I don't give a goddamn about the score. You may lose. You may win. I care how you hold your heads up."

Walsh's voice was shaking when he finished. The players had never heard him like this before, and they ran on the field with purpose and energy. And then they got slaughtered.

Mark Butterfield was playing quarterback now, and that was a Bill Walsh nightmare. It wasn't that Butterfield was a bad quarterback. It's just that Butterfield's appearances had been limited to those times Stenstrom was separated from his senses, and Butterfield had attempted only fourteen passes. Now he was thrown to a defense that was out for blood.

On Stanford's first series of the second half, Walsh tried to keep the drive going on fourth and two at his own 45-yard line. He called for a simple run up the middle by Ellery Roberts, who would be preceded into the hole by Nate Olsen. Unfortunately, after taking the snap from center, Butterfield held the ball out too far, like a man dropping a used Kleenex into a garbage can, and Olsen, who was charging toward the hole, knocked it out of his hand. Washington recovered the fumble and scored a touchdown three plays later.

The score soon ballooned to 34-7. Mark Butterfield was supposed to be having a learning experience, but it was more like shock therapy. On one play, he couldn't decipher the hand signal from the sideline and had to run almost all the way to Walsh to get the call. The stadium was such a riot of noise that his linemen couldn't hear his signals. Butterfield had been instructed to defeat Washington's stemming— their moving into a different formation after he called signals—by yelling "Ready down," and then calling the play. But in the confusion of the moment, Butterfield reversed the procedure, first calling out the play and then shouting "Ready down."

The strangest moment occurred when he called two different plays in the huddle. He called a quarterback run, and then he doubted that was the right play, so he called a pass to J. J. Lasley. The plays had totally different blocking schemes, and no one knew which way to go. As the Cardinal broke the huddle, Lasley grabbed Butterfield and asked him to clarify his call. Butterfield told Lasley to run to the flat for a pass, but it was too late to tell anyone else. When the ball was snapped, the Stanford team found itself in chaos, everyone running in different directions, players slamming into each other. Butterfield threw a pass to Lasley that fell incomplete. Later Scott Schuhmann laughed about the play and said he wished he could be with the coaches at USC, Stanford's next opponent, when they looked at that play on the game film. "They'll probably scratch their heads and tell each other, 'That's Bill Walsh being a genius again.'"

Some moments were less comical. Early in the fourth quarter, Cardinal cornerback Darrien Gordon slugged Huskies receiver Jason Shelley in full view of the 70,821 spectators in the stadium. Shelley was a freshman and had been waving his arms and celebrating all day, and some of the Stanford veterans thought he was in bad taste. The officials thought Gordon was in bad taste, and ejected him from the game. The other ten men on Stanford's defense were disgusted with Gordon. They had held Washington on third down, and now, because of the penalty, Washington could keep the ball and would score its final touchdown on that drive.

Walsh was more than disgusted with Gordon. He was beside himself. As Gordon came off the field, Walsh confronted him and poked his finger three times into Gordon's chest while he shouted, "I've never seen Ronnie Lott do that. I've never seen Carlton Williamson do that. Why do you do it? Why don't they do it? Give me that answer."

Gordon had broken one of Walsh's basic rules. He'd let emotion get the better of him, lost his head. It was an unfortunate moment of self-indulgence, and it cost the team; not that it affected the outcome of the game, but that wasn't the point. Walsh expected his players to be composed even when the team was getting killed. Days later, Fred vonAppen was still upset. "Who gave him the right to do that to the whole team?"

Rain was pouring down in the final minutes. It was as though, just to make matters worse, the skies had opened and emptied their contents on the Cardinal. Special teams coach Bill Singler ran up and down the sideline telling the players, "They're an upper-echelon team. They and Miami are up here." Singler put his hand over his head. "And then there's all the rest." Singler put his hand near his waist. "The important thing is we can beat USC."

When the final gun went off, the Cardinal players shook hands with the Huskies at midfield. "They didn't rub it in. They were cool," Dave Garnett said. Tom Williams said, "They were very cordial. They didn't do anything illegal except kick our ass."

Walsh congratulated Don James and walked briskly through the tunnel to the locker room. He did not appear upset, although it was hard to imagine he wasn't. He stood at the door of the locker room as the last of his players filed in. Then Walsh turned to several members of the Stanford party who were coming up the tunnel. He looked at Gary Migdol and Pat Broun, who were handling public relations, Jim Stump, the team chaplain, the team doctors, and team managers.

"If you're not on the team, you can't come in the locker room," Walsh said.

Then he shut the door.

This was the most important moment he would face all season— more important even than the time he addressed the team after the John Sims affair. The Cardinal had lost two of the last three games and had free-fallen out of the race for the Rose Bowl. Walsh had to turn things around this very moment or the season and his comeback might end in failure.

The players jammed inside the locker room. Some sat on the few available benches, but most stood or crouched on the floor waiting for Walsh's words. He walked to the front of the room, stood next to the chalkboard. His voice was clear and direct, without a hint of criticism or disappointment.

"OK, men, we took a beating. We came unraveled, no use blaming anybody. I wish we'd done better the second half—we came out meaning to do better. But halfway up this walk I'm thinking USC."

He looked around the room, taking his time, making eye contact with the players.

"Southern Cal is the biggest game of the year. We all know that. Let's say we've learned a hell of a lot today about ourselves. We're six and three, nothing to be ashamed of. It's still a good season. When I was here before, we lost 49-0 to Southern Cal, and then won three in a row. So we can come back. Now, let's bow our heads for a second and remember we're in this together. We're a pretty good bunch of guys. We're going to finish this season well, or we're going to bust our asses trying."

It was a good speech, looking forward, stressing the positive, and when the season was over, the players remembered this as the moment Walsh prevented the team from disintegrating. Only once did he show his disappointment. He stared at Fred vonAppen, who stood at the back of the room near the door leading to the labyrinth of rooms in the rear. For a moment Walsh's voice filled with anger.

"Coaches, hear me. At halftime, I don't want players to come sauntering in here. We're not divided. We're one team. When I call for the defense I want the coaches to get their asses in here."

It was clear to every person in the room that he was criticizing vonAppen in public, although he never mentioned him by name. Von-Appen leaned against the wall, staring straight ahead, never moving, registering no more emotion than he would have if Walsh were reading a shopping list.

Walsh's relationship with vonAppen was almost too paradoxical to comprehend. Most of the time he was in agony in order not to offend his defensive coordinator. He would debate for days whether or not to criticize vonAppen, would scheme how to broach a touchy subject, finally coming up with a broad remark that just as easily could apply to Scott Schuhmann or Terry Shea. The comment would be so generic that vonAppen wouldn't even know it was directed at him.

Just the other day, Walsh had wondered how to criticize vonAppen for playing without a free safety at the end of the Oregon State game. "I'm going to sit down today and I'm going to pick my words carefully," Walsh confided to a friend. "I don't want him to get upset. I'll say, 'Fred, now if you were the head coach, would you have wanted a free safety there?' Then he'll be objective. See, it's an assistant coach syndrome, because whether it's conscious or subconscious, he doesn't take the full responsibility when the game's over. He might feel bad, but there's one guy who takes the heat."

Then in one angry, impulsive moment, Walsh would forget about vonAppen's feelings and skewer him in front of everyone, as he was doing now. What complicated the issue was the layout of the locker rooms at Washington. The dressing cubicles were spread out over several rooms and it had taken time at the half for vonAppen to gather all his players, then round up the wounded from the trainer's room.

"He was wrong," vonAppen was to say later. "It's like with your family. You'll take it out on them because you know they can take it. It's that way between him and me. I think we have a special relationship. When he's frustrated, he lashes out at those around him. He knows that. Our first couple of years together, he would do something like that and then he would come around and say, 'Don't take it personally. I was making my point to the team.' He doesn't have to tell me that anymore. He's a very complicated man. I've been around some distinguished coaches, Frank Broyles, Lou Holtz, and I've noticed there's a fine line between greatness and the guy being right on the verge of loony."

To Walsh, the issue wasn't whether vonAppen had been casual about arriving with his players for the halftime meeting. It cut deeper than that. "It smacked of a split in the squad," Walsh was to say a few days later. "And I couldn't have that. It's been troubling me a little bit all along. Not major. But I had to say it. It was important to be assertive, because that's where leadership has to show itself. I didn't think, 'Well, I should be a leader now.' I just did my job."

After the season, Walsh would identify the moment he nailed vonAppen and the defensive coaches as the exact instant he took complete control of the team.

"I didn't feel I was in control as I should have been. But we were all still learning from each other, hadn't been through that kind of situation, hadn't really been beaten badly. So we had to experience it once to know just where the authority and the direction should come from right at a critical moment. And I wanted to make sure I told the coaches, in front of the players, that I was running it. It took some adaptation on everybody's part for me to become the head coach, because my style is different. So people had to see the other side of me."

The other side was the shadow side of Walsh's face, the power behind the politeness, Walsh the sovereign.

After Walsh met the media for the postgame press conference, he showered and dressed and walked slowly to the bus. The weather had cleared. Walsh sat in a front-row seat, next to the window on the right side, his usual place. He absentmindedly chewed a sandwich. He looked tired.

At the airport, he kept to himself. He boarded the plane and sat in the first-class section sipping a diet soda. A few minutes out of Seattle, he turned to Terry Shea and began talking football. Shea got out a yellow legal pad and so did Walsh, and they started drawing plays. In a few minutes, they were smiling. By the time they landed in San Francisco, they were well into the game plan for USC.

WALSH HAD A way of looking fragile. It was how his hands shook, how his head listed to the side when he was weary, the slight stoop to the shoulders. Someone who had worked with him on the 49ers remembered his tendency to depression. "At those times, he wasn't a complete Bill. You could sense it, and you'd try to give him space and hope he'd rally."

But none of that showed up now, even though the day after the Washington game he had come to the office later than usual and recorded an interview for a radio station, listlessly telling the interviewer, "I have nothing to say. Just ask me whatever you'd like."

Walsh's kind of depression, a tendency toward dreamy immobilization, usually came in anticipation of failure, as it had before Notre Dame. But there was no time for introspection now. Three games remained, sitting there like targets in an arcade, and although Walsh was telling people he might lose all three, he secretly believed he could beat the University of Southern California. The Rose Bowl was out of the question with Stanford's 6-3 record, 3-2 in the Pac-10, but the character of the season, its very meaning, was still wide open, still to be determined. Lose three, and the season and Walsh's comeback would be flops. Win all three, and Stanford could go to a January 1 bowl game.

At the press conference the previous January announcing his appointment as Stanford's head coach, Walsh had found an opportunity to take a playful hit at SC. "Being a teacher, an educator, does have redeeming value," he said at the time, "unless it's at USC." And before the Pigskin Classic against Texas A&M, he'd told the media, "If you had to list the top five or six programs in the country, A&M would be one of them. I'm not sure USC is or not. We're still trying to decide."

Although Stanford's traditional rival was the University of California, Walsh rarely mentioned Berkeley to his players. But he always talked about SC, which he often referred to as "that think tank on Figueroa." Estevan Avila remembered the first time he met Walsh. Avila was in the weight room with a bunch of other players when Walsh walked over to introduce himself. "I'm your new head coach," Walsh said. "You know we've got to have a good year and we've got to beat SC."

"That was the only school he mentioned," Avila later recalled. "At the time we were like, 'Why SC?' No one knew why. Those kinds of comments continued throughout spring, throughout the beginning of the season. He would say A&M or Notre Dame, and he'd always add USC. It was like Coach Walsh hates SC, we hate SC, too."

Walsh didn't actually hate USC. *Resent* would be a better word. Before the season started he told someone, "I hope USC finishes last."

"Why?"

"Because they lord it over everyone else."

Although USC currently ran a clean program, that wasn't always so, and Walsh's misgivings were, more than anything, based on old moral grievances. He once sat in his office trying to explain his feelings.

"I grew up down Vermont Street from USC and used to go through the kids' gate to watch the Trojan's games, so a part of me has affection for them. But they have been the neighborhood bullies for years. They have a way of getting the best players, and it hasn't always been aboveboard. For years they went on and on about their program only to find out that it was compromised to the fullest extent, where players were taking phony classes, where players scalped complimentary tickets. And when all this came out, people were fired and people left."

Walsh leaned forward. He was frowning. "And why is it so important to the alums to have this kind of a program, where there's tremendous pressure on everybody to win? There's way too much emphasis on their football for their very acceptance as an educational institution. We're two private schools and I don't want to be holier-than-thou at

Stanford, but the fact that they've dominated Stanford for years is totally understandable."

He got up from the table, leaned his hands against the back of a chair. "So for me to tease them, and for them not to laugh right along with me, shows you there's an underlying insecurity on their part. I don't tease them to provoke them, although if it does, it does. Because, hell, if they beat Stanford every year anyway, what am I going to do? They can add another touchdown to the score if they want. Maybe that would make them feel better. But when they'd come in and beat us 42 to 7, 54 to whatever, huge scores, and then strut away like they've accomplished something, when in fact this whole thing's been so loaded for them for years against every school in the conference. It's sort of"—Walsh paused, looked off into space—"I'm trying to think of the right word. It's so superficial and so fabricated."

Recently Walsh had stayed home one night watching television, and happened to see *Quo Vadis*, Mervyn LeRoy's 1951 epic about the fall of ancient Rome and the rise of Christianity, starring Robert Taylor, Deborah Kerr, and Peter Ustinov as wacko Emperor Nero. After a while Walsh began to focus on the costumes. Robert Taylor was parading around in a golden helmet with an industrial-size red scrub brush on top. He sported a variety of fancy skirts like a ballerina's tutus and golden sandals with leather straps that wound around his legs.

Walsh pointed at the screen and blurted out to Geri, "Look at that big gladiator with the great big long sword and that funny-looking outfit, and listen to all that music. You know what that is, that's the USC band." It struck him so funny, he stamped his foot. "You hear those trumpets blare, and they come out with those little outfits on, and I swear that's USC."

As he watched Peter Ustinov burn Rome to the ground, Walsh decided on his theme for the game. USC's marching band, with its musicians dressed in skirts and sandals and wearing helmets, not to mention that mascot, the white Trojan horse called Traveler IV, well, it all amounted to an old Hollywood extravaganza. It was dated. Strictly cornball. Walsh had to laugh out loud as he thought about it.

When he came to work Monday morning, he was cheerful, actually confident, although SC had won four in a row, was ranked second in the Pac-10, eleventh in the nation—and Stanford had fallen to twenty-first. Walsh believed SC had better athletes than the Cardinal. In this he was certainly correct, even if he believed that just about any team he played, with the exception of Northwestern and Oregon State, had better athletes. But Walsh saw the Trojans as a talented squad that played sloppy, undisciplined football. He knew exactly how to take advantage of their hyperactive defense—of the way they failed even to account for the fullback on passing downs—if only he could get his own offense to play to a minimum level of efficiency. And that meant getting his line to protect.

"All these plans can be so effective," he confided to a friend that morning, "but we have to play effectively on the fundamental stuff, which we have yet to do all year. I mean we're terrible, all related to our offensive line. One play out of five works because the rest blow up in our face, and it's so frustrating during the game. You almost have to chuckle sometimes, it's so bad."

Down the hall, Fred vonAppen sat alone in his office working on the defense's game plan while Beethoven's *Emperor Concerto* boomed in the background. Through the first six games of the season his defense had saved the Cardinal, but over the last three the defense had slumped, surrendering 83 points.

Even though his players were tired and overworked, vonAppen was not in a sympathetic mood. He stood up behind his desk, threw down a pencil, and explained to a visitor what he intended to tell them. "Just how fucking tough are you now? Are you tough enough for this shit?"

VonAppen walked to the door, headed back to his desk, sat down, took off his glasses, then put them back on. "The whole team has gotten progressively more fragile with our psyche," he growled. "People look to others for the answer. We're the answer. What gives anyone the right to shut down because things go badly? At this point they're fragmented—they doubt themselves and their coaches. If they buy into thinking they're stale, tired, and worn-down, they'll be stale, tired, and worn-down. Who gives a shit?"

VonAppen was shouting, and down the hall, Jane Walsh peeked her head out of her office. "Hey, call somebody who gives a shit," vonAppen was saying. "Most people want to know how you did. You lost 41-7. They kicked your ass. If you're not tougher than that, you'll get more of the same."

When Walsh walked into the Hall of Fame Room for the team meeting he was not thinking about getting tough. He was thinking about Steve Stenstrom, wondering whether to replace him with Mark Butterfield against USC. True, Butterfield would get confused sometimes—Walsh had only to think of the two plays he called in the huddle to be reminded just *how* confused—but Walsh also knew that Stenstrom was getting pounded, and he thought it might be bad for Stenstrom's confidence to continue that way.

Walsh wasn't sure what to do, not that he had to decide right away. Stenstrom was too beat up to practice, so Butterfield would take all the snaps, at least for a few days, while Walsh thought things over. If he decided to start Butterfield—and Walsh understood this would represent a momentous change—he would use it as an opportunity to teach, telling Stenstrom, "Stand by me on the sideline and let's watch Mark." Even if Stenstrom started, Walsh would replace him with Butterfield if things did not go well. This was the first time Walsh would substitute quarterbacks for performance instead of injury.

But Walsh shoved all of that out of his mind as he faced the team. "Assess where we are," he told the players. "At one point we won five in a row. Last week's score means nothing. We lost a game. There's not a chance Stanford ever will win every game it plays. You can say that about every team except about five who have a lock on the talent. The bottom line for us is at the conclusion of the season. We want to look back and feel good about what we did. This is the moment of truth. We play three tough teams and maybe a bowl game waits out there. It's still there for you, everything's right in front of you. When it's said and done we want to say we busted our ass. We're not bad. In fact, we're damn good. As coaches it's a study in people—which guys follow it through. Don't let yourself lose interest."

Walsh fell silent and stared at the players, who sat quietly like students in a lecture hall. "We're in over our heads a little against this USC team. They're loaded. But, hell yes, we can beat them. Listen to your coach, even if you're bored to death with what he says—'This damn coach, there he goes, he said it again. All he knows is football.'"

The players laughed and so did the coaches, and when the team broke up for offensive and defensive meetings everyone seemed relaxed.

Walsh was on the spot at his Tuesday press conference. He knew he'd be asked about his putdowns of USC and coach Larry Smith, and he'd decided to defuse the situation with humor. Asked if the Trojans would be able to use his remarks to motivate themselves, Walsh replied, "Well, they can if they choose. I don't know if they need it. I hope they think they need that kind of stuff to play us." He paused, allowed a second to pass. "I apologize, by the way."

His tone was ironic; he was obviously ribbing the Trojans. A smile was plastered on his face. He got a big laugh out of the reporters in the room. After that, he evaluated the USC team. "They were inconsistent a year ago, and they've brought it all back together. They're right back to where they used to be as one of the great football dynasties of the country." He paused again, let another second pass for dramatic effect. "Does that sound OK?" he asked, while the look on his face had passed beyond a smile to a leer.

Walsh liked to play games with USC, didn't care if he came off as insincere. But it disturbed him that some of the newspapers reported his apology without including the irony.

"I thought I was funnier than hell when I said I apologize," he explained privately. "I thought I was a riot. And they took it seriously. I didn't apologize. I just gave another needle. God, you'd think that the reporters would realize Walsh has been around. He knows how to have a sense of humor and how to tease people. Why would I, with my background in coaching, have to apologize to people? That's silly. And I could have added something like, 'I promise never to say anything like that again.' But they still would have taken it all seriously. I've just got to remind myself that the writers that we get here are not as sophisticated as the guys that covered the 49ers."

For a brief moment, Walsh was allowing himself to romanticize his relationship with the 49er writers. He'd had more misunderstandings with them, especially his last few years, than he'd ever had with the Stanford press corps, which took a laissez-faire attitude toward him. But that was beside the point. This press conference was in a sense a test of the media, although the writers and broadcasters who were present had no way of knowing that.

Walsh was dropping hints about Stenstrom all over the place, seeing if the media could pick them up. At the beginning of the press conference Walsh was asked about Stenstrom's status.

"We expect he'll be able to play," he replied.

"Will Stenstrom practice?"

"He'll practice, probably tomorrow. It's his left arm, so we're OK there. Butterfield is looking better each day. He had a good practice yesterday."

Walsh had changed the subject from Stenstrom to Butterfield, literally substituted Butterfield for Stenstrom in the middle of the paragraph. If the media could press him, pin him down, he'd have to admit he might start Butterfield. A part of him wanted exactly that. But the press let it pass. The next question concerned offensive lineman Chris Dalman, but a few minutes later, someone drifted back to Stenstrom.

"Bill, how do you see your quarterback position? How far has Steve come physically, and what would it take for Mark Butterfield to . . . "

Walsh cut him off in his eagerness to leap back into that subject. "Well, uh, Steve's been chased around quite a bit this year, and he's had some outstanding moments. And I expect he'll continue this way." Walsh's syntax was ambiguous. It wasn't clear if he meant Stenstrom would continue to be chased around, or to have outstanding moments.

Again he changed the subject to Butterfield, almost begging the reporters to drag the truth out of him.

"Mark Butterfield showed signs of maturing as a quarterback in the Washington game. Signs. I think yesterday he had more confidence, it appeared, in practice, because he had played a significant amount of time against a top team and sort of held his own. He had some bright spots. He can throw the ball with great velocity. So he's improving. I think Mark's a full year away from really being a viable starter. But he very well will see action this week."

The press finally was on the right track. Someone asked, "Do you think the week-after-week pounding Steve has taken has reduced his effectiveness at all?"

"Well, it's possible. Sure. It's quite possible."

"Might Butterfield play in place of Stenstrom?"

"Right, he's getting closer to our being able to substitute him, voluntarily. And a lot of it's just his knowledge of what we're doing, his command of it. There are signs he's growing into the job."

"Are you talking about bringing him in on some of the plays where maybe Steve's banged up?"

Actually, Walsh was talking about a lot more than that, but what he said was, "We'll have to decide what to do about it, say Thursday or Friday. We just don't know. Steve hasn't practiced yet. Depends on how he looks, how Mark's come along. So I can't report very much yet."

This was the first time Walsh ever had put Butterfield on the same level as Stenstrom, but the next question from the media had something to do with linebacker Coy Gibbs.

Walsh felt disappointed. He had laid it all out there, practically dumped a news scoop in their laps, and they had whiffed. Later on,

Walsh joked about the risks he'd taken in the press conference. He imagined putting out the same bait when he was with the 49ers, and Ira Miller of the *San Francisco Chronicle* harpooning him. Walsh made his voice sound like a prosecutor's: "Are you saying that Stenstrom won't start against the Trojans?" Walsh laughed. "Does that mean Butterfield is the new starter?"

But no one ever inquired that directly, and the issue of Stenstrom losing his starting job was never addressed again.

Later that day, at one o'clock in the afternoon, Chris Dalman and Steve Hoyem, two of Stanford's best offensive linemen, walked out of the locker room where they spent most of their time during the football season and headed for the courtyard in the front of the gymnasium. It was the third of November, but the temperature still hovered in the seventies and the sky was blue.

Dalman and Hoyem had come to meet a local journalist, to discuss being members of an offensive line that was under attack in the newspapers and was perceived by the coaching staff as disappointing. Stanford quarterbacks already had been sacked thirty-nine times, the most in the conference.

Dalman and Hoyem sat on the steps in front of the building, and, if you could ignore their size—Dalman was six four, 290; Hoyem, six eight, 300—they seemed like any other undergraduates wearing Bermuda shorts and enjoying the beautiful weather. Except for the frowns on their faces. This had been a difficult year for them. Dalman was a fifth-year senior—he had graduated the previous spring and remained at Stanford, taking just one course, for the opportunity to work with Walsh. He was the most competent lineman of the bunch, was as broad as a refrigerator, and had struggled all season with a nerve problem in his neck.

Hoyem was the more gentle of the two. Dalman brushed aside the criticism, but Hoyem took it to heart. He used to weigh 310 but had dropped ten pounds because Walsh wanted him to move faster. During games he constantly fought against dehydration, and after the scene in South Bend, getting an I.V. on the floor while water from the showers sloshed against his prone body, the team doctors had decided to head off any problems by regularly giving him an I.V. at halftime. Hoyem had learned to accept suffering as the price he paid to pursue his passion.

Hoyem played right tackle and Dalman usually played right guard, and their moves were choreographed together—they were a tiny team unto themselves. Along with the other linemen, they lived in Delta Tau Delta fraternity, and being part of the offensive line had come to form the core of their lives. Just the other day one of Hoyem's comments had been quoted in a newspaper: "Every Monday we watch film of the game, and we're always disappointed with our individual performance."

Dalman felt just as glum. He had stayed in school to improve his chances of landing a job in the NFL, but now he wondered if his marketability had gone down. After especially bad games Walsh would tell the linemen they were messing up their future, taking money out of their pockets, and Dalman, the only starter on the line who would be leaving after the season, was worried. He had only three games remaining as an undergraduate, four if the Cardinal played in a bowl game, and he saw his performance this season as his resumé, a job application preserved on videotape. When Walsh told the press the offensive line was slow, Dalman interpreted that as a failing mark on the resumé. "After a bad game, it's hard for me not to get down on myself, because I've directly affected what I've worked for my whole life."

An informal code had developed among the offensive linemen. They never criticized each other. "Actually, we try to help each other," Hoyem said, a sad smile on his young face. "We're kind of like a big support group. It seems like all we have sometimes is each other."

Dalman nodded in agreement. Hoyem began to knead his hands and spoke about the humiliation of giving up a sack. "You feel like everyone is watching you get beat," he whispered. "When I see a guy make a move and all of a sudden get by me, and I see Steve with the ball still in his arm, cocked, and ready to throw, looking for a receiver, my first instinct is to yell, 'Look out, Steve! Get rid of the ball!'" Hoyem raised his voice, yelled as if Stenstrom was actually there. "But you just watch. No matter how you do the rest of the game, those things stay on your mind all week."

"Exactly," Dalman said, eager for this chance to explain his feelings. "I gave the sack last Saturday and I'm still pissed off. I was playing against D'Marco Farr, and he set me up perfectly. He was working on the outside shoulder, four or five plays in a row, and then, all of a sudden, he took a step outside and I overplayed the outside, and then he snaked inside and came free and sacked Mark. I was swearing in the huddle. You're not supposed to get down on yourself in the middle of the game, but it's a terrible feeling, just looking back and then seeing the guy get Mark and then do a stupid sack dance. I guess they replayed my sack on television, focused on me. You start to think about people back home, watching. On the offensive line, the only time your name gets mentioned is when you screw up. Where's Dalman? The next thing you know Chris Dalman just got beat by Farr."

Hoyem looked over at Dalman and smiled. When he gave up a sack it felt to Hoyem as if everyone in the huddle was staring at him. "When Coach Walsh came, there was an air of confidence that, even after the A&M game, we couldn't be beaten, that we were as good a team as there was," Hoyem said. "That started to be eroded, even though we were winning. We won five straight games, but we weren't winning by enough. Our quarterback was getting beaten up. Milburn wasn't rushing for two hundred yards a game. And we just couldn't take pride in anything. We're the type of guys who like to run block. If a guy passes for over three hundred yards, well, that's a reflection on the quarterbacks and the receivers. The offensive line can have mediocre blocking and get that done. But if you have a guy rush for two hundred yards, then you know the offensive line is doing a good job."

Hoyem fell silent. It was time for the afternoon meeting, and they stood up, dusted off their pants, and headed for the locker room. Both had lost confidence during the last few months, although that was the last thing they expected when Walsh took over. It seemed as if everyone was asking Hoyem and Dalman what was wrong with the offensive line, and lately, they'd begun to ask themselves the same question.

Early Thursday morning, the entire coaching staff gathered in the conference room. Walsh leaned back in his chair with his right foot on top of the table. Although the SC game was only two days away, Walsh had called everyone together for a presentation by Guy Benjamin on recruiting. As part of his graduate studies, Benjamin was working on a project to determine how Stanford could attract better players.

Benjamin passed out booklets with his data and conclusions and made a long speech to the staff, going into detail about his methodology. He explained that his research asked four questions: 1) Who are we getting, and are they the same as our assumptions? 2) Who aren't we getting? 3) How do we look for them? and 4) How do we recruit them?

Benjamin said the pond in which they fished for players was smaller than the ones in which other schools fished. Stanford's pond was limited by academic requirements and, in terms of income, didn't represent the lower 50 percent of the population. "The prevailing wisdom is that we can only get certain players because of our admission standards," Benjamin said. "That may not be true."

The other coaches were listening hard to Benjamin talk about ponds. But time was passing, and the eyes of a few coaches began to glaze over.

"If there are three ponds and you only fish in one, you'd better fish as well as you can," Benjamin was saying. "You might be able to catch fish in other ponds, but you don't go to them because you were successful in the first. Or, other ponds' fish don't like our bait."

Benjamin told the coaches to turn to a page that contained mathematical figures and explained he was using something called a Bayeseral Curve to interpret the data in his recruiting study. By this time, Walsh had a queer smile on his face, as if he were receiving a translation of Benjamin's remarks in French.

"I'm sweating and I'm getting a headache," Fred vonAppen groaned in mock agony.

Walsh laughed.

VonAppen said, "Let's find the pond with the running back, and fish the shit out of it."

Al Matthews, who was consumed by USC, hissed under his breath, "I want to win a fucking ball game."

Walsh ended the meeting by thanking Benjamin and telling him to keep up the good work.

Walsh decided to start Steve Stenstrom after all. He held Stenstrom out of practice until Thursday afternoon, and Al Matthews was sure it was premeditated, a tactic to motivate Stenstrom, make him hungry to play. Walsh believed Stenstrom would handle the beginning of the game—the tension, the noise, the jitters—better than Butterfield. After that, if Stenstrom couldn't find open receivers or get away from the blitz, well, Walsh was ready to make a change. As it turned out, this wasn't necessary, and Stenstrom never knew how close he'd come to losing his job.

The game wasn't scheduled to start until 3:30, an accommodation to television, and most of the coaches gathered in their locker room on the south side of the gymnasium to drink sodas, chew gum, and wait. VonAppen, worrying as usual, said to Scott Schuhmann, "Gee, I wish we were playing someone shitty."

Walsh was still in his office studying the game plan. Al Matthews told some of the others he was worried about the look on Walsh's face—tight, pale, preoccupied. But when he came out for warm-ups, Walsh seemed relaxed. He stood quietly near the end zone, watching his players and studying the crowd, which contained a large contingent of USC rooters decked out in crimson and gold. The USC marching band, dressed like extras from *Quo Vadis*, was playing a martial tune and seemed serious about the music and the enormity of the occasion. Across the field, the Stanford band eyed them. Some of the Stanford band members were pointing and laughing.

For anyone who's been brought up in the tradition of college marching bands with perfectly formed lines, neat military uniforms, majorettes, the whole works, the Stanford band is difficult to categorize. It's not so much a marching band as a swarming band. It consists of a bunch of iconoclasts—some might say slobs—wearing weird hats and dirty sneakers with their shirttails hanging out of their pants. The band's mascot is not even from the animal kingdom. It's a tree, some sort of shapeless evergreen with big goggly eyes that runs around the field looking and acting goofy. The Stanford band isn't actually a band; it's an anti-band, a put-on of the whole concept of marching bands.

When the members of the Stanford band got a look at the Trojan marching band, they cracked up. They piled on top of each other just outside the south end zone. A tuba rolled free on the grass. The Tree stared at the Trojans. Walsh saw what the band was doing and laughed.

And then it was time for the teams to leave the field. As USC jogged past the Cardinal locker room, Ron George stood in the way, staring down the Trojan players. They had to run around him like an obstruction in the road. The Cardinal players admired his bravery, but Walsh later said, "That's exactly what I don't want. I prefer players to be unemotional, not to make it personal."

When all the Cardinal players had filed into the locker room, Walsh entered, his posture erect. "There shouldn't be a nervous guy here," Walsh said as he walked among the players, laid hands on their shoulders. "The game is too big for that. You've got to think clearly."

He stopped and a strange grin took possession of his face. When he spoke, his voice was a verbal sneer. "This team we're playing is yesterday. Look at that band—silly-ass outfits with skirts on guys who play those stupid tubas. It's a team of the sixties trying to hold on to the past. Knock their ass off and take pride in it. You can't be awed by that sorry group—hairy legs, little skirts, and those tubas. They're like an old movie you see at midnight. You're watching *Quo Vadis* or something. See their ridiculous alums out there. They all want to think they're from Hollywood. Look how they're dressed. Fifty-year-old women with miniskirts."

By the end of his speech, Walsh's voice was filled with disgust for everything USC represented. Of course, right in the middle, he'd had to turn around and take a deep breath, because he was about to break out laughing. Even he knew he was laying it on thick. He'd caught vonAppen's eye at that moment, and the two smiled at each other, but the players, who were prepared to kill, never noticed.

Walsh told the players to drop to one knee. He looked around the room. "Somebody said we don't have any confidence. Jesus Christ. That's what we're winning on." He dropped to a knee. After a long silence, he asked Steve Stenstrom to begin the prayer. It was a nice touch, almost amounting to anointing Stenstrom in front of everyone, giving Stenstrom the feeling that he would be leading Stanford in battle against this fading army from Los Angeles.

When the prayer ended, Walsh stayed down for almost a minute. There wasn't a sound in the room. Finally, everyone got up. It was almost time to take the field, but linebacker Tom Williams stepped forward. When Williams had something to say, everyone listened, even the coaches. "We're the least confident six and three team I've ever seen," he said. "I'm going to play as hard as I can, and I challenge every single player in this room to play his best."

Listening to Williams, Dave Garnett wanted to rush out on the field and hit someone. He felt his arms and legs begin to tingle. "It was like Tom was questioning our heart," Garnett was to say later. "Fuck that."

Against USC Walsh called his best game of the season, and his offense finally came of age. One of Walsh's talents involved self-scouting, the ability to diagnose the patterns he'd fallen into in his play-calling, and then to call a game completely counter to those tendencies. This is exactly what he did against the Trojans. His offense had featured Glyn Milburn as both runner and pass receiver, and Walsh correctly anticipated that USC would funnel its defense toward Milburn. So he planned something off the wall. He would spread the ball around a group of receivers and backs, and he'd focus on J. J. Lasley, someone from the supporting cast.

Walsh brought in four wide receivers on Stanford's first play from scrimmage—he called it the Eagle Formation. The USC coaches wouldn't expect that and Walsh told himself it would "cloud their minds." Stenstrom completed a seven-yard pass to Mike Cook. Walsh went without a huddle for the next play, which gave the USC coaches even less time to consider what he was doing. Walsh's call was a trap up the middle to Lasley, something else USC couldn't have expected. Now SC had to deal with two unusual plays in succession, and Walsh literally had put the defensive coaches on the defensive, forced them to adjust to one play while Walsh was coming at them with another.

Walsh went without a huddle for the third play, an incomplete pass, and came back right away with a twenty-yard completion to Lasley on a Bingo Cross. At the snap of the ball, Lasley and Milburn crossed in the backfield, Lasley running from left to right behind Stenstrom, Milburn from right to left. The USC defense took off after Milburn and lost sight of Lasley, who was so open he seemed like a spectator.

As the drive progressed, Walsh used a formation with two tight ends, another with one running back and Nate Olsen as a blocker, yet another with three wide receivers. He was trying to break down SC's basic rules of coverage and he was succeeding. The drive ended with a forty-seven-yard Eric Abrams field goal.

Through the first two series, Walsh did not repeat a single play. The second drive ended with Stenstrom throwing the ball to Lasley, who broke several tackles and tumbled into the end zone for a thirty-eight-yard touchdown.

Lasley had prepped for the SC game by posing nude in the *Stanford Daily*. Well, not exactly nude. The day before the game, a photo had been printed in the *Daily* showing Lasley completely in the buff except for his strategically placed helmet. He was staring straight ahead, his chest flexed, his legs spread, his belly button out there in plain view. It was pure softcore beefcake. The caption read, "Running back J. J. Lasley, now a fifth-year senior, has been a consistent performer for the Cardinal on both the football and rugby fields since his arrival on campus."

The picture had caused a stir around the football offices, mostly of amusement. Walsh didn't say anything about it. He was in his office going over the game plan with Stenstrom in hushed tones, both men formal with each other, when Lasley bounded up the steps and stuck his head into Walsh's office. "I'm sorry about the photograph," Lasley called out. "I didn't mean it as a putdown of the program." Walsh, whose mind was elsewhere, told him not to worry.

The tough guys on the defense appreciated Lasley, believed he was the one offensive player who was like them. Although he was the starter at fullback, he was small for the position and had only carried the ball forty times. Mostly Lasley blocked for Milburn or stayed in the backfield to protect Stenstrom. Although he wanted to play in the NFL, he didn't mind doing grunt work.

He grew up in South Central L.A., a gang-ridden neighborbood, and many of his friends were dead or in jail. Later he moved to the San Fernando Valley and became a high school football star. He had come from a mixed marriage, white mother, black father, and hardly got to know his father, who left the house when J. J. was two. Lasley and his mother, Susan, lived on welfare until she got a job cleaning houses. She had two children from a former marriage, and one of them, who was ten years older than J. J., acted like a father to him. He taught Lasley about the periodic table of elements, introduced him to Plutarch and Aristotle, and made it clear he was expected to attend college. USC pushed hard for her son, but Susan Lasley steered him to Stanford and insisted he stay there even when it was clear he would not be a star. So far this season Susan Lasley had attended every Stanford home game, getting up early Saturday morning, driving six hours to Palo Alto, and arriving just before kickoff. She'd spend the night at a motel and drive home on Sunday so she'd be ready to clean toilets early Monday morning.

The half ended with Stanford ahead 13-0. The only unexpected development involved cornerback Vaughn Bryant, who got into a fight with USC receiver Curtis Conway and was penalized fifteen yards for a personal foul. At the time, the Trojans were facing fourth and twelve at their own 5-yard line, and now Bryant had given them a first down. It was a repeat of what Darrien Gordon had done against Washington, and as Bryant came off the field, Walsh buttonholed him. "Why, after last week?" he yelled. "Why?"

Bryant's teammates were even less understanding. Estevan Avila told him, "You want to make that happen again, don't even come back in." Later on Avila explained, "Vaughn got into that little pushing match, which was worthless. It was fourth down. It was after the play. And then it was first down again. Hey, we don't need to make stupid mistakes like that, I mean maybe a late hit, but not stupid personal fouls."

After that, Ron George got into a fight with SC offensive tackle Tony Boselli, who had ripped off George's helmet during a pileup. George knocked Boselli over and jumped on top of him, and got ready to clock him. Then George stopped. He knew he'd be called for a penalty, not that he was particularly bothered by that prospect or the lecture he'd receive from the coaches. But he couldn't face the look he'd get from his teammates in the huddle. George later explained, "The look would mean, 'We were so close to being out of it. Why did you do that?' It's the look I can't stand." George didn't think Boselli, whom he referred to as Number 71, was being malicious. "I give him the benefit of the doubt because he's a football player. Anyway, I won't be an asshole. Let him be an asshole."

In the second half, Walsh switched from an all-passing offense to an all-running one. The idea was to take time off the clock but also to baffle SC, which was pretty baffled to begin with. The USC coaches would have adapted to a passing game, and now they'd have to face something entirely different.

Leading 16-9 with 7:02 left in the fourth quarter, Walsh called ten runs in twelve plays, taking almost six minutes off the clock and taking SC right out of the game. He'd found his rhythm. "This is when you're going to win the game right here," he whispered to himself. "You've got it. You feel it."

The final score was 23-9. Stenstrom had played beautifully, avoiding sacks by rolling out and throwing on the run and getting rid of the ball quickly. The offensive line played its best game, actually had protected, which resulted in Stenstrom making it through without the usual knockout. This was the first time Stanford had beaten USC at home since 1970.

When the excited Cardinal players entered the locker room, Walsh was standing at the door with a big grin on his face. He kept repeating, "Notre Dame, UCLA, SC."

John Lynch said, "Whaddaya say J. J. gets naked every week?"

Walsh said, "We beat Yesterday U."

He led the team in prayer. Then, although he had trashed SC all week, he told his players, "Listen up. Say good things about these guys."

Walsh lingered longer than usual at his postgame press conference, then did several interviews, and finally disappeared into the trainer's room with KZSU, the student radio station. Sports Information Director Gary Migdol stood outside shaking his head. He'd never seen a Stanford coach do a postgame one-on-one with a student station. When Walsh came out, he was grinning. He asked Migdol if anyone else wanted an interview.

C H A P T E R

WALSH ALLOWED HIMSELF to enjoy the victory over USC until 4:00 A.M. Sunday morning, when he woke up with a start and said to himself, "We have to win one more game."

He tried to calm down and go back to sleep but couldn't. One more win would guarantee the Cardinal at least an 8-4 season and a pretty good bowl game. He wanted that. It was one thing when it looked as if the season would go down the tubes; he could relax and watch that happen like a man at his own hanging. But now he had something to gain or to lose, depending upon how he looked at it from one moment to the next, and what that had brought him to, at this very moment, was a pounding heart and an overactive mind in the middle of the night.

So he got up and walked around the house thinking about Washington State, Stanford's next opponent. He was still adjusting to the realities of college coaching. In the pros, he could cut, draft, or trade players. And there was no one better at that than Walsh, at knowing when another team's former superstar, who seemed washed up, would be perfect for the 49ers. He proved that in 1981 when he got Fred Dean from the Chargers, who then led the defense in the 49ers' first Super Bowl season. But now Walsh had to play the hand he was dealt.

He poured himself a cup of coffee and watched the sunrise. By the time he got to work Sunday morning he looked tired and drained, which is not what anyone was expecting the day after beating the Trojans.

Walsh often looked exhausted from his work schedule, which was unrelenting. When he wasn't writing the game plan or directing practice, he was giving speeches or interviews, always running from place to place, while Jane Walsh desperately informed him where he had to be and if he had to wear a tie or if a Stanford T-shirt was OK. He needed every minute of his day to be filled, even if it meant that his sinus infection never went away, even if he sometimes wanted to sit down and pant like a dog. No matter what the physical and psychological consequences of his new existence, being busy, directing his micro-universe, was preferable to what he had tried the last few years at NBC when his life seemed to drift and at times he couldn't find proof that he actually existed, at least not in any way that mattered to him.

Walsh was reminded of the impermanence of life as a television commentator later in the morning, after he had watched film alone in his office. He found he couldn't focus so he came out, wandered by the conference room, and noticed that a friend was sitting at the table looking at the Raiders play the Eagles on television. Walsh sat down and watched, then sighed. "I'm glad I'm not doing that," he said.

"Coaching in the NFL?" his friend asked.

"No, TV."

In his search for permanence, Walsh had recently bought a new home in Woodside, a wealthy community a few minutes north of Palo Alto at the base of the coast range that separates the southern San Francisco Peninsula from the Pacific Ocean. During his time with the 49ers and afterward, Walsh and his family had lived in Menlo Park, in a modest home Geri had decorated and made beautiful, although, according to one reporter who visited there, "It was not a place you would expect Bill Walsh to live in."

Now Walsh was making his statement. He had gone through so many incarnations in his life—angry teenager, boxer, assistant coach, frustrated assistant coach, professional head coach, Super Bowl champion, sportscaster—and now he had made himself into something of a country squire who had retired to a small estate while he coached amateurs at one of the most prestigious learning institutions in the world.

During the football season he had brought an endless procession of visitors to his new spread, which was in the process of a complete renovation that had not yet been finished. His assistant coaches, school administrators, retired coaches, childhood friends, even reporters were treated to tours of the grounds, which were planted with pinot noir and chardonnay grapes and had a magnificent view of the mountains. Walsh didn't actually live in the house yet; he would not spend his first night there until the Wednesday before Stanford played Washington State. But he visited constantly to oversee the workers and to gaze at the hole in the backyard that would become the swimming pool, and to see how his grapes were doing, and to admire the chandeliers Geri had installed, and to look at his bedroom that connected to a bathroom with a sunken tub, and right beyond that to Walsh's very own workout room. It was glorious, more than he'd ever imagined. All those years he'd been paid a fortune by Eddie DeBartolo, Jr., Walsh had felt no need to acquire possessions or to buy a new home, because he wasn't at heart the least bit materialistic. He was an artist, and he was happy if he had a scratch pad and a pencil with which to draw plays.

But now he was sixty, so he allowed himself this indulgence. And it felt good, although with so many last-minute details to attend to and the movers coming to his old house on Wednesday, it was harder than usual to concentrate on business. Sometimes after he had taken a visitor to the new house and when he was driving back to campus, he would think about what the place meant to him and he would realize that the house had assumed a symbolic meaning in his life. It had been built in 1927, and it must have been something to see in its day with its tiled roof and the ceilings with exposed wood beams, ceilings so high that when you looked at them you felt you were gazing at the ceiling of a cathedral. The walkway to the front door was sheltered by a tiled roof held up by wood posts, and right there on the wall next to the front door was a tile mural done by California artist Benny Bufano; although it was unsigned, Geri had contacted Bufano's son, who confirmed the authenticity of the work.

Through the years the house had fallen into disrepair. It was as though someone had cast a spell on it. The first time Geri dragged Walsh to the property, he was appalled. The external adobe walls were sooty gray, the wood beams, inside and out, blackened with a dark stain. The whole place was gloomy, ugly. Rosebushes, untended for almost thirty-five years, grew to outrageous heights and dominated the landscape.

A woman who died at the age of ninety-two had willed the home to Stanford. It was put on the market at two million dollars and had sat there even when the price was cut in half. Walsh wondered what he was getting into. But Geri told him she would sandblast the wood beams and clean the walls, and the house would be beautiful. And she was right. The external adobe shone pink and new, the beams were blond, the house was light and cheerful.

Walsh saw this place as his last stand. "The minute I took the home I knew I wasn't going anywhere else," he told one of his visitors. "I can say this with conviction because some people have a suspicion that maybe I'm maneuvering to go somewhere else. All they have to do is look at my age, and they've got to know I'd be out of my mind to be thinking of anything else. So this will be it. I think my last job would be helping someone coach their team, a sort of consultant."

A few months after Walsh started living in the house, he took a journalist for the grand tour. It was completed now, down to handmade white rugs in the living room and a display case for Walsh's Super Bowl memorabilia, which included a trophy in the shape of a regulation-size football made of crystal that DeBartolo had presented to him. Walsh walked the property and every few seconds he gushed, "Some house, isn't it?" He went to his vineyard and stretched out his arms toward the grapes and the mountains. "Can you imagine a football coach having all this?"

In a way it all seemed too grand to him. Sometimes when Al Matthews came over and they'd talk about the past, they'd wander around the house looking for a place to set down their beer glasses. Walsh had recently gotten two black-and-white border collies and built them a kennel on the side of the house. The dogs would wag their tails when he let them out to run through the vineyard, but when he called them in a stern voice, "Come here," they'd look at him as if he were nuts and keep running and barking. Walsh may have had clout in the world of football, but to them he was merely the guy who kept them locked up.

Recently, Walsh had driven east across San Francisco Bay, past Oakland, and out to the town of Walnut Creek to the house Geri's father built for his family in 1949. Walsh found the pink dedication stone her father laid when the house was completed, and on the stone were inscribed the names of everyone in the family and the year 1949. Walsh dug up the stone and took it away to his new home, where he placed it in the front garden. He surprised Geri with it, and for him, it represented a kind of covenant. He would live out his life in this house.

*　　*　　*

Washington State was an excellent team on the rise when it met Stanford. If the Cougars could defeat the Cardinal and then beat Washington the following week, Washington State might go to the Rose Bowl, which seemed entirely possible considering that the Cougars' quarterback, Drew Bledsoe, was just about the best in college and a few months later would be the first player chosen in the NFL draft.

Fred vonAppen, of course, saw only doom the morning of the game. He was killing time in the coaches' locker room, imagining every conceivable disaster. "You just have these thoughts that nothing you call will work," he groaned. "They'll run right through you. You get the feeling you might get a stroke on the sideline."

Walsh, however, was sure he could beat Washington State, and part of that certainty was rooted in the fact that this would be the last home game in the careers of seniors Ron George, Dave Garnett, Estevan Avila, Tom Williams, J. J. Lasley, and Glyn Milburn. Walsh believed there was no way they would lose a game like that.

"You've got to be at your best," Walsh told the team in the locker room just before kickoff. "We've got some guys who came down that runway for the last time. The rest of you have got to do the job for them. They busted their ass for four years, some for five, in this program."

Walsh paced back and forth in front of his team. "It's a hell of a feeling coming down that road knowing you'll never do it again. The rest of us better appreciate it."

Walsh looked to the left where the defensive players sat. "You've got to have patience on defense," Walsh said. "This big lug Bledsoe is going to make some plays, this big son of a bitch." Walsh looked back at his offense. "The offense is going to have to do it today."

Walsh told the team it needed to score 31 points to win. The Cardinal would go on to score 40. The way the defense played, four would have been enough.

The Cougars had their excuses. They were delayed on their way down to Palo Alto Friday night when an emergency slide inflated on their charter plane, which was parked at the boarding gate. The team had to kill three hours before taking off, some of the players wandering through a nearby mall. Washington State didn't arrive at San Francisco International until eight o'clock, much too late for a workout in Stanford Stadium. So the team bused to the hotel, where the coaches put the players through a brief workout on the tennis courts.

Cougars coach Mike Price maintained an even disposition through the whole calamity. He was happy with his team's progress, and he liked the idea of matching his skills against Walsh's. A few days earlier, when he talked to the Bay Area press on a speakerphone, he found himself answering the usual questions—mostly about whether Drew Bledsoe would leave school a year early—and suddenly he interrupted the flow of questions to say, "Hey, how come you guys haven't asked me what it's going to be like to coach against Bill Walsh? I mean, that's what everybody's asking me around here."

Someone in the Hall of Fame Room obligingly shouted toward the speaker phone, "So what's it going to be like, Coach?"

"Well, I don't know," Price said chuckling. "I've never coached against him. But I think about midway through the second quarter, I'm going to look over and say, 'Hey man, that's Bill Walsh over there!'"

Against Washington State Walsh seized complete control of his offense, calling plays in sequences so convoluted that the Cougars' coaching staff couldn't keep up with him. Stanford piled up 394 net yards, 193 of them on the ground. For several weeks Walsh had been encouraging Stenstrom to throw on the run so that blitzers wouldn't know where to find him; now Stenstrom got the message, was more elusive, and ended up throwing for 198 yards and two touchdowns.

Walsh was feeling so comfortable he was able to use trick plays, strange plays, anything to keep the Cougars confused. On one, wide receiver Justin Armour, who had been a quarterback in high school, got the ball on a reverse from Stenstrom, dropped back and threw a pass to, of all people, Stenstrom, who caught the ball for a three-yard gain.

On another, John Lynch fielded a punt and lateraled to Glyn Milburn, but Lynch, also a former quarterback, heaved the ball over Milburn's head and it skipped out of bounds.

Another play, called Speed Reverse, was Walsh's favorite. He hadn't used it since his days with the Bengals, but called it late in the third quarter with Stanford at the Cougar 31. Stenstrom faked a hand-off to J. J. Lasley, while Glyn Milburn also ran toward the quarterback. Then Milburn abruptly pivoted and cut to his left as Stenstrom tossed him the ball. Two Washington State defenders converged on Milburn, but now he was in the open, perfectly positioned to use his moves. He spun away from the defenders and dashed down the left sideline for a touchdown. In the fourth quarter, Milburn ran a mirror image of the first Speed Reverse to the opposite side, this time going thirty-three yards.

Walsh had worked hard to sell the Speed Reverse to the team, and he almost failed. The problem was that it didn't succeed once in practice, mostly because the defense knew what was coming and didn't go for the initial fake. "Trust me," Walsh said, "it will work in the game."

"The play does not draw up very well," Walsh said later. "In this game it fit, but everybody practiced it like, 'Oh boy.'" Walsh yawned for effect to show how bored the players had been. "The only way the coaches and players could accept it was to have faith in me," he said. "I've been coaching for thirty-something years, and I still have all the equations for football right in my head." He pointed at his temple and smiled.

Beating Washington State should have been an unqualified success for Walsh, but it wasn't. Not the final score, 40-3, or Stanford's 8-3 record, or Stenstrom outplaying Drew Bledsoe, or Milburn scoring three touchdowns, or Fred vonAppen's defense mystifying a Washington State offense that had averaged 29 points a game—none of this helped take away the sting of what happened in the first half with the offensive line and Scott Schuhmann.

Steve Stenstrom was sacked on Stanford's first two series, and the coaches later said Walsh was raging over the headsets, wilder than he'd ever been. He thought he'd solved the problem with the line, but obviously he hadn't.

And then with only eight seconds remaining in the half, on one of those meaningless plays when you expect a team to run out the clock and head off toward the locker room, all hell broke loose. Instead of taking the snap and falling to a knee, Stenstrom dropped back to pass. Walsh wanted one shot at a long bomb into the end zone. But Stenstrom got sacked. It was the fifth of the half, and for some reason, this one blew all of Walsh's circuits. As the gun went off, Walsh was going off on Schuhmann, screaming into the headsets, all the coaches silent interlocutors to what he said.

"We can't throw the ball," Walsh was yelling. "We can't protect. They're shoving our guys around. This is the worst I've ever seen. How can you put up with this?"

Schuhmann ran off the field white-faced, crushed, and Walsh, who realized that he had stepped over a line, made the matter personal, hurried over to him in the locker room. "I have to apologize," Walsh whispered. "I'm so sorry."

"I was glad he apologized," Schuhmann later told a friend. "But it still hurt."

It hurt so much that Schuhmann did something completely out of character. He phoned 49er offensive line coach Bobb McKittrick, whom he knew only as an acquaintance. McKittrick told Schuhmann he understood how he felt. He'd been Walsh's whipping boy on the 49ers.

"Well, how did you handle it?" Schuhmann asked, desperate for guidance.

"I told him off," McKittrick shot back.

McKittrick was a tough guy. He'd shaved his head, which looked as if it could crack marble. He'd served as an officer in the Marine Corps, and on the coldest days in towns like Green Bay and Chicago would walk up and down the sideline without a jacket. He was the kind of man who took absolutely no crap. But Schuhmann was gentle, affable, and wouldn't have known how to yell at Walsh if he tried.

McKittrick told Schuhmann to hang in there, that Walsh had high standards for the offensive line and things were bound to improve. Guy Benjamin told him the same thing. Every day, Schuhmann drove to work with Benjamin and poured out his heart, about not pleasing Walsh, about his fears of getting fired. Benjamin would soothe him, tell him not to worry. Walsh was volatile, Benjamin said. The fits of temper meant nothing.

Schuhmann tried to take comfort from this, telling himself that if Walsh yelled at him only on Saturdays, he could survive.

When the game ended, Walsh entered the locker room grinning.

"Wasn't that something?" he asked the players over the shouting and the celebrating.

Some of the players were chanting, "Beat Cal," a reference to Stanford's final game of the regular season, the Big Game in Berkeley the following Saturday. But Walsh held up his hand. "Let's not worry about that right now."

The coaches walked the quarter-mile to their locker room and, as they changed and gathered their gear, began speculating about the Cardinal's bowl possibilities. Teams were already beginning to position themselves for postseason play, and the coaches had been told that representatives from the Hancock, Freedom, Copper, and Holiday Bowls had showed up in the locker room after the game. Stanford

Athletic Director Ted Leland stuck his head into the coaches' locker room, and naturally everyone wanted to know what bowl Stanford would go to if the Cardinal could beat Cal. Leland said it could be the Blockbuster Bowl against Penn State or the Fiesta Bowl against Syracuse.

That was all Fred vonAppen had to hear. He was sitting at his locker drinking a soda, and he almost hiccuped Sprite across the room. Syracuse had an option quarterback, a big guy named Marvin Graves who scared vonAppen to death. VonAppen got up and started pacing. It was no more than thirty minutes since Stanford had beaten the Cougars. The Cardinal still had to prepare for Cal, and after that there would be weeks of maneuvering before Stanford was locked into a bowl, but none of that mattered. Stanford might have to play Syracuse.

"It's hard to defend that quarterback. He's a stud," vonAppen said. He sat down and stared at the floor, his day ruined.

While vonAppen imagined Marvin Graves taking apart his defense, Walsh entered. He spoke to no one. He sat at the round table in the center of the room, reached into the box containing hundreds of packs of chewing gum, grabbed a piece, peeled off the wrapper, popped a slice into his mouth, and began chewing. He looked up at the ceiling, seemed to enter a dream state. Finally, he looked down and let his eyes scan the coaches. Then he smiled and announced to no one in particular, "If we can only win one more game."

CHAPTER

16

WALSH DIDN'T STAY late in the office on Sunday. He watched film, but left before dinner to help Geri set up the new house and decide what to do with their grand piano, which didn't fit in the living room. He was trying to conserve energy for what would be the most demanding week of the year.

The game against the University of California is an annual tradition, a friendly rivalry that divides the Bay Area into Stanford and Berkeley camps. In every other part of the country the game may seem like just another season-ending contest between regional rivals. In the Bay Area it is known as Big Game, and Walsh and Cal head coach Keith Gilbertson were scheduled to appear at luncheons and dinners almost every day of the week preceding the game. When he was younger Walsh wouldn't have minded giving speeches and shaking the hands of hundreds of eager alumni, but now he had to husband his energy. Besides, he was preparing for his twelfth game now, and it almost seemed like an NFL season. The whole process was beginning to feel redundant. Later, after the season was over, he would need several months away from football before he could stand discussing Xs and Os again.

After he went home, his coaches worked on the game plan and put together the playbook and discussed Cal. In public, coaches like to give the impression they are indifferent to what happens at other schools: "We play them one game at a time. We can't concern ourselves with what's happening at Cal." But of course that's not true.

Football coaches gossip like anyone else, and now was the time for Cal gossip. The coaches had heard about strife on the California coaching staff.

The news had come down that Cal head coach Keith Gilbertson had recently engaged in a wild, eye-bulging, vein-popping shouting match with his defensive coordinator, Artie Gigantino. This was good news for the Stanford coaches. Now, they weren't sure there had been a fight, and it wasn't as if they could call up the Cal Berkeley Athletic Department and ask for a clarification, but what made them reasonably certain was that the story had circulated through the coaches' grapevine, from one Pac-10 school to another. The Stanford coaches believed those stories a lot more than, say, the ones they read in the papers.

Not that they were indifferent to stories in the newspapers. Just a few weeks before, after Cal lost to Oregon 37-17, the *San Francisco Examiner* ran a story in which some Cal players accused others of quitting. This article was a big hit on the second floor of the Stanford Athletic Department. Even Walsh, who usually remained aloof from these conversations, said, "They celebrate after each play. They're down 21-10 to Oregon and they're celebrating." The Stanford coaches wondered if Gilbertson was fully in charge of his team.

The parallels between Gilbertson and Walsh were interesting. Both men were in their first year. The announcement of Gilbertson's hiring at Cal, in fact, had come just one day before Walsh's hiring at Stanford. Just as all the sports editors in the area were telling their writers to grind out Gilbertson profiles, here came the news that the Genius was back, and Gilbertson and Cal quickly found themselves an asterisk to the biggest sports story in years.

Walsh immediately put his stamp on the Stanford program. Dennis Green had laid the groundwork but no one ever doubted that what was happening on the field was pure Walsh. But some of the Stanford coaches wondered if that were the case at Cal. They speculated that Gilbertson had been told to leave things alone, that Cal was loaded with talent and would almost certainly go to a bowl game if he didn't rock the boat. So Gilbertson had not seized control as he should have. The result was that Cal, which had come off a 10-2 season in 1991 including a victory over Clemson in the Citrus Bowl, was slogging along with a disappointing 4-6 record and had lost five of its last six games.

Cal gave every appearance of being an undisciplined squad that played below its talent level. As proof, one of the Stanford coaches pointed out how both teams had reacted to losses at Washington. Cal did better in Seattle than Stanford, losing 35-16 on October 10, but after that the Bears won only once more. Somehow, Gilbertson could not bring his players together. Walsh, on the other hand, had surged to two straight victories and had his team playing its best football of the year.

Guy Benjamin had his own theories about the problems at California. Gilbertson came to Cal from Washington, where he worked as an assistant coach for three years, the last as offensive coordinator. But when Benjamin studied the Bears media guide he noticed that Gilbertson's roots went back to the University of Idaho, where Gilbertson had been offensive coordinator for two years, head coach for three. Delving deeper, Benjamin discovered that four assistant coaches on Gilbertson's Cal staff also came from Idaho. Benjamin was not impressed and drew this conclusion. "It's very hierarchical. There's no spark, no challenge. But Bill's staff is electrifying. I wake up every day and thank God I'm in this situation, this staff, this team."

Benjamin doubted he'd find in Gilbertson's conference room the lightning-fast exchange of ideas that surged around Walsh's large rectangular table—Scott Schuhmann suggesting formations, Terry Shea writing as fast as he could on the greaseboard, Walsh sometimes sitting there taking it all in, merely asking, "Do you think it will work?" or "What if we do it this way?"

"Everyone contributes in our meetings," Benjamin said. "Ideas fly. There's sometimes conflict, but that's OK. It's creative. Bill asks for suggestions because he's a teacher. Too many of the football coaches are not teachers. They're just football coaches."

At 2:30 on Monday afternoon, Bill Singler held his special teams meeting in the Hall of Fame Room. Sometimes the other coaches would attend, sitting quietly in the back on bridge chairs. Fred vonAppen had come down early from his office and was lurking in the shadows, pacing back and forth, visualizing Cal's offense. Singler was saying to his punt return team, "If you see a punt bouncing wildly, back off and yell to each other, 'Peter! Peter! Peter!'"

VonAppen, who had a love for etymology, came over to a visitor and said, "The derivation of Peter is interesting. It means don't touch it. It's derived from 'Don't play with your peter.' It came down from some old coach somewhere."

At three Walsh appeared, walked to the front of the room, and almost in a monotone told the players, "There's no need to talk. We just need to play damn well. Cal's got the talent. Just look at the tapes. They're capable of self-destructing and they're capable of playing great. My guess is they won't self-destruct. We'll have to beat them."

Then Walsh adjourned the meeting, just like that. There wasn't much to talk about and the players knew it. Beat Cal and the Block-buster or Fiesta Bowl was out there, waiting for them. Lose, and . . . well, that was inconceivable.

On Wednesday morning, Walsh came into the staff conference room wearing a white shirt, dark tie, and a suit jacket. In a few hours he had to attend the Guardsman Luncheon at the St. Francis Hotel in San Francisco, but he had work to do first. The Guardsman was the most prestigious of the pre–Big Game functions, and although he'd prefer to stay in his office perfecting the game plan, such devotion to duty would have been interpreted as a snub to the alumni of both schools. Besides, Gilbertson had indicated he would be there.

Head coaches didn't always attend. In 1986, his last year at Cal, Joe Kapp stayed away from the luncheon, said he was too busy to show up. The fact that his team had only one victory might have contributed to his absence, although in an attempt at realism, someone had placed a life-size photo of Kapp in front of the dais. Kapp's absence was not par-ticularly noticeable considering that Stanford's head coach, Jack Elway, also skipped the luncheon. Cal won Big Game 17-11 and the Golden Bear players carried Kapp off the field on their shoulders. The admin-istration had already told Kapp he was fired, and he cried in his players' arms.

At his weekly press conference, Walsh had humorously shrugged off the whole Big Game phenomenon. He walked into the room and said to the media, "We have Big Game this week. Some of you writers might note that. Well, we're excited about the game, we're looking forward to it. There's a lot of excitement surrounding Memorial Sta-dium, it's a great place to play a game, great setting. It's been a privi-lege to be here, thank you, good evening."

But now he was dead earnest as he went over plays in the confer-ence room. At 11:15 Jane Walsh told him his town car and driver were waiting outside to take him to the Guardsman Luncheon. Walsh wiped the chalk off his hands, gathered up his playbook, and walked downstairs for the ride to the city. The November sun shone brightly into the car, and Walsh put on sunglasses. In the light of day, he looked pale. He hadn't played tennis for weeks, and his sinus infection was the worst it had been all season.

He took off his sunglasses and said to a friend, "I look in the mirror, I have big circles under my eyes. I don't know why, really. I don't feel tense. I'm no more nervous about this game than any other."

Walsh set down the playbook on the seat. "Big Game has some meaning, but until today at our luncheon, I won't even think about that. Now, for Gale Gilbertson." Walsh paused, creased his brow. Something about what he'd just said didn't sound right. "Gale Gilbertson," he repeated, then he laughed because he had forgotten the name of his rival coach, or more precisely, he'd combined Keith Gilbertson's name with that of Gale Gilbert, Cal's quarterback in the early eighties. So many coaches had come and gone in Walsh's life that he could barely keep track of them. Sometimes they all seemed to meld together into The Opponent.

"Keith Gilbertson," Walsh corrected himself, chuckling. "Keith might just be frazzled with the idea that this is the Big Game and everybody's making an issue of it, whereas I've been through a lot of games like that. I appreciate it, but I don't give it much of my time."

At the banquet, Walsh sat quietly at the dais, sometimes seeming to inhabit a world elsewhere. He was locked into his game plan, and nothing, not this banquet, not his dinner commitments, not Geri's latest additions to their new house, would seem real until Big Game was over.

Keith Gilbertson was a hit at the Guardsman Luncheon. He was forty-four, a chubby, smiling man who looked like a young Buddy Hackett. Gilbertson told the audience it would have been impossible to put on a luncheon for the game between the University of Washington from Seattle and Washington State from Pullman: "The wheat farmers would be throwing food at the stockbrokers."

Walsh laughed at the joke and smiled at Gilbertson, and when it was all over, the shrimp salads and the white wine and the stand-up comedy and the applause, Walsh and Gilbertson shook hands. Gilbertson seemed genuinely pleased to be coaching against Walsh, to have a chance to match his skill against this legend. Walsh walked through the lobby and got back into his town car as people rushed past him in Union Square, stopping, then pointing. Walsh picked up his playbook.

He sighed, settled back, and began to read, and as the car pulled away from the curb, the Guardsman Luncheon, for him, was already insubstantial, a million miles away.

After practice the Thursday before Big Game, the team always gathered on the field, away from reporters, so that the freshmen could imitate the coaches. The tradition was part catharsis, part homage, and the big hit this year came when defensive end Jason White had the temerity to do a takeoff of Fred vonAppen. In vonAppen's gravelly voice, White yelled at the team, "OK, men, swing your dicks over this way. Remember, men, everyone on this field's an asshole except you and me, and I'm not so sure about you."

VonAppen said he could vaguely recognize himself in the portrayal.

That night the undergraduates attended a bonfire on the Stanford campus. It was an annual Big Game ritual. Observing the bonfire was defensive end Tyrone Parker. "This is everything college football should be," he said. "It's all old-fashioned traditions, the fight songs, the seniors coming out on stage for the last time. It's everything, growing up as a kid, that you think college football is."

Parker might have had a greater appreciation of Big Game than the others. Stanford opponents liked to portray the Cardinal players as rich kids who drove BMWs, but Parker was the furthest thing from that stereotype. He had grown up in Coney Island, and after his mother died when he was thirteen was raised by a half-brother named Lester. When Parker got home from school in the afternoon he'd clean the apartment and cook dinner for Lester, who was out working. "It wasn't lonely," Parker once said. "We lived in a big apartment house and I had childhood friends all around me. And I never had any problems. I can say my mother did such a good job raising me that by the time I was thirteen, she pretty much taught me all I needed to know."

During the bonfire the coach was expected to introduce his graduating seniors and explain why Stanford would beat Cal. Walsh got into trouble right away when he had to introduce his players. He was terrible with names to begin with. He sometimes forgot the names of his coaches' wives, and from time to time when he was being interviewed in his office with the door closed, Jane Walsh would knock quietly and pretend to slip Walsh an urgent note—in reality the name of the journalist conducting the interview.

Now Walsh was on the spot. He had twenty-two seniors to introduce, and he felt the pressure. He could recall all the offensive players, sure, but he was not as confident about the defensive team, and as he turned and looked at the line of players standing behind him, he immediately noticed that he'd drawn a blank on the big, good-looking kid standing right in the middle. It's not as if Walsh didn't know who he was. He was the nose guard. That was obvious. But try as he might—and he was trying with all his wits to come up with the name—he couldn't. So he did the only reasonable thing. He started at one end of the line and began to introduce his players, hoping that the nose guard's name would pop into his head at the appropriate moment. He came down the row, graciously introducing the players until it was the turn of the player with no name. Walsh stared at him, hoping to find the right words, but they didn't come, so he looked down to the other end and began working his way back to the middle once more, and the nose guard. Finally the moment had come. Walsh called out, "Jason Fisk."

Going strictly by the odds, Walsh had a 50 percent chance of being correct. Jason Fisk was indeed a nose guard on the Cardinal. In fact, he was the starting nose guard. Unfortunately he wasn't this particular nose guard, whose name happened to be Aaron Rembisz. Walsh was informed of his error, and he turned red. Rembisz, of course, Rembisz. It was that old quirk in Walsh. He could remember a play he had called almost thirty years ago at Washington High School—the down and distance, even the weather. That was all vivid to him, but sometimes his current life, everything that went on around him, seemed less real.

Walsh was still in the spirit of the bonfire when he met with the team in the Hall of Fame Room late Friday morning. He began to go over a play for J. J. Lasley when suddenly he stopped and, grinning, peered into the room from his raised platform. "Where's J. J.?" he asked. Lasley raised his hand. "What a spokesman for the university," Walsh said, his words loaded with irony. "He just cuts through all the bullshit. Did you hear him at the bonfire last night? 'Fuck Cal. Cal, fuck 'em.' I was standing with the president of the university, telling him how smart you guys are."

Later that evening, when the team gathered at the hotel for meetings, Walsh wasn't as giddy. He methodically went over the first twenty plays—the first call a quick slant pass to Mike Cook to nullify the blitz everyone knew was coming. When he was done, he simply ended the meeting. No pep talk, no infusion of spirit. He might have been going over the monthly sales figures at a real estate brokerage.

"That's it. You guys need any extra coaching? I think you're in pretty good shape."

It was a nice touch, theatrical in an understated way. Without actually saying it, Walsh was telling his players they had prepared an entire season for this game and he had nothing to add.

The players went back to their rooms, and Walsh, who was in a nostalgic, philosophical, melancholy mood, invited a friend to the hotel bar. They sat at a table in the rear, Walsh keeping his red playbook right in front of him. He ordered a margarita and, with all his work completed until he had to run the game, allowed himself to relax. He nibbled on the salt near the rim of his glass and sipped the margarita. His hands shook slightly. "I'm so happy not to be in the NFL," he whispered. "If we win tomorrow, we'll be nine and three, and that's great. If we lose, we're still eight and four and we go to a bowl game. In the NFL, you have to be Number One. You're always afraid Washington may win and only be a game behind, and then you have to worry about home-field advantage."

The waitress, a woman in her early twenties, asked Walsh if he wanted another drink and he said no, and then she gave him a napkin to autograph. When she left, he ran his hand through his hair. "I'm not doing as good a coaching job as in 1981 with the 49ers," he said. "I was inspiring then." He drank from his glass. "In college you have to bring them back, focus all that emotion. I can do that, but I've changed." He stared at the cover of the playbook, struggling to complete the thought. "I'm not inspiring anymore."

The winner of Big Game gets custody for the next twelve months of the Stanford Axe, a red axe with a blade broad enough to chop off heads. In its press release the week of Big Game, Stanford had this to say about the Axe:

The history of the Axe dates back to 1899. Stanford yell leader Billy Erb purchased a broadaxe with a fifteen-inch blade, painted with a Cardinal "S" to decapitate an effigy of a bear. On April 15, 1899, Erb brought the Axe to a baseball game between Stanford and Cal to lead the Stanford crowd in the Axe Yell. However, after the game, the Axe was stolen by several Cal students and remained at Cal for the next 31 years. The Axe, which was held in a bank vault in Berkeley, was brought out only once a year for a baseball rally. Then in 1930 a group of Stanford students pulled off the second theft of the majestic blade following that rally and brought the Axe back to the Farm. That group is known to this day as the Immortal 21. Three years later it was agreed that the Axe would become a trophy that would go to the winner of the Big Game. Since the original thefts, however, the Axe has been stolen five more times—twice by Cal and three times by Stanford—and the security around the Axe is always extremely tight.

The Stanford-California series, which Stanford led 46-37-11, was one of the fiercest rivalries in college football. Forty-four of the ninety-four Big Games had been decided by one touchdown or less, and only 73 points separated the two teams during the series, which was discontinued in the war years of 1915–1918 and 1943–1945. Big Game had come to symbolize, more than anything, improbable finishes. In 1972 Vince Ferragamo hit Steve Sweeney with an eight-yard touchdown pass as time expired, giving Cal only its third victory of the season by a score of 24-21. Cal never even attempted the extra point because the crowd spilled onto the field and the officials couldn't restore order.

In 1990, Stanford scored nine points in the final twelve seconds to win 27-25, the clincher coming on a 39-yard field goal with no time showing on the clock.

But the craziest ending, the one that most strained credulity—at least for Stanford rooters—came in 1982, and has been known since then simply as "The Play." With 1:27 remaining and Stanford behind 19-17, the great John Elway led the Cardinal to a go-ahead field goal. Elway had kept that drive going with a make-or-break twenty-nine-yard completion to Emile Harry on fourth and seventeen, and it looked as if, based on that comeback, Elway was headed for the Heisman Trophy as the climax to his brilliant college career.

With four seconds remaining, Mark Harmon kicked off to Cal, and then began the strangest combination of laterals and runs anyone had ever seen. Kevin Moen fielded the kickoff at Cal's 44 and ran to the 48, where he lateraled to Richard Rodgers, who didn't gain anything. Rodgers lateraled to Dwight Garner, who ended up at midfield and pitched back to Rodgers, who lateraled to Mariet Ford after reaching the Stanford 45. Ford advanced to Stanford's 25 and, when he became trapped by Stanford defenders, hurled the ball blindly over his shoulder to Moen, the player who had started everything. Moen caught the ball, headed for the end zone, and steamed through the Stanford band, which had come onfield to celebrate Stanford's victory and was happily playing "All Right Now." Moen ran through the high-fiving band members, knocked over a trombone player named Gary Tyrrell, and scored the winning TD. There were five laterals in all, and afterward Stanford claimed that Garner's knee was down (lateral #2) and the play should have been called dead. The officials didn't see it that way, and Cal was declared the winner.

Elway finished second in the Heisman voting to Herschel Walker. Stanford head coach Paul Wiggin, who was fired following the next season, took his family to Williamsburg, Virginia, in the days following The Play, thinking no one would know him there. But in a visitor's center, someone tapped him on the shoulder and said, "Hey, Coach, tell me about that play." The four Cal players became cult heroes in the Bay Area and were introduced at the Oakland A's Opening Day, and a Los Angeles television producer presented Tyrrell with a new trombone.

This was the tenth anniversary of that game, cause for celebration in the Bay Area. The principals were invited back for the game, and local newspapers ran detailed accounts of The Play. Both the *San Francisco Examiner* and the *Chronicle* printed diagrams of The Play drawn on mini-football fields, and went so far as to number each lateral, labeling dramatic moments—"Garner's knee down?" The University of California band planned to reenact The Play during halftime, positioning its members at the critical points on the field, going through all the laterals and the runs, and finally having a surrogate Kevin Moen run through a surrogate Stanford band.

But, as he rode up to Berkeley on Saturday morning, November 21, 1992, Bill Walsh couldn't have cared less about all that. On the bus ride from Palo Alto he wasn't thinking about The Play, he was thinking about *plays*, the specialty plays he meant to install but never got a chance to because of the banquets and other functions he'd attended all week. He and Terry Shea sat next to each other in the front of the bus furiously drawing up the plays—what to do on third and three; on fourth down; with two minutes left. As it turned out, they didn't have to hurry. The Stanford buses arrived late at Memorial Stadium, caught in traffic in the narrow Berkeley streets. Wide receivers coach Mike Wilson, who had driven to Berkeley on his own, waited at the gate, wondering what happened to the team.

When the Cardinal finally arrived, Walsh was frazzled—everything was behind schedule. His mood was not enhanced by the state of the visitors' locker room.

Cal's Memorial Stadium is one of the most beautiful in the country. It is a bowl that sits in the lush country of Strawberry Canyon in the Berkeley hills. Looking west, fans can see the Bay Bridge and the Golden Gate Bridge and San Francisco sparkling like a jewel. But the stadium was constructed in 1923, and the facilities in Stanford's locker room looked as if they might have been original. When Walsh set foot in the cramped, dingy locker area, he frowned, took a friend by the arm, and led him on a tour. "This is an insulting locker room," Walsh said, walking into the bathroom, which contained a small, troughlike urinal and only two stalls, both without doors. "It's a sophomoric trick to present a team with something like this, so inadequate for today's large squads. The Pac-10 should tour this facility and say you have two years to bring it up to standard and we never want to see another stall without a door. But they don't care about the players. They wonder where they can hold their meetings next year."

Walsh walked into a hallway. Players had already lined up, waiting for a turn to use the bathroom. A dirty stream of water flowed from the bathroom, past several tables on which players were being taped and examined by doctors. One of the doctors, Gary Fanton, was finding it difficult to work. Space was so cramped that whenever someone wanted to walk past, everyone else had to jump on the tables. "This is disgusting," Fanton told Walsh.

Stanford did not play well at the start of the game. Although Walsh expected this, knew Cal would come out in a fury to redeem its disappointing season on this warm fall afternoon, he still found himself complaining into the headsets when his team could not manage a first down on its first two possessions. Cal scored a field goal and led 3-0.

Stanford got a break near the end of the first quarter after the Cardinal was forced to punt. Cal's returner, Ike Booth, ran under the punt, a high pop fly, but lost it in the bright sky—the official game notes said he became "disoriented." The ball fell through his hands and bounced high in the air off the artificial turf. Poor Booth looked every which way for it as it hovered over his head. By the time he located the ball, it was too late. Stanford had recovered on Cal's 46.

Stanford scored on the very next play. Cal had switched into what football people call a Two-Deep Zone. All that means is that two defensive backs were playing behind the coverage like a pair of out-fielders. The minute Stenstrom saw the zone, he called an audible that Walsh had drilled into him. He sent two receivers deep, tight end

Ryan Wetnight and Justin Armour. Wetnight drew the two defenders to his side of the field, leaving Armour free down the middle for the catch and the TD. Keith Gilbertson, of course, had warned his players what to do on a Two-Deep Zone, to keep both receivers in sight, but Stanford fooled Cal anyway.

Stanford scored another touchdown in the second quarter on a strange series of plays that represented the quintessential Walsh. On first and ten Stenstrom pitched the ball to Glyn Milburn, who started to run a sweep. At least that's what Cal thought. The Cal defenders began to sprint after Milburn, and their pursuit was orderly and well conceived. The only problem was that Milburn had no intention of running. He stopped dead, looked downfield, and threw a wobbly pass for a sixteen-yard gain to Justin Armour.

On the next play Stenstrom faked a handoff to Milburn but gave the ball to wide receiver David Calomese, who ran a reverse for fourteen yards. On the next play, and this was the craziest of all, Walsh deployed his offensive tackles like split ends. They lined up several yards away from the center as if they were disassociating themselves from their teammates, and beyond them were the wide receivers. Stenstrom's pass was batted away, but that didn't matter. Walsh had run three trick plays in a row—the run-pass, the reverse, splitting out the offensive tackles. Now the Bears were off balance, wondering what he would come up with next, and Walsh was doing exactly what he wanted—breaking them down psychologically.

Mike Wilson happened to look through his binoculars at Cal's defensive coordinator Artie Gigantino about this time, and the way Wilson saw it, Gigantino had thrown up his hands. "He had his greaseboard, but he didn't write anything," Wilson said later. "Can you imagine trying to prepare for this offense? We run more than two hundred formations."

Stanford scored a few plays later on another TD pass to Armour, and scored on its next series on a two-yard run by Ellery Roberts. That touchdown was set up by a twenty-one-yard completion to Milburn—for that play Milburn, a back, had lined up as a wide receiver, while Mike Cook, a wide receiver, had lined up as a running back.

This was Walsh's most imaginative, most daring game of the season. High above the field in the press box, Al Matthews was smiling, and under his breath he whispered, "Yes, Bill, be yourself. Let it all out."

*   *   *

As Walsh left the field at halftime with the Cardinal leading 20-3, he was amused by what he had observed on the Cal sideline. "In the early stages, the coaches at Cal were jumping up and down and screaming and high-fiving with their players and going to the crowd to come on and cheer," he told a friend. "*Coaches* were doing that. And about fifteen minutes later, it quieted down to zero."

But when he entered the locker room, his face grew dark and his mood changed. When he addressed the team, he sounded as if Stanford, not Cal, were getting blown away. "There's not a chance we can win unless we score ten more points," he shouted at the offense. "This will be the most physical thirty minutes of football you've ever played in your life." His face was red, his voice angry. "They're embarrassing us with their goddamn blitzes. We're humiliated offensively. They're destroying our offensive line. We've got to get more points on the board or we'll lose the Big Game. We'll be the sorriest goddamn team in the country if we don't score ten more points."

In other situations, Walsh might have been acting, trying to work up his team for one great half of football. He wasn't acting now. He looked as if he had gone into shock. He came over to a friend and whispered anxiously, "If we win this game, it's a fucking miracle. The other team's so much better than us physically."

He went over to Fred vonAppen and whispered, "They're going to throw."

Who knows what fear went into that statement? Walsh expected Cal to come out bombing, and he didn't want the defense to take chances, to blitz wildly, although vonAppen had not played a risk-taking style since early in the season. Behind Walsh's worry was the feeling that he couldn't lose now, not with a 9-3 record right there for the taking.

"Jesus Christ, if you let down a bit, you lose this game, I promise you," he warned the whole team. "Let's not lose concentration, especially defense. They're going to be throwing the ball all over the place."

As the team filed out, down a flight of wooden stairs, through a tunnel, and out to the field—one player had to urinate in the tunnel because he couldn't get into the overcrowded bathroom—Walsh went over to an old wooden bench in the locker room, sat down, and put his head in his hands until the last player was out the door.

While Walsh had been working on his team at halftime, on the field, the Cal band reenacted The Play, and then the perpetrators of all those laterals were introduced to the crowd. The mood was gay until two men leaped out of the stands, ran over to the Stanford Tree, knocked it over, and pulled the tree costume off the stunned student who had been wearing it and who was now lying on the ground. One guy got away, but the Stanford band members surrounded the other man and began kicking him. Ushers rescued him and dragged him to the Cal side, where he was cheered. The cops showed up, handcuffed him, and led him away. The fans booed.

None of Walsh's fears were realized in the second half. In the third quarter Stanford ruined Cal as Stenstrom threw a touchdown pass to J. J. Lasley, and Glyn Milburn fielded a punt, cut to the left sideline, and ran upfield for a seventy-six-yard TD. The score was now 34-3, and Cal was only going through the motions. The night before the game Walsh had told his team, "If you keep the heat on the other team, it will start to crack ten minutes into the third quarter." His prediction was correct almost to the minute.

When Stanford went ahead 41-9 with about seven minutes left in the game, Walsh told the coaches in the press box to come down to the field, the game was over. He took off his headset and Stanford cap, straightened his hair, and prepared to enjoy the rest of the afternoon. He inserted Mark Butterfield at quarterback and took out most of his starters on offense and defense. Glyn Milburn was on the sideline mugging for the TV cameras, and cornerback Darrien Gordon was so relaxed he had taken off his jersey and his shoulder pads and was casually talking to fellow cornerback Vaughn Bryant on the sideline.

Then everything went wrong. In the next few minutes, Stanford fumbled a punt and muffed two onside kicks and Cal scored two quick touchdowns, making the score 41-21 with less than two minutes to go. Darrien Gordon put on his shoulder pads and jersey and went back in. Glyn Milburn stopped talking to the TV cameras. Walsh was pacing back and forth along the sideline muttering to himself, "Son of a bitch."

Walsh reinserted the regulars, including Steve Stenstrom, and they brought order to the game, final score 41-21. When it was over, Cal fans streamed over the wall that separated the stands from the playing field. Someone tore a Stanford banner from the hand of a Stanford rooter, and Cal fans ran across the field to confront the Stanford fans. Two Stanford security men had to escort Walsh from the field. Looking down on the chaos from the press box, Stanford Athletic Director Ted Leland told himself, "The idea of a barrier has been eliminated at Cal. Fans feel they can come right on the field." Leland worried what would happen if Cal lost future Big Games—the Bears hadn't won in the last six years—and he told himself that if the Cardinal continued to dominate California, Stanford's Big Game might end up being against Notre Dame.

As Fred vonAppen entered the locker room, he threw down his hat and said, "Twenty-one points to these peckerheads."

Walsh was more cheerful. He had completed his schedule in the Pac-10, the toughest conference in the country, winning his last three games by a total score of 104-33. As he gathered his team in the tiny dressing area, he was grinning. "Hell of a year," he shouted, "Hell of a year. I just want you to know you're Pac-10 co-champions because Washington lost to Washington State today." The players cheered. Walsh held up his hand. "We came unraveled at the end. We can't let it happen again for this school or this team."

He shook hands with some of the players, walked back to the coaches' locker room, and as the others showered and as more water streamed onto the floor and meandered into the corridor, he sat staring into space. The staff made plans for a party that night at Dave Tipton's and Walsh absentmindedly said he would show up, then looked away. In all the tumult of the victorious locker room, he sat there brooding.

Everyone else dressed and went out to the buses. Walsh lingered. He changed into his street clothes, tied his shoes, then knotted his tie. "It was almost a perfect game," he said to someone who'd stayed with him. He began to leave, but abruptly sat down again. He couldn't get over the ending. It was as if someone had substituted a Three Stooges movie for the last act of *Hamlet*.

"It loses its artistic sense," he whispered. "Now it's not a thing of beauty. It's just a victory."

CHAPTER

IN THE DAYS following Big Game, Walsh turned his attention to recruiting. It would be almost six weeks before Stanford would appear in a bowl game, and during much of that time Walsh would be on the road trying to convince blue-chip high school seniors of the virtues of Stanford's football program.

He was eager to land Scott Frost, the quarterback from Wood River, Nebraska, who had shown up in South Bend when Stanford beat Notre Dame. But there were problems. Tim Carey, a fine drop-back passer from Seal Beach, California, had already committed to Stanford, and now coaches from other schools were warning Frost that he wasn't Number One in Walsh's plans. Walsh had to find a way to convince Frost he was important to Stanford. That was simple. Walsh would fly to Nebraska. That would be the clincher: Bill Walsh getting off a plane, renting a car, and driving over to Frost's house. And if somehow that didn't work, Walsh would play his hole card. He'd tell Frost's parents—the father was head coach on the high school football team, and the mother coached wide receivers and the offensive line—that if Walsh had a chance to tutor their son, Scott might end up as the first quarterback taken in the NFL draft, which could mean a difference of a million dollars in bonuses and salary.

Before leaving for Nebraska, Walsh had to swing by the local office of the Department of Motor Vehicles to get a new driver's license. The old one hadn't expired, Walsh had just lost his wallet again—around the football offices, the staff had lost count of how many wallets he'd gone through that season. He had scheduled a coaches' meeting for 2:30, but the coaches had to kill time because Walsh got mired in the endless lines at the DMV. And when he finally returned, Walsh had to dash over to the Hall of Fame Room for a 3:30 team meeting. He gave out various awards to the players—he was a big believer in awards and plaques, tangible rewards for service.

Then he began talking about recruiting, reminding the team that high school players would visit Stanford in the next few weeks and would size up the place and pump team members for information. Walsh implored the Cardinal to be positive about Stanford. "Some guy just lost his girlfriend, so he tells a recruit Stanford sucks. 'I wouldn't recommend this goddamned school.' Don't take it out on Stanford just because you've been rejected socially," Walsh pleaded. "This is the best school in the country. We will be the best team in college football soon. And this is an honest program, which you already know."

Then Walsh began talking about how to prepare for a bowl game. He reminded his players that they had "mixed results" in the Aloha Bowl the previous season. "Mixed results" was, of course, a Walsh euphemism for losing. Nothing mixed about that. There had been talk among the players that the minute they got to Hawaii they lost their "discipline" and "focus," which are sports clichés for having too much fun.

"This is not something you've earned like three weeks vacation," Walsh told them. "It's not a holiday, not a chance for us to see beautiful Phoenix or Miami. This is a working business trip. You'll do this many times in your lives. You rehearse it and go down there to make the deal. If we end up playing Syracuse or Penn State, can we win it? Hell, yes. We bring it home, and what a hell of a year." Walsh raised his hand over his head, indicating the heights they could attain. "There's nothing better than flying home with ten wins, it's the best Stanford's ever done. We had the hardest schedule in college football and now we have to prove we're championship material."

Walsh went to visit Scott Frost the first week in December. While he was gone, Bill Singler and Guy Benjamin would sit for hours in the conference room with recruiting secretary Jan Souza, plotting strategy. On the greaseboard, Souza would draw circles representing tables at various dinners for recruits during their visits to Stanford and write in the names of who would sit where, which recruit was lucky enough to be at the Walshes' table, where Athletic Director Ted Leland and his wife would be. If a certain recruit seemed shy, she'd remind the coaches to draw him out. She even helped plan the menu.

At one end of the room was a greaseboard that was always covered, hidden, as if it were the holy of holies, and in a sense it was. It contained the names of the recruits Walsh absolutely wanted, and next to each name, tiny notations indicated when the coaches last had phone contact with him and what they thought their chances were of bagging him.

On Wednesday, December 2, Jan Souza worked over her preparations for the upcoming weekend. Three recruits were coming to campus, and she wanted to make sure everything went smoothly. But only *three* recruits. That bothered her. She'd been told that Notre Dame was having twenty-five the same weekend, including Frost, and Notre Dame was legendary for really laying it on thick, even treating recruits to a training-table breakfast with legendary ND-monogrammed waffles. She was convinced Stanford had more to offer, but a lavish Notre Dame banquet and all that tradition might turn the heads of teenagers. She quickly went over in her mind the schools against which Stanford competed for players: Notre Dame, UCLA, USC, Washington, and Cal. Cal didn't bother her—the Bears had flopped and she didn't see them posing a threat. Neither did the Washington Huskies, not with all those stories about Pac-10 sanctions looming over the program.

But Notre Dame, well, that was a problem. What made things worse was that the Frosts told her they were coming to Stanford December 19 through 21. That made her anxious because as of now, no other recruits planned to be on campus that weekend. Souza was afraid the atmosphere would seem grim and unfriendly, especially after all the hoopla in South Bend. She'd even told the Frosts that Scott would be the only recruit in Palo Alto when they visited, and although they assured her they understood, she worried anyway.

While Souza worked on the preparations, Terry Shea sat in his office going over film of recruits. Fred vonAppen had just returned from the college bookstore, where he'd gone to break the tension of recruiting. He bought the collected poems of Howard Nemerov for sixteen dollars, and headed for his office and shut the door.

And where was Walsh? Bill Singler looked at his watch. "Bill's in Wood River, Nebraska, and right about now, he's trying to convince Scott Frost he's Number One."

*   *   *

Walsh believed his trip to the Frosts in Wood River was a success. Although the parents hadn't given any indication they would send their son to Stanford, they didn't say no, either, and Walsh was sure he had made a good impression on them.

The day after he visited the Frosts Walsh was scheduled to fly back to San Francisco and give a speech, but with the change in time zones and all the excitement, he'd slept later than he meant to. The hotel clerk told Walsh about a shortcut to the airport, and Walsh stood there attentively taking it all in.

Then Walsh jumped into his car and got lost. It was still dark outside and Walsh got all turned around and confused, and pretty soon he found himself slamming the dashboard and screaming at himself, "You dumb son of a bitch!"

It was in this state of mind that Walsh wandered into a grain store for help. The man behind the counter, who clearly had no idea who Walsh was, took one look at this frantic stranger and said, "Sit down, relax, have a cup of coffee." Walsh felt grateful that someone was taking charge of the situation. The two of them looked up United Airlines in the phone book, "And of course it wasn't listed," Walsh said a few days later. They finally got the number and dialed, and as the guy from the grain store began speaking, over their heads, they heard the plane flying away. So that was that.

With time to kill, Walsh drove back into town and strolled into a kind of general store. He found himself running his hands over the denim and plaid work shirts and Ben Davis overalls, and then he bought some. Walsh was enjoying himself. "You know, you really can get nice shirts for ten dollars," he told his coaches when he got home. Finally, he routed himself through Denver to San Francisco. He called Jane Walsh and told her he could still make it to the lecture. But Denver was snowed in and the plane couldn't land. Then after it landed, it couldn't leave. So Walsh didn't get home until late that night.

The next day, Walsh joked about what had happened to him. He assembled the coaches in the conference room and told them the whole story of getting lost and buying the shirts and getting snowed in. But his mood changed as he told the staff that Arizona's Dick Tomey had been voted Coach of the Year in the Pac-10, and that bothered Walsh. Tomey had lost his last two games (and would lose a third against Baylor in the John Hancock Bowl). Walsh said Mike Price from Washington State deserved the award, and if not him, then Rich Brooks from Oregon, who had salvaged a pretty good season with inferior talent. Thinking about what he had accomplished with the Cardinal, Walsh said he deserved the award, too.

"It was an insult to the coach at Washington State," Walsh said. "Any number of coaches deserve the award, including me." Tomey got the award, Walsh said, because he was in the good-old-boy network. "I haven't been welcomed the way I thought I would. I'm not in the loop."

Another time Walsh told the staff, "We haven't been accepted by the other Pac-10 coaches. We're new on the block. We showed them up all over the place and outcoached them. People are pissed off because we were successful the first year out."

One Stanford insider had a theory on why the other coaches did not vote Walsh Coach of the Year. "They compete against him for recruits right now. And they should anoint him king again? Perhaps there's a feeling that he won three Super Bowls, what does he need to be Pac-10 Coach of the Year for?"

Scott Frost's visit to the Stanford campus seemed to go well, except that for dinner Jan Souza had ordered chicken cordon bleu and she was afraid the Frosts didn't like chicken cordon bleu. She had heard the family went out for Burger King afterward. Walsh, meanwhile, had developed a roaring cold, and he looked pasty. He'd lose his voice on and off, and sometimes found that he could only communicate with the Frosts by whispering.

Losing his voice wasn't the biggest problem he faced that weekend. It came out later that Scott Frost and Mike Mitchell, a running back from a high school in Phoenix, had gone over to Walsh's house, where they ran into Joe Montana. This was a sticky situation for Walsh. If Walsh had arranged for Montana to be there as a way to impress Frost—"What I did for this guy I can do for you"—that was a recruiting violation. Walsh insisted that Montana had dropped by to discuss his future, something Montana was doing quite a bit with Walsh those days as he weighed his options with the 49ers. Walsh said Montana had accidentally bumped into the recruits, who arrived thirty minutes early, and stayed around for a half-hour making small talk. Even though Montana supported Walsh's story, the incident was embarrassing for Walsh and Stanford.

Walsh also had to answer questions about talking to Frost on October 3, after Stanford had defeated Notre Dame at South Bend. Any contact with Frost then was illegal, and the Stanford coaches were expected to invoke what the NCAA calls the Bump Rule: If coaches bump into a recruit at a time they are not allowed to have contact with him, they are supposed to say hello and move on. But Walsh and his assistants had stood in front of the bus gabbing with Frost and his father, and that was a clear infraction.

Walsh committed other violations in the recruiting period, all minor, but in the aggregrate they troubled the Pac-10. One involved running back Adam Salina from Berlin, Connecticut. Salina had already verbally committed to Stanford, and when Walsh and Bill Ring arrived at Salina's house, reporters were there. Without his knowing it, photographs and some of Walsh's comments praising Salina's skills ran in a local newspaper. This was a no-no. The only thing Walsh was allowed to say on the record was that he was recruiting Salina.

After they left, Walsh and Ring realized they'd made a mistake and reported themselves to the Pac-10.

But they weren't done yet.

That night they drove to Wellesley, Massachusetts, where they met fullback Greg Comella and his family, high school coaching staff, and friends at a pasta takeout restaurant owned by the Comella family. The next morning Walsh was informed that a press conference had been set up at the high school and was asked to participate. He said yes because he always said yes. At the press conference he talked about Comella's athletic ability, again going beyond NCAA guidelines. In addition, he'd now had contact with Comella on two consecutive days. Coaches in Division 1-A are allowed only one day of off-campus contact, so that was another violation. Walsh self-reported this incident also, and the Pac-10 treated Salina and Comella as one case.

These infractions may have seemed inconsequential to Walsh—after all, he wasn't doctoring transcripts or paying off recruits—but Stanford suffered because of what he'd done. Shortly afterward, a columnist in Sacramento suggested that Walsh had an undue influence on the admissions department and had arranged a backdoor admissions policy to get players who did not meet Stanford's requirements.

The charges were unfounded. The NCAA tracked football players entering in 1983, 1984, and 1985, and according to its figures Stanford graduated 91 percent within six years, compared to 74 percent at Cal, 75 percent at Penn State. The average SAT score for entering football players at Stanford was usually around 1100. By comparison, for the class entering in 1991 University of California players averaged under 900 on the SAT, Notre Dame about 1000, San Jose State under 800. Stanford football players entering in 1991 averaged a 3.55 grade point average compared to 2.75 at Cal and 2.97 at Notre Dame.

A spokesman for the Stanford Admissions Department said, "Academically, Bill Walsh's fall 1993 recruiting class compares very favorably with others in recent years." Stanford did not alter its standards for Walsh. All recruited athletes were required to submit a full Stanford application including high school transcript, SAT scores, counselor evaluation, two teacher recommendations, and responses to five different essay questions. Applications from football recruits were read by at least two deans in the admissions office, some by as many as three or four. However, the Admissions office would speed up consideration of a recruit's application, mostly because other schools were telling high school seniors that Stanford took too long to make a decision.

The Admissions office allowed Walsh to make a case for borderline students, sometimes postponing a rejection until Walsh had a chance to make his presentation. But the Admissions office did reject some of Walsh's recruits, and he responded philosophically. Just after he had taken over as coach of the Cardinal, Admissions turned down a wide receiver Walsh wanted, and a few days later the receiver announced he would attend a large midwestern university. Walsh's only response was that if he had met the receiver earlier, he could have convinced him to work harder in school.

The Pac-10 did not penalize Stanford for Walsh's recruiting violations because the conference determined that Stanford was adequately handling its problems on its own. Eager to comply with regulations, the university asked the NCAA to review its record. A representative from the NCAA came to Stanford for two days and met with Walsh, explaining that Walsh needed to have people from his staff research his trips in advance so screwups wouldn't happen in the future. The NCAA rep left a checklist that Walsh could consult before going on the road. The list was detailed down to which door of the high school he would enter and whether the press would be there.

The Pac-10 was satisfied with Stanford's safeguards, although earlier the Pac-10 Compliance and Enforcement Committee, displeased by Walsh's peccadillos, arranged a conference call, which he took at home. The call was lengthy and tense, and after a while Walsh told the committee, "I'm growing weary of this."

David Price of the Pac-10 was not sympathetic. "They do not pull punches when they quiz about violations," he said. "If Bill felt it was an inquisition, that would not deter them. When the other coaches see Bill Walsh doing all these things, they wonder if he even knows the rules."

CHAPTER

18

STANFORD ACCEPTED AN invitation to play in the Blockbuster Bowl against Penn State at Joe Robbie Stadium in Miami on January 1. This was a dream matchup of great coaches, Walsh against Joe Paterno, and the newspapers already were calling the game "The Genius vs. the Legend," which made Scott Schuhmann laugh. "You couldn't imagine those two guys sitting down and playing chess against each other," he said. To Schuhmann, Paterno was a good coach who cared about his players and, like Walsh, had all the right priorities when it came to university life, but no one ever would compare Paterno to Walsh as a tactician. Give Walsh extra time to prepare for an opponent—in this case almost a month—and he was unbeatable. He'd already proven that with three Super Bowl victories and two bowl wins in his previous tenure at Stanford.

But before Walsh could get down to the serious business of the game plan, he had to deal with two sensitive issues on his team. He was disappointed in reserve tight end Tony Cline, a good-natured, whimsical, talented young man who seemed strangely detached from the urgency of the football team. He was sometimes late for meetings—would wander in while Walsh or Terry Shea was busily explaining plays—and remained unaware of how the team perceived him or that he was unintentionally mocking the cornerstone ideals of discipline and solidarity. Walsh had not come down on Cline, even after Cline was late for the bus before the Oregon State game. Walsh held the bus until he arrived.

But now Cline had gone too far. He arrived late for a practice a week or so before the team flew off to the Blockbuster Bowl, this after Walsh had delivered his stern lecture about the bowl game being a business trip, not a vacation. Walsh remained calm. He waited for practice to end, then called the members of the Committee over to the side of the field, out of earshot of Cline and the rest of the team. He told the Committee what Cline had done and suggested a punishment: Cline would not be allowed to fly to Florida on the team charter but would remain on campus several more days, finally traveling on a second charter for coaches' wives and children and guests and friends of the university. Being ostracized from the team would be a tremendous loss of face for Cline.

Walsh explained all this to the Committee members, then told them to talk it over among themselves for ten or fifteen minutes and he would honor their decision. Then he left.

The players were surprised that Walsh gave them that much clout. So often players complain about coaches being unfair, and here Walsh had allowed them to prejudge one of his actions. It took no time for the Committee to back Walsh. Tom Williams and most of the others believed Cline wasn't remorseful and should be punished. But this wasn't the kind of punishment that would embitter him toward Walsh or the squad. He'd still be able to play in the game and, with all those players wandering around the hotel and practice field, the press would probably never even notice that he was missing for a few days.

What impressed the Committee members was that Walsh's solution seemed so rational, so well modulated to the circumstances. They had all heard stories of hard-ass coaches issuing hard-ass decrees, banning players from bowl games, making examples of them. They could imagine Lou Holtz telling Cline he was through for the season, but Walsh didn't overreact. He fit the punishment to the crime, making it clear that when Cline arrived in Florida he'd be handed his playbook and welcomed back into the fold. And that's exactly what happened. Cline was reabsorbed into the team with no outsiders knowing what had happened.

A few days before the game, Walsh was interviewed at the team hotel by Ted Koppel on "Nightline" and talked about Cline's case without mentioning him by name.

After the broadcast the players referred to Tony Cline as "Nightline Cline." The nickname was not a putdown. It was a way of bringing him back, of showing him he belonged.

*   *   *

The Committee solved another problem that was not as delicate. A week or so before leaving for Florida, the players were told that Stanford would provide them with dinners in Florida, but they were on their own for breakfast, lunch, and entertainment. That didn't go over very well. The players believed there was no way they should be spending their own money in Fort Lauderdale. Some suggested practicing in Palo Alto, then flying to Florida the day before the game. The Committee talked to Walsh, who considered the complaint, then promised the players $200 apiece for the week.

The players appreciated the money, but the first night in Florida, they attended a barbecue with the Penn State players, and of course the Cardinal wanted to know how much Penn State got to spend on the trip. Word spread through the team that the Penn State players received a travel allowance of $700. Since many of the Nittany Lions were able to drive to the bowl or book cheap flights, some of them pocketed the money. That ticked the Cardinal off all over again.

The team arrived in Fort Lauderdale late in the afternoon on Saturday, December 26, and bused to the local Marriott, where the players checked in and were immediately summoned to a meeting in an oversized conference room on the first floor. It was a dark, sleepy room with red carpets, and through the windows the players had a fine view of the hotel pool and, beyond that, a wharf with sailboats bobbing in the water.

Walsh was standing at the front of the room behind a podium. "By the way," he began, "this is as close to the ocean as you're going to get. We intend to keep you busy. So take a look." Walsh gestured toward the wharf the way the warden at San Quentin might point out to a lifer the penitentiary wall and beyond that the lights of San Francisco.

"What we're going to do tonight is get down to business," Walsh continued, "to the two-minute offense and the four-minute offense. I'll be the guy who keeps telling you to pay attention. When we leave Florida, either this will have been a wonderful experience or a godforsaken one."

Walsh's voice was weak. He'd come down with yet another cold, a chronic affliction for him preceding big games. This may only have been a bowl sponsored by a videocassette rental company against a mediocre Penn State team with a 7-4 record, but Walsh wanted to win, badly. He told the players they had a 1:00 A.M. curfew with no bedcheck. He would treat them like men, trust them to police themselves. He walked away from the podium.

Up stepped a Broward County sheriff named Jim Herbert, who'd been assigned to the team. He was cheerful and well-meaning, and the first thing he told the players was not to wander west of I-95. "If you get beyond that, you start getting into our crack areas," he said, like a tour guide pointing out the Grand Canyon or the Alamo. Herbert said he would be there all week as the team's link to other law enforcement agencies. "I won't make any busts, but I can't guarantee I can help you if you break the law. Our drinking age is twenty-one. If you get into a little problem with alcohol, call me. I'll pick you up."

Walsh interrupted the sheriff. "I'll be the one to pick you up," he said. Walsh was smiling, but he wasn't happy. In the back of the room, Guy Benjamin was muttering to himself. He'd been through the Sun Bowl with Walsh following the 1977 season and knew how Walsh thought. "That's exactly the message we *don't* want to give them," Benjamin whispered to the other coaches. "That makes it all right if they drink."

Walsh continued. "I just want to warn you—anybody gives you a hard time, don't be brave. Get the hell out. I don't care if she's attractive or unattractive. Turn and run. No way you're a match for three or four guys."

Herbert chimed in: "There are a lot of guns around here. They'll shoot you for flipping them off on the highway." He waited for that to sink in, then added, "This is known as the AIDS capital of Florida."

The players were silent. Walsh got ready to speak. He and Herbert were taking turns working over the Cardinal like a couple of tag-team wrestlers.

"Don't wear a Stanford shirt," Walsh warned. "Be careful. You could hurt the university and you could get hurt."

By now Walsh and Jim Herbert had scared the players to death. As he broke up the meeting, Walsh told them, "Hey, have a fun time in Fort Lauderdale."

The team attended an outdoor banquet that night at Penn State's hotel—Walsh and Geri posed for photos with Paterno and his wife—and when the banquet was over, Walsh told the players to get on the buses for the trip to Saint Thomas Aquinas High School, where they would work out at Brian Piccolo Field. On the bus ride through town, the players were yelling at each other, "Are we on the good side or the bad side of I-95?" The mood was playful, but when they arrived at practice Walsh worked them hard. It was dark and warm and humid, and Walsh stood in the middle of the field like the ringmaster at the big top calling out situations. "There are fourteen seconds left," he'd say, or "There's a minute and fifteen seconds left and you have three timeouts." After each play, he'd call the gain or loss, or make believe someone was whistled for holding, or a field goal attempt was blocked, or a running back had fumbled. He was preparing for every possible situation, and as he called out his plays he was smiling.

But the next morning, Sunday, he didn't show up for a 10:00 A.M. staff meeting. This was awkward. Terry Shea and Fred vonAppen and the others waited around the ballroom drinking coffee and killing time. Walsh would sometimes walk in late, but after a half-hour it was clear he wasn't coming at all. That was too bad. Twenty-five players had missed curfew the first night, and Terry Shea was hoping Walsh would lay into them.

When the players came to the room for their 11:00 A.M. meeting, Shea told them Walsh wouldn't be there because he was ill. Then he lectured them on curfew, appealing to their "honor."

"Nothing good happens out there after one A.M.," he told them. Reserve center T. J. Gaynor didn't hear Shea's appeal to honor because he had overslept. When the coaches realized he wasn't there, Mike Wilson called his room from a house phone and rousted him. A few minutes later, Gaynor slouched in, puffy-eyed and embarrassed.

Walsh appeared at noon. "I couldn't possibly get up at ten," he told the offensive coaches, who were watching film. He was coughing and his nose was running, and along with those symptoms, he'd developed an upset stomach, all of which added up to a classic cold-flu combo five days before the Blockbuster Bowl. Everything was on schedule.

He walked over to a chalkboard to write down the week's schedule for the coaches, but stopped. "What day do we play the game?" he asked.

"Friday," the coaches told him.

He wrote the schedule with his left hand, while he held a wad of tissues in his right. His mind was fuzzy from the antihistamines he was taking. Later that day, team doctor Jeff Saal asked what medication he was on. "I don't know, it's a long white pill," Walsh said. Saal had to laugh to himself. "White is good," Saal told Walsh. "If your condition gets worse, we'll have to change to red."

Walsh wasn't feeling any better the next day. In fact, the long white pills made his legs cramp at practice. Fred vonAppen stared across the field at Walsh, whom he had affectionately taken to calling "the Old Man," although not to Walsh's face. "Football has been his life's work," vonAppen told a spectator. "Bill knows that he's recognized as a great coach, but that's not a static concept, it's a dynamic one. When he put himself back into the arena, he had to perform to greatness. And he did. This was a zany year, but he pulled it off. And he can give all the credit he wants to Denny Green and the assistant trainer from last year. That's all very magnanimous. It's nice of him to throw bouquets to other people, but those fuckers, none of them were here. He had to run the show. Somebody else could have come in, and the same thing that happened at Cal could have happened here. Very easily."

At that moment, Walsh blew his nose.

Walsh made dinner plans with his family that night, but first he had to meet the other coaches at 7:00 P.M. in the ballroom, which had become Cardinal headquarters. After taking a nap, he felt better. He was dressed in a suit and tie, and the purpose of the get-together was to call eight recruits and keep the pressure on. The methodology was interesting. Walsh would sit on a chair in the middle of the room, while one of the assistants called the recruit from a wall phone. The assistant would make small talk for a few minutes—"How are your grades? Oh, that's great." And then he'd say that Coach Walsh was in the room and would like to say hello. It was a form of phone-selling, and Walsh was the big man, the closer of the deal.

He would take the phone and in his most cheerful, positive voice tell the recruit that he was excited about the prospective freshman class, that fifteen had verbally committed, many of them high school All-Americans, and that it was conceivable Stanford could go to the Rose Bowl next season—although privately Walsh did not believe that was possible until the 1994 season, when many of these recruits would be sophomores. Where appropriate, Walsh told the recruit not to close his mind to Stanford until after his campus visit. When he spoke to Tim Carey, the impressive quarterback from Seal Beach, California, he mentioned that the incoming freshman class would be "a great bunch of guys we're going to surround you with." Walsh was careful not to mention the name of Scott Frost, who had verbally committed earlier that day, which did a lot to cure Walsh's cold.

After Walsh had spoken to a recruit, he'd give the phone back to Bill Singler or Keena Turner or Scott Schuhmann—to whichever coach was the conduit to that recruit—and sit down until he was needed again. He enjoyed recruiting players. It was like putting together the 49ers from scratch using draft choices, and everyone knew he had been brilliant at that.

"I was a hell of a recruiter," he told a visitor between phone calls. "I recruited Craig Morton, so you know that really dates me. I recruited John Elway." He laughed. "This is fun, but years ago, recruiting went on until the day the kid came to school. So you'd be calling in spring and summer." Walsh put an invisible phone to his ear and pretended to talk to a recruit. "So you broke the rake. Oh, too bad. Well, you can get a new one at Ace Hardware. Oh, sure. And your little sister is seven and a half now. How terrific!" Walsh laughed again. "We'd talk about ridiculous stuff just like that."

The next morning he looked healthy, his old self, and he devoted the entire team meeting to trick plays. He had a horror of seeming predictable or dull, and in the last few days the fountain was flowing. He had come up with almost a dozen new plays that he wanted to use against the Penn State defense:

Hitch and Lateral—Steve Stenstrom throws to a wide receiver, who then tosses the ball back to Stenstrom, who throws the ball downfield.

Oski Pass, named after Oski the Bear, Cal's mascot. Walsh had installed this for Big Game but never got a chance to call it—Stenstrom fakes a reverse to Milburn, but keeps the ball and throws a long pass downfield.

Triss Pass Right—this was Walsh's pièce de résistance. He had named the play for one of the team's managers, Triss Chantrill, who brought in water for the players during timeouts and retrieved balls during workouts. Why? Because she'd asked him to. Stenstrom would fake a screen pass over the middle to wide receiver Mike Cook. Walsh expected the defense to follow Cook, and when that happened, Stenstrom would toss the ball to Milburn in the right flat.

Walsh was certain he could confuse Penn State with his trick plays and his no-huddle offense and with everything else he brought to a football game. He even said so in the press conferences he held at least once a day at the hotel, although a person listening to him had to decipher Walsh's rhetoric to know what he really meant. When Walsh spoke about Penn State he always compared the Nittany Lions to Notre Dame. This sounded like high praise, but Stanford had scored thirty-three unanswered points against the Irish once Walsh had steadied the foundering ship. When Walsh looked at Penn State's defense he saw a team that depended on good athletes playing a conservative zone, although Penn State's athletes weren't as good as Notre Dame's. Walsh loved a defense that played zone. Walsh performed surgery on zones. But he wasn't the only Stanford coach who liked what he saw.

After studying tapes of Penn State's defense, receivers coach Mike Wilson called it "vanilla." Wilson was certain that Paterno would blitz—everyone else had—but Paterno never disguised his blitz. That was a mistake against an intelligent quarterback like Stenstrom. Wilson noticed that Penn State's blitzer would usually be a cornerback who had to travel so far that Stenstrom would have no trouble getting off the pass. The University of Washington had blitzed nine men against Stanford—and that was the way to attack Walsh, send so many men his offensive line wouldn't know where they were coming from— but Penn State wouldn't be that daring.

Wilson read through the Penn State media guide and noticed that most of Paterno's coaches had either gone to school at Penn State or had been with Paterno for years. To Wilson that meant the football program had stability, continuity, and a philosophy, which he respected. What it lacked—especially on defense—was freshness, an infusion of new ideas. This made the Lions vulnerable.

Monday night, Stanford's offensive coaches had gone to the ballroom, turned off the lights, and studied film of Penn State's 42–17 victory over Tennessee in the previous season's Fiesta Bowl. What Penn State did one year, the coaches believed, was pretty much what Penn State would do the next.

None of this was to demean Paterno's achievements, which were massive. He'd won two national championships, coached four teams that were unbeaten and untied, was the fourth-winningest coach in college football history—behind only Paul "Bear" Bryant, Amos Alonzo Stagg, and Glenn "Pop" Warner, each one a legend—and had the most victories of any active college coach. He'd won fourteen bowl games in twenty-six seasons, trailing only Bear Bryant, who had fifteen bowl victories, for the most in history.

Paterno, who wore black shoes and rolled up the cuffs of his pants so they wouldn't get muddy during games, was a no-frills coach whose game plans were monuments of simplicity, of doing the basics but doing them perfectly. He believed in power football, running the ball and daring an opponent to stop him. Paterno and Walsh were opposites who represented the endless, unresolvable tension between tradition and change.

The Stanford coaches respected Paterno, a small, energetic man with thick gogglelike glasses—Walsh made a point of telling the staff that he liked Paterno—but the Stanford coaches believed they were centuries ahead of him and his staff in football theory.

So did the Cardinal players. "Paterno's good," Estevan Avila said, "but we have Coach Walsh. Everyone else is literally just everyone else."

This should have been the best time of Walsh's life. He was back in football, doing what he loved, without the pressure of the 49ers weighing on him every minute. But something else weighed him down.

What was he going to do about Scott Schuhmann? Or more precisely, *how* was he going to do it?

Walsh had just learned that Monte Clark was willing to be his offensive line coach. After that it wouldn't have mattered who else was the coach. He wanted Clark. But that decision created problems. Schuhmann would have to be told, and then Walsh would have to address the issue of Schuhmann's future, and somehow Walsh would have to do all this without looking like the bad guy.

Walsh put off any action until the team arrived in Florida, and even then he acted reluctantly. The chain of events began with Fred vonAppen, who went to Al Matthews and said Scott Schuhmann probably thought the crisis had passed. Someone had to tell Schuhmann the truth, and soon, because of something that was happening on the Penn State staff.

Penn State assistant Jim Caldwell had just been named new head coach at Wake Forest. Caldwell would begin assembling a coaching staff right after the bowl game—he might be in the process right now. Caldwell and Schuhmann happened to be friends, and vonAppen didn't want Schuhmann to lose this chance for a position. It was important to let Schuhmann know how things stood at Stanford, even if that seemed cruel in the short run, so he could approach Caldwell.

VonAppen asked Matthews to explain the situation to Walsh. After all this time vonAppen still felt a mixture of awe and dread in Walsh's presence, and trusted Matthews, Walsh's old friend, to find the right words, use the proper tone.

Matthews went to Walsh Monday, the day vonAppen approached him, and said, "Bill, you've got to do something about this Schuhmann situation." Walsh heard him out, but didn't reply with anything definite. Before Tuesday's practice, Matthews went to Walsh a second time. After speaking to Walsh, Matthews got vonAppen alone at practice and said, "Coach wants you to sit with him on the bus."

"Ah shit, is he going to fire me?" vonAppen asked, joking.

"No, he wants to discuss a situation with you," Matthews said.

On the bus, Walsh asked vonAppen to drop the bomb on Schuhmann. VonAppen agreed to do it, although it made him sick at heart. Schuhmann was his friend.

Besides, something that had happened in vonAppen's office a few weeks earlier made this request resonate in his breast. VonAppen was alone, happily listening to the classical music station on his radio, when Walsh entered. Walsh wanted to know if vonAppen was interested in applying for the head coaching job at a certain university. Walsh told vonAppen he was well connected at the school and could help.

VonAppen didn't know what to say. If he answered no, it might seem that he lacked ambition. But that's what he wanted to say. No. He went home and thought about Walsh's offer, and as it got later and as his feelings grew more tender, he wondered if Walsh's words contained a hidden message. Maybe Walsh didn't think vonAppen had done a good job, was looking for a way to unload him. VonAppen told himself that was ridiculous, but he couldn't push the fear out of his mind. It was a reasonable fear with Walsh, who rarely came right out and said what he meant. He dropped hints and expected his assistants to be bright enough to understand them. The ability to decode was an unwritten part of the job description.

The next morning, vonAppen drove to work, temples throbbing. He ran up the stairs, hurried to Al Matthews's office, and told him what had happened. "Bill's words festered all night long," vonAppen said. Matthews laughed and told him not to worry. Later, vonAppen explained to Walsh he wasn't interested in the job, and the matter died there.

But now vonAppen had to confront Schuhmann, and he knew in advance exactly how Schuhmann would feel. For a moment vonAppen, too, had seen the abyss.

*   *   *

After speaking to Walsh on the bus, vonAppen came to Matthews. "I'm going to tell Scott that Bill wants to talk to him about his contract," vonAppen said.

"You can't do that," Matthews said. "He's your friend. You won't be able to live with yourself unless you tell him the truth."

After the team lunch on Tuesday, vonAppen asked Schuhmann to join him in the ballroom. Under a gaudy chandelier the two men sat alone in that large room to talk about the direction of Schuhmann's life, although Schumann did not know that at first.

VonAppen had trouble coming to the point. "Scott, this is a serious situation," he said. "You've got to protect your ass. Look for other jobs."

That's about as far as vonAppen got. He couldn't bring himself to tell Schuhmann that Walsh wanted to replace him. Schuhmann, who could not entirely take in what vonAppen was saying, asked if von-Appen and Walsh had talked about his situation before and vonAppen said yes. Then Schuhmann left and made an appointment with Walsh later that afternoon.

And that's how it came to be that, about an hour later, Al Matthews was pacing back and forth on the dark red carpet in the hallway outside the ballroom. When someone asked Matthews what he was doing, he replied in a whisper, "Bill's doing it right now, relieving Scott of his duties." Matthews paced some more. He was muttering to himself, his forehead bathed in sweat. "This situation is so tough," he said. "We all love Scott. If he was a prick it would be easy, but he's a great guy."

Walsh arrived in the ballroom before Schuhmann. He sat in a chair in the middle of the vast room and put his playbook on the chair next to him. Through the window he could see the sunshine and the sunbathers, but in the room it was dark without the lights.

He was nervous, wasn't sure what to say, didn't know how Schuhmann would react. His mind drifted back to 1985 when he had outmaneuvered Paul Hackett, his offensive coordinator on the 49ers. Walsh wanted to move Hackett on, was concerned about his maturity, but he didn't want to ruin him. So he recommended Hackett to the Dallas Cowboys. Walsh sold the job to Hackett by telling him Tom Landry wasn't going to coach much longer and he might be Landry's heir. Hackett went to Dallas and the problem was solved without anyone getting hurt.

But as he sat there waiting, Walsh couldn't find the tactic that would make everything come out right for Schuhmann. He'd set forces in motion and now he was being swamped by a situation he'd created. He thought about Schuhmann's wife and kids and the house he was buying, and the fact that Stanford had a good season and Schuhmann never would be expecting something like this. He had to admit to himself that even now he had mixed feelings about his decision. Schuhmann had worked hard and the line was improving. Walsh's back felt stiff and his head ached. It was one thing to find the solution to Tony Cline's lateness, quite another to hold a man's life in his hands. He was struck once again by the difficulty of being a football coach and maintaining normal human relations with people he cared for. Walsh sighed and looked at the large double doors and wished Schuhmann would come in and they could get it over with.

After he'd left vonAppen, Schuhmann tried to make sense of what he'd been told. He convinced himself that vonAppen, and through him, Walsh, were talking about loyalty. Sure, that was it. Schuhmann had gone to dinner with Jim Caldwell from Penn State earlier in the week, although he never tried to hide that fact, didn't see a need to because everyone knew he and Caldwell were old friends. But clearly a misunderstanding had developed. Either Walsh thought he was consorting with the enemy, or thought he was trying to land a job behind his back.

When Schuhmann pushed open the heavy doors to the ballroom at the appointed time, his heart pounding, his mouth dry, and when he saw Walsh waiting for him—the white hair, the head slightly bowed—he blurted out, "I'm loyal, Coach. I want no other job."

It was a brilliant stroke of inadvertence, and it saved Schuhmann's career.

The last thing Walsh expected was this surrender, this total coming clean. It is not clear just what Walsh expected. Every time he tried to imagine this scene, a door would shut in his mind before he reached the denouement. It was odd being unnerved like this. Walsh was a man of tactics, both in football and in his life. There was a tremendous homogeneity to the man. In football, he disguised power with finesse, and finesse with power. But sitting in that room, Walsh had run out of tactics. Schuhmann had just announced he was loyal and was saying something about loving Stanford, never wanting to leave, and without meaning to he had put Walsh on the defensive by throwing himself on his mercy.

Walsh suddenly held up his hand like a cop stopping rush hour traffic. He motioned for Schuhmann to sit down next to him. Schuhmann walked across the room, slumped into a chair, and stared at Walsh.

"I'm thinking of hiring another offensive line coach, someone closer to my age," Walsh said. "I have two friends out there, Mike White and Monte Clark, but I want you to understand this has nothing to do with your performance. You've done a fine job."

Walsh's mind was running a million miles a minute, trying to find a way to make this come out right. Schuhmann just sat there, saying nothing.

Suddenly Walsh heard himself tell Schuhmann, "We'll see about making you recruiting coordinator."

Walsh had not yet spoken to Athletic Director Ted Leland about this—he only that moment had thought of the idea—but it was so obviously the right solution. Schuhmann was friendly and upbeat, the perfect representative of the university to recruits and their parents. Walsh was sure he could sell this idea to Leland.

And that's why when the double doors swung open and Schuhmann walked out, forcing a smile, Al Matthews, who'd stopped pacing in the hallway, heard Schuhmann say in an unsteady voice, "Thank you, Coach."

As Schuhmann stepped into an elevator and rode up to his room to tell his wife what had happened, Walsh walked out of the ballroom. He saw Matthews, hurried over to him, and lowered his eyes. "I couldn't do it," he said. "George Seifert would have done it."

What he couldn't do was fire Schuhmann. He knew dozens of coaches, tough guys, who'd have cut Schuhmann loose with no sweat, and Walsh blamed himself for not living up to their code.

He drifted down the hallway wondering if he had done right. When the news spread that Scott Schuhmann had been saved, every single member of the staff felt relieved.

Walsh never let on in public the anguish he was experiencing behind the scenes. The next afternoon he attended a press conference with Paterno at the Fort Lauderdale Convention Center and explained exactly how the game would go. Stanford had twelve plays Penn State hadn't seen before, and he would use as many as possible. He expected the Nittany Lions to blitz their cornerbacks whenever they could. "I don't think we'll be surprised. Whether we stop them is another story." Paterno seemed to be listening, although it's not clear if he believed Walsh would be so honest.

Walsh came to breakfast at nine Thursday morning, the day before the game, and sat with the coaches at a large round table and told them about attending a black-tie dinner with Paterno the night before. Paterno, he said, had become very friendly by the end of the evening and was calling him "Billy." Walsh said there had been a circle dance with each person taking a turn at a solo in the middle. Paterno went first. "He's a great guy," Walsh said, "but he is not a pretty dancer." When it was Walsh's turn, he held his arms out and did the dance from *Zorba the Greek* that Anthony Quinn and Alan Bates had made famous. Walsh was having a good time until Geri gave him the hook.

Apparently talking about the dancing got him in the mood again, because he got up from the breakfast table, spread his arms, and started hoofing it. Fred vonAppen blushed. Walsh danced again at the ten o'clock team meeting, right in front of the players. He knew how to beat Penn State, and he had solved the Scott Schuhmann problem, and at last the world was a place for dancing.

After the regular team meeting, Admiral Jim Stockdale came into the ballroom to talk to the players on special teams. He had been Ross Perot's running mate when Perot ran for president, was a senior research fellow at Stanford's Hoover Institution on War, Revolution and Peace, and was friends with Walsh. Stockdale was one of the most highly decorated officers in the history of the U.S. Navy. Among his twenty-six personal combat decorations was the Medal of Honor, awarded him in 1976 for his leadership of American prisoners of war in Hanoi during nearly eight years of captivity. Stockdale had endeared himself to the entire nation during the televised vice-presidential debate when he decided he'd heard enough of the shrill arguing between Al Gore and Dan Quayle and turned down his hearing aid.

Walsh saw Stockdale as an American hero and would invite him on road trips and let him sit in on team chalk talks, which Stockdale called "briefings." Bill Singler had asked him to speak to his players, and now introduced him as "a special person for special teams."

Stockdale walked with a limp, a reminder of the tortures he'd suffered in Vietnam, and when he spoke he sometimes talked around a subject, giving the impression that he might lose the thread. The Stanford athletes would not be impressed with him just because he had been a hero in some war they'd only read about. He had to earn their attention.

"I'm going to talk about how you control yourselves under pressure, how you control those demons that assault your heads," he said. "Get your head out of the box."

Some players shifted in their chairs. What box?

"Don't be preoccupied with your predicament and think the whole world is caving in on you. Don't get hemmed in by these goblins. Control yourselves in such a way that you wouldn't be forced to do things you'd be ashamed of later."

Stockdale came closer to the team.

"The way to get around that was taught to me in survival school by men who had been prisoners of war in Korea. One time, a guy put me in a tiny black box with the lid closed. I panicked. I had the feeling I couldn't get my breath. They beat on the box." Stockdale pounded on an invisible box with his fists. "The worst thing is to lose your composure and push against the box. The man got me out of there and said, 'You've got to mentally get your head out of the box. The noise won't hurt you.'"

Stockdale limped to one side of the room, then came back to the center. "When getting closed in by these pressures, remember your childhood, getting dressed, going to school. After a few moments, you'll realize you're the same guy who walked to school when you were a kid."

The players were listening intently now. Stockdale told them how to project themselves out of the box. When he was a prisoner of war, he would reconstruct entire days from his childhood as a way of vaulting out of intolerable circumstances. "Don't imagine dangers that aren't there. I learned to cope with pain. It's not bad. It's not going to kill you. You become familiar with it." He paused. "Most students go through Stanford and never learn about this subject—pressure and fear."

When Stockdale finished, the room went dead quiet. From the front row, linebacker Vince Otoupal suddenly jumped up and shouted, "Head out of the box." In the back of the room, J. J. Lasley stood up and repeated, "Head out of the box." Then he ran to join Stockdale and Otoupal. One by one, the players yelled, "Head out of the box," like worshipers at a revival meeting, and came forward until they were all crowded around Stockdale. They joined hands, and with Stockdale in the center of the circle looking determined, his jaw set, they shouted one more time.

In the afternoon, the team bused to Joe Robbie Stadium for the first time, went through a light workout, and then posed for a group photograph. When they returned to the hotel, Walsh revealed his first twenty plays to the coaches. Nine were no-huddle plays. He didn't want Penn State's defense to have a chance to adjust to what he was doing. On one play called Wham, short for *whammy*, a running back would double-team the nose tackle with an offensive lineman. The Lions wouldn't expect that blocking scheme, and the other running back would be free to shoot up the middle. Walsh was proud of that play, but his stomach flu had returned, which forced him to leave the room several times during his presentation.

The Cardinal players didn't like the Nittany Lions, although it's not unusual for one team to dislike another before a big game. Whenever the teams bumped into each other at night in restaurants or on the streets of Fort Lauderdale, the Lions acted superior, as if the Cardinal were a bunch of neophytes. They actually called them "rookies," and said they had no business appearing in a January 1 bowl game. The Cardinal had a 9-3 record and they believed if anyone's credentials were suspect it was the 7-4 Lions, who had lost four of their last six games, going 0-3 against ranked opponents Miami, Boston College, and Notre Dame.

The Nittany Lions, in fact, didn't have to do much to get into the Blockbuster. Penn State would be joining the Big Ten the next season, but in its final year as an independent it had been shut out of the newly formed coalition that assigned bowl berths. So Penn State had arranged to play in the Blockbuster the previous spring, needing only six victories to guarantee an appearance in Miami. Stanford players felt Penn State had no right to its arrogance. "Nothing against Penn State," Ron George said, "but we didn't make any deals at the beginning of the season. We had to earn our way here."

Walsh, of course, knew how his players felt as he walked to the front of the meeting room on New Year's Eve, the night before the game. He was wearing burgundy-colored Stanford shorts and a T-shirt, and he needed a shave. "I haven't said much about the game," he said, his voice tense and angry. "Now I want to give you my true feelings."

He paused a moment, and looked around the room. When he spoke, he was almost shouting. "I think Penn State wanted us to go to this bowl because we're a soft touch. Who the hell are we kidding? They think they can kick our ass without trying. That's why we're here."

He stopped, stared at the players. "We're a setup, a fucking setup. This is a setup if there ever was one. They don't think we're physical. They think we're a bunch of gentlemen. Why do you think their athletic director picked us? Dr. Saal went to a beach party and a bunch of their players said we're not up to playing on New Year's Day instead of the day before. If the players repeat it, you can be sure the coach said it."

Players shifted in their chairs and muttered to each other. If at that moment they had been told Paterno was in the hotel bar, quietly enjoying a cocktail with his wife, they might have run down, grabbed him by the seat of his pants, and tossed him into the swimming pool.

Walsh was on to something good and didn't let go. "I mean, we could play on December thirty-first, but if we play on January first, we'd collapse? They think the fight's fixed. We'll go down in the third quarter. We've got to kick the shit out of them. I just want you to know how I feel."

He turned to Chris Norte, who was in charge of video for the team. "OK, Chris, what the hell do you have for us?" he shouted.

"Big Game highlights," Norte said faintly, afraid of becoming the object of Walsh's anger.

Walsh watched the highlights film from the side of the room. The film caught shots of seniors Glyn Milburn, John Lynch, and Ron George, while the musical refrain "We are the champions" repeated in the background. Without the players observing him, Walsh slid out the door and walked to the end of the hallway. He experienced that old problem of becoming overemotional. He had to choke back tears.

After the highlights, during which the players were stomping and yelling louder than they did with Stockdale, Walsh walked back into the meeting and said, "Penn State will be sleeping easy tonight. I hope you won't sleep easy. I hope you'll want to play these guys and knock them on their ass. I hope you'll knock one of their players into their goddamn little coach."

Scott Schuhmann, forever faithful, leaned over to a guest and whispered, "Bill's only trying to motivate the players. He really likes Paterno."

Walsh stormed out of the room, leaving the team to Terry Shea and Fred vonAppen. He paced back and forth in the corridor, unable to come down from the high he'd felt while exhorting the team. Someone asked if he were serious in that angry speech. Walsh leaned against the wall. "I begin to believe it," he admitted. "There's a kind of truth to it. They do think we're an easy touch. It was like that in the Sun Bowl in 1977. LSU had an off year and wanted a win in a bowl, so Charley McClendon called me and asked if we'd be interested in playing. He thought, 'Stanford, we'll get a win.' And of course, we kicked their ass."

A few hours before the Blockbuster Bowl, Walsh arrived at Joe Robbie Stadium and walked into the coaches' locker room, a small cubicle painted in the aqua blue of the Miami Dolphins. He put down his red playbook, smoothed his hair, and stared at the bathroom. He peeked into the shower, large enough to hold an entire coaching staff at one time, scanned the lockers, and sat down in front of the one designated for Scott Schuhmann.

"What an adventure this season was," he said to a friend who had joined him in the locker room. "I never expected to be back here, not after *that* game."

That game was Super Bowl XXIII on January 22, 1989, and it was the last time Walsh ever coached for the 49ers, who beat the Cincinnati Bengals 20-16. After that win a burned-out Walsh stepped away from his NFL career, and now he was back in exactly the same little room getting ready to coach in a bowl in his first year back at Stanford. An incredible symmetry attended to this moment.

None of the other coaches had come in yet, and Walsh sat there allowing his thoughts to flow back to that game. He recalled how, after the 49ers won, the team came off the field and charged into the locker room. The first thing Walsh saw was Eddie DeBartolo, Jr., hugging players and shouting, but in spite of himself Walsh could not join him. Instead, Walsh positioned himself against the wall like an outsider, which in a sense he was.

"I realized this wasn't my team anymore," Walsh explained. "The players didn't know that yet. After a while, I got into that shower." He pointed across the room. "I was in there alone, and Kenny Anderson and Dan Fouts came in to congratulate me, and they were the only ones. They weren't even my players. Of course, I orchestrated it that way. I didn't tell anyone I was retiring, but as I stood in the shower I asked myself, 'Why did you do it that way?'"

He thought about DeBartolo and George Seifert. "Am I saying Eddie and George didn't come through for me? Yes. Do I mind? No, they're human."

Walsh stopped speaking. He was taking in the locker room, trying to experience the present and the past as parts of the same moment. His voice was somber.

He had not been that way a few hours earlier. When he'd come down to the team breakfast that morning, he'd acted impish, trying to show his coaches and players that this day was supposed to be fun. He said to Fred vonAppen, "I don't mean to embarrass you in front of your friends here, but one time I was leading a faculty group to practice, many of them women, one who'd never been to an athletic event, and I was explaining to them how football broadens character, teaches values, and shows you how to control anger." VonAppen, who saw where this was leading, began to chuckle. "Just then we turned the corner, and we heard you yell, 'Hey, get your thumb out of your ass!'"

Walsh's face grew red from laughing and vonAppen laughed, too, even though, for the briefest moment, he wondered as usual if Walsh's story contained a hidden message.

But all the laughter was behind Walsh now in the coaches' locker room. The other offensive coaches walked in, and they all crowded together going over plays. Walsh told Bill Ring and Scott Schuhmann to remind their players where to be in certain formations, and then he stopped himself and said to the others, "It's funny, we practice three weeks for a game and we're sitting here going, 'You tell them this. You tell them that.'"

Walsh scribbled adjustments for two plays on a pad. He couldn't help himself. He was like the mad lapidary who, if given the chance, would polish a stone until it no longer existed. Then he walked into the main locker room and drew the adjustments on a chalkboard. When he came back to the coaches' room, the others had gone to the field. It was time for Walsh to leave, too, but he lingered. "I don't get nervous for games anymore," he said. "That's neither good nor bad. I just don't get nervous."

One of the officials came in and asked Walsh if he planned to run special plays. Walsh looked up, his expression vague. It was so hard to drag himself into the realities of this day, this moment. He mentioned the one in which the tackles split off from the line. "We like to play around with that. We don't expect much from it," Walsh told the official. He also mentioned his play-action passes, and later told someone, "That's so the officials won't screw it up."

Outside on the field, the warm-ups, usually routine exercises, were becoming tense. Penn State had set up camp at Stanford's 40-yard line, an acquisitive act that was supposed to establish dominance. Analogies include a boxer before a championship fight loitering in the other boxer's corner, or a tomcat spraying urine along the borders of his territory. Stanford's defensive line coach Dave Tipton asked Penn State to move across the 50-yard line, which the Lions reluctantly did, but Penn State had established a sour tone for the game. "It was the ultimate act of disrespect," Tom Williams said.

After the warm-up, the team returned to the locker room to hear Walsh's last pregame speech of the season. He was casually sitting on a bench next to vonAppen, in no hurry to make his remarks, a sharp contrast to the Texas A&M game when he had spoken too soon. Finally, he stood up and came forward.

"If you're not used to handling the ball, don't get cute," he told his players, his voice soft, measured. "Don't pick up a fumble and run. Protect it. You've got to have patience. The game will ebb and flow. You'll look great. You'll look lousy. Also the other side thinks it's a fucking fixed contest. They think it's already done—'Let's play Stanford, a bunch of pussies out on the West Coast.' They think they're the big time and we're not. They think we can't stand the pressure of a big game."

After delivering that final jolt, Walsh told the players to take the field, and they ran out of the locker room ready to kill.

As he walked to the sideline and put on the earphones, Walsh told himself the Lions would not be ready for this game. Penn State had started the season thinking national title, and now it was playing in the Blockbuster Bowl against a team that by its very nature could never be a perennial power in college football. Walsh assured himself that Penn State would not be intense, and that certainly seemed to be the case when Stanford drove down the field on its first possession, scoring a touchdown on a two-yard pass from Steve Stenstrom to tight end Ryan Wetnight.

The quarter ended with Stanford ahead 7-3. The Cardinal might have scored more points, but Walsh, who always tried to call his trick plays before the other team, had Justin Armour throw a pass off a reverse that was intercepted.

Late in the second quarter, J. J. Lasley scored a touchdown on a "Slow Draw Right," although the play didn't develop as planned. Stenstrom dropped back and faked a downfield pass. At the last instant he scooted behind Lasley, who was pretending to block, and tried to tuck the ball under Lasley's right arm. That's how the play was supposed to work in theory. But Lasley didn't raise his right arm to take the ball. He raised his left. Stenstrom and Lasley fumbled with the ball for a few seconds, while the entire Penn State defense began dropping back for the pass that never came. Finally, Stenstrom had to jam the ball under Lasley's right arm and Lasley took off along the right side, which was completely free of Nittany Lions, and went in for the score.

Up in the press box, Terry Shea was puzzled at Penn State's lack of preparation. The Lions consistently misaligned on Stanford's forma- tions—simply lined up wrong. Shea wondered how this could happen after the Lions' coaching staff had the benefit of twelve full game tapes to study. He assumed Walsh had shown so many formations during the season that the Penn State staff had been overwhelmed, was unable to track them. On several plays Stanford outflanked the Lions at the line of scrimmage, which meant Stanford backs went into their pass routes completely uncovered.

Penn State's offense wasn't coping any better with the Stanford defense. When Stanford's defensive coaches studied tape of the Lions' offense they had no trouble picking out what they called the Penn State "keys," which the coaches and players considered obvious. When the tight end wearing number 18 entered the game, it was always a pass play. Any other tight end in the lineup indicated a running play. This made things a cinch for Stanford's defensive line.

That wasn't the only key. The Stanford defenders noticed that Penn State always started its offensive plays with the tight end next to number 71. So if the tight end lined up on the other side of the line next to number 66, Stanford would not adjust its defense, because everyone knew the tight end would move to the other side of the for- mation before the snap. This was Mickey Mouse stuff, which would have amused the Cardinal defenders if they hadn't taken such a serious dislike to the Lions players, whom they considered worse trash talkers than USC.

According to Tom Williams, Penn State's All-American receiver O. J. McDuffie was strutting around the field saying, "I'm an All-American, baby."

"Fine, just look at the scoreboard," Williams said.

To which McDuffie replied, "I'm an All-American, baby."

"Like, we'll just roll over and die now," Williams told him.

At halftime, Stanford leading 14-3, the doctors had to give Steve Hoyem and Ron George I.V.'s to keep them from getting dehydrated. It was hot and muggy on the field, and George, who sometimes went into games verging on the hyperkinetic, had worn himself out. Judged by his own lofty standards, he was having an average day.

Walsh, as usual, was calm, methodically going over plays on the chalkboard, his voice droning. "We're going to run our Slow Draw again," he said. "I don't think they knew what the hell we were doing. J. J. made sure of that." Walsh urged the offense to make first downs. He wanted to give his defense a rest, believed it was wearing down in the heat and hadn't been able to rush the passer on the last series. Just before the team went out for the second half Walsh told the offense, "Thirty minutes left to the season. Make it the best half you've ever played. Control the ball. Move the ball."

Eric Abrams kicked a twenty-eight-yard field goal with about six minutes left in the third quarter, and on Stanford's next possession Walsh was at his most whimsical. He knew he was going to win and wanted the aesthetic pleasure of running another of his trick plays, in this case Triss Pass Right—the play named for the student manager.

Stanford faced a second and ten at Penn State's 40. Stenstrom dropped back and faked a pass to Mike Cook, who was running right to left across the middle. Walsh reasoned, correctly, that the Lions' overanxious linebackers would take off after Cook, and then Stenstrom would toss the ball to Milburn, who'd be standing off to the right like a commuter waiting for a bus. The play worked perfectly. Cook slashed across the middle and even waved his arm at Stenstrom, indicating he was open. It was an extra little frill Cook invented on his own, and the Penn State defense bought it. Stenstrom looked at Cook, then turned to Milburn, threw him the ball, and there was Milburn sprinting untouched into the end zone. "I got the ball and there was one guy," Milburn said, "and after that, there was no one."

The game ended 24-3, although Walsh believed he could have scored two more touchdowns. After the final gun Tom Williams went over to shake hands with O. J. McDuffie, who rebuffed him. "He was very All-Americanish, very standoffish, very babyish," Williams said later.

The team ran into the locker room, and it was noisy for a few moments, but then the oddest thing happened. A calm settled over the team. The players had expected to win, had come of age weeks before after the loss to Washington, and now they methodically peeled off tape and showered as if this were any other game.

After Walsh led the team in prayer, he talked to the media near the locker room door. Geri was there, and every once in a while he'd break away and give her a kiss and then return to the media and talk some more. He had succeeded, was in his bliss. He'd hoped for seven wins and now he had ten, the first time any Stanford football team had done that since 1940, when quarterback Frankie Albert led Stanford to a 10-0 season by defeating Nebraska in the 1941 Rose Bowl.

A writer asked if a loss in the Blockbuster would have damaged recruiting, and Walsh giggled. "If we'd lost, we'd have been on the phone with recruits saying we lost the game plan on the way to the stadium." He stopped. An impish gleam came into his eyes. He raised his right index finger to emphasize what was coming next. "We'd have said we were taking midterms."

It was his final shot at Lou Holtz, who'd blamed his loss to Stanford on exams.

The Stanford charter flight arrived at San Francisco Airport at 6:30 the next night. Walsh always insisted the charter park away from the terminal, usually in a cargo area, where the players would be met by buses and transported to campus.

Everyone came down the stairs from the plane and waited for the luggage. It was windy and chilly, typical San Francisco weather, and it felt good compared to the heat and humidity of southern Florida. The buses arrived and everyone began to board. Off to the side stood Berni Schuhmann, Scott Schuhmann's wife, with her two children. She was a small woman with a ponytail, who from certain angles still resembled a teenager. She had an open, easy disposition and usually smiled, but it was said that a few days earlier, after Scott told her about his meeting with Walsh, she flew into a rage, expressing all the anger her husband had repressed.

She wasn't taking the buses to campus with everyone else. The Schuhmanns lived in a town just south of San Francisco, near the ocean, and she would be driving home without her husband, who had gone to a football coaches' convention in Atlanta. Her luggage was late in arriving, and she seemed alone and unprotected on the dark runway with the wind whipping her hair.

Everyone boarded the buses except for Walsh, who finally grabbed his attaché case and began to get on. At the last instant he turned around, saw Berni, and stopped. He stared at her, then set down his case and walked over to her. She didn't say anything. He put his arm on her shoulder and placed his lips on her cheek. She allowed him to kiss her.

He turned around, walked back across the tarmac, and boarded the bus, its engine revving, exhaust fumes pouring into the cool air. The door closed, and the bus drove away.

FIVE DAYS AFTER Stanford won the Blockbuster Bowl, Monte Clark flew to the Bay Area from his home in Detroit, drove to the Stanford campus, and made his way to the football offices. Bill Walsh set him up in the conference room, where Clark spent several hours watching tape of the Cardinal offensive line. Clark was fifty-five, a large man with a large head, and he seemed to fill up the conference room all by himself. Walsh left him alone, and when Clark finished, they met in Walsh's office with the door closed.

A week later Stanford issued a press release announcing that Scott Schuhmann had been named the school's recruiting coordinator. In the release Schuhmann was quoted as saying, "I have been pondering a career change for some time. I am excited about beginning a new career and bringing the recruiting office to the standards of Stanford's athletic teams."

Three days later Stanford issued a second release announcing that Clark had been hired as offensive line coach.

On January 30, the day before the Super Bowl, Walsh was elected to the Pro Football Hall of Fame. For weeks after that he bustled around the football offices telling his coaches and Jane Walsh and friends, "This ring I will wear."

His skin looked healthy, almost glowed, and his sinus infection had gone into temporary remission.

"I've had a hard time getting over the 49ers," he admitted to a friend in his office one day. "I barely could watch their games. I'd be thinking, hey, that's my team and those are my plays. I felt abandoned, in exile. But now that I've been elected to the Hall of Fame the bitterness has passed. I've made peace with the 49ers in my heart."

Only one thing worried him. How was he going to get through the induction ceremony, the physical act of giving a speech and accepting the award, without breaking down like a baby? He'd walk up and down the halls buttonholing Mike Wilson or Terry Shea or whoever walked by, "Do you think I can do it without crying?"

He would spend hours visualizing the awards ceremony, seeing himself talking in front of a crowd of NFL dignitaries, and he'd imagine himself getting through it without weeping—except for the times he couldn't pull it off, and then he visualized himself sobbing while the people in the audience looked away and cleared their throats. At times like these he considered seeking advice from a therapist on how not to cry.

But when the day arrived, a sunny Saturday in July in the small town of Canton, Ohio, he got through the ceremony without shedding a single tear.

He considered that a victory, a sign that he could change, even at the age of sixty-one.

Walsh was grateful for many things as the 1993 season approached. The editors of the *Stanford Daily* picked him as the person who'd made the largest impact on the school in the first year of its second century. In choosing Walsh, they ignored new president Gerhard Casper. "Bill Walsh has had more of an invigorating effect on campus than the president," one *Daily* editor said. "Casper hasn't come out with anything that's gotten people real riled up or real excited."

One booster, who was dazzled by getting Walsh as head coach, had gushed, "We were looking for Moses to lead us out of the muck and mire, and we got God."

Walsh appreciated the honors heaped on him, but mostly he was grateful for the freshman class he'd recruited, which was ranked in the top five in the country.

But the 1993 season turned out to be a trial for him and the other members of the staff, especially for Fred vonAppen, whose defense had graduated seven starters, four to the NFL: Ron George, Atlanta; Dave Garnett, Minnesota; Darrien Gordon, San Diego; John Lynch, Tampa Bay. VonAppen had to shove inexperienced players into battle and the defense ended the season ranked last in the Pac-10 in every important statistical category, giving up more than thirty-five points a game.

Walsh's offense lost key players to the NFL as well: Glyn Milburn, Denver; Chris Dalman, San Francisco; Ryan Wetnight, Chicago; Mike Cook to the developmental squad of the Phoenix Cardinals. Steve Stenstrom remained, and although he broke John Elway's Pac-10 record for most passing yards gained in one season, without Glyn Milburn Walsh had no running game. The Cardinal ranked last in the conference in rushing.

Denny Green, it turned out, had willed Walsh one great class, and now that it was gone, Walsh was left with a football wasteland. Sometimes it seemed to him that he was going to battle with a bunch of freshmen, a team of eighteen-year-olds in a world of men. The Cardinal finished the season 4-7 and got blasted in Big Game 46-17. The night before Big Game Walsh had a cold and stomach flu, and his hands shook worse than ever.

But Big Game wasn't the low point. By then Walsh knew what to expect. The defining moment for the team had occurred a month earlier, on October 16 in Tucson, when the Cardinal met the eleventh-ranked Arizona Wildcats. Stanford's record was 2-3 and if the team could pull itself together, it still had a shot at a bowl game.

Stanford surged ahead 17-0 early in the second quarter, but by the half, Arizona had cut the lead to 17-14. The Wildcats tied the score with a field goal in the third quarter and then the teams traded touchdowns. When Stanford got the ball for the last time at its own 14-yard line with 1:04 to go and the scored tied at 24, Walsh decided to play for a tie.

And then the game turned into a disaster.

On third and nine from the 15, Steve Stenstrom dropped back to pass, got sacked, and fumbled the ball at Stanford's 8-yard line with forty seconds to go. On the sideline Walsh felt himself getting ill. What the hell was going on? He hadn't called a pass play, not with the Cardinal so close to its own end zone. He'd be insane to pass. He expected Stenstrom to run with the ball to take time off the clock.

Arizona recovered the fumble, kicked a gift field goal, and won 27-24.

Afterward Walsh, who seemed to be in shock, said Stenstrom called the wrong play. "It was supposed to be a running play. Steve was going to run to the outside and run the clock."

It was an unfortunate statement; it made it seem as if Walsh was blaming the loss on his quarterback. In fact, Walsh himself had made a strange call, considering the circumstances. Sure, Stenstrom was supposed to run, but the play also contained the option of a pass if Stenstrom thought it was open. Walsh knew that. It's just that he never expected Stenstrom to pass in a situation like that.

For three days after the game, Walsh could not sleep past three A.M. He'd lie in bed and feel his heart pounding against the mattress. He walked around the football offices like a zombie, sometimes passing Fred vonAppen and Al Matthews without noticing them. Matthews told someone, "For those three days I thought Bill was going to throw himself off a goddamn bridge."

When he finally calmed down, Walsh confided to a friend, "I blame myself for what happened. I never should have called that play. I don't know what I was thinking of."

He called Stenstrom into his office, told him they both needed to work on "finishing off games." Then he went over the play in a neutral voice, matter-of-factly using it as a diagnostic.

Stanford's next game was at home against Arizona State. The night before, Walsh ate dinner with the team in a large ballroom at Rickey's Hyatt House in Palo Alto. Then he and Terry Shea walked to his suite, sat at a small round table in the living room, and worked on the game plan. Walsh had asked Shea to draw up his own version of the first twenty plays. This was the first time he'd ever allowed Shea to do that. Walsh also drew up a list of the first twenty plays, and for the next hour, the two of them sat in the room merging their lists. Shea couldn't keep a grin from spreading across his face, he was so pleased to be included at this level.

But there was more. It wasn't just that Walsh finally had decided to involve Shea in scripting the first twenty plays, which always had been his domain, was in fact one of the innovations he introduced to football so many years before. Walsh had decided that Shea would run the offense during the game, would actually call the plays from his perch in the press box.

This was an astonishing change. Walsh prided himself on his in-game performance, his ability to judge the risks and come up with the right calls. He had run the offense on every team he'd worked for starting with the Bengals. And now he was passing the torch.

Later that night after the team meetings, Walsh went to the hotel bar for a glass of wine before bed. "I'm supposed to be a mentor to the players and the assistant coaches," he told a friend. He sipped the wine, leaned against the back of the booth. "That includes teaching Terry also."

He set the glass on the table. "Am I afraid? Yes. There's the unknown. Terry will feel the pressure because he knows I'm there observing and he'll be less daring than I would be, at least for a while. But it's got to happen sometime."

He smoothed his napkin, ran his hand across the playbook. "I've been thinking about Abraham Lincoln lately," he said. "I've read so much about him and I admire him. And what I admire most was his ability to internalize stress, to suffer and move on." Walsh paused. He looked tired in the half-light of the bar. "But it takes its toll. I had to quit the 49ers after only ten years. Less sensitive men go on longer. They're not as scarred."

Walsh gathered up his playbook, got ready to leave. Then he pointed to his chest. "When I couldn't sleep this week, I worried about my heart. I asked myself, 'How many times can you go to empty?'"

Walsh did not wear a headset the next day and that led to lasting repercussions he could not have foreseen. He stood on the sideline like a visitor, clearly out of the loop, while Shea called the game from upstairs. Not one member of the media noticed Walsh's lack of involvement. Sportswriters had been habituated to Walsh calling the plays, and when he wasn't calling plays, the writers simply could not see reality.

At the very end Walsh put on headsets and ran the game, trying to pull out a victory. It didn't help. The Cardinal lost 38-30. For the remaining games of the season Walsh would allow Shea to call the first quarter before taking over.

Some of his coaches were not pleased with what he had done against Arizona State. It was fine to be a mentor to Shea, but not after that horrifying loss to Arizona the week before, with Stenstrom fumbling near his own goal line. This was the time for Walsh to take over, not to step away.

"It wasn't passing the torch," one coach said. "It was wiping his hands of it. After what happened in Arizona, it was like he said, 'I'm not involved anymore. I'm through.' The players see him standing there and they feel he gave up on them."

Another member of the staff said, "He should have worn the headset even if it was disconnected."

The coaches might have shown more sympathy for Walsh if they'd known what had prompted him to take off the headset in the first place. Walsh had been calling plays as usual during the Arizona game, feeling the rhythm, when all of a sudden he began forgetting things.

He could visualize which plays he wanted, but he couldn't remember their names. He searched frantically on his card, but the clock was winding down and sometimes he made the wrong calls.

A few days later, he told a friend, "It was so frightening. I couldn't remember the names of plays I created, that I'd been using for years. I began wondering if I was losing it."

Walsh had forgotten plays before, even in the Super Bowl years, but now the Cardinal was playing poorly. Losing put him in a desperate state of mind.

A former offensive lineman on the 49ers once told this anecdote about Walsh: "Bill was a good coach during games, but even he'd get rattled by the pressure. They all do. Sometimes Joe would get the call from the sideline and then he'd come back to the huddle laughing and say, 'You're not going to believe this shit.'"

Walsh's friend told him that story and Walsh laughed, seemed relieved. At least he wasn't losing his mind.

Two days after the season ended, Mark Soltau of the *San Francisco Examiner* interviewed Walsh privately. The other coaches saw the two of them go into Walsh's office and they saw the door swing shut, but they didn't think much about it. Earlier in the day the staff had talked about recruiting, and everyone was feeling good about preparations for next season. Soltau stayed with Walsh for about thirty minutes and then Walsh left to play nine holes of golf.

The next day an article appeared in the *Examiner* with the headline WALSH MAY NOT RETURN. This floored the coaches. They knew Walsh was having trouble with all the losing. Over the headsets he would cry out, "I'm being humiliated." And sometimes he would talk about the sixties being "a crisis decade" in a man's life. When he walked off the field after Big Game he heard someone yell, "You're no fucking genius." Later he told a friend, "The catcalls hurt. I wonder why I need to put myself in a position to hear things like that. After we played Oregon, someone in Eugene, for God's sake, yelled the same thing. People look at me and they think I'm failing."

In his office, he would wax nostalgic about Montana and Jerry Rice and John Taylor, about having men who could turn routine plays into huge gains. It was obvious Walsh still had trouble adjusting to college players, was judging his team and himself by the standards of the NFL. He had begun the 1993 season with a cumulative three-year

Stanford record of 27-10 and now he worried that his record was becoming ordinary.

But no one realized it had gone this far.

The article said, "Walsh hasn't felt well for several weeks and will undergo tests shortly. If doctors tell him his health is at risk, he'll quit."

Walsh was not around when the article appeared. Coaches took copies into their offices and behind closed doors got on the phone to their wives. They wondered if they would have jobs. It was two days before Thanksgiving and no one felt like rejoicing.

The assistants were deep into recruiting and this article would hurt. "How selfish of him," one coach said. They all had visions of Cal or Notre Dame or USC sending copies of the article to recruits, stealing away blue-chip players who were leaning toward Stanford. Many of the coaches wondered why, if Walsh was thinking of quitting, he would go to an outsider instead of first leveling with them.

Some members of the staff wondered if Walsh intentionally planted the story about his health in case he needed an excuse to step away later. Other coaches thought Walsh was merely exhausted from the season and spoke without thinking.

When he realized what he had done, Walsh phoned each of his coaches individually and explained that he had no intention of stepping away. The reporter had asked under what circumstances he'd consider leaving and he'd answered honestly. He'd leave if his health were at risk. But he had no plans to quit and was beginning to feel like his old self again.

The staff assembled in the conference room the Monday after Thanksgiving and Walsh apologized to all the coaches for the article. Then, to show his dedication, he led a three-hour recruiting meeting, discussing in detail every high school senior on Stanford's list.

He refused to go out a loser. He'd proven that over and over again with the 49ers.

"I signed on," he told the staff. "Nobody forced me. I have to act with dignity."

We will not be a wildebeest.

He smiled. He would turn sixty-two the next day and, again, he was starting over. He did not find this frightening. He had spent his entire life starting over.